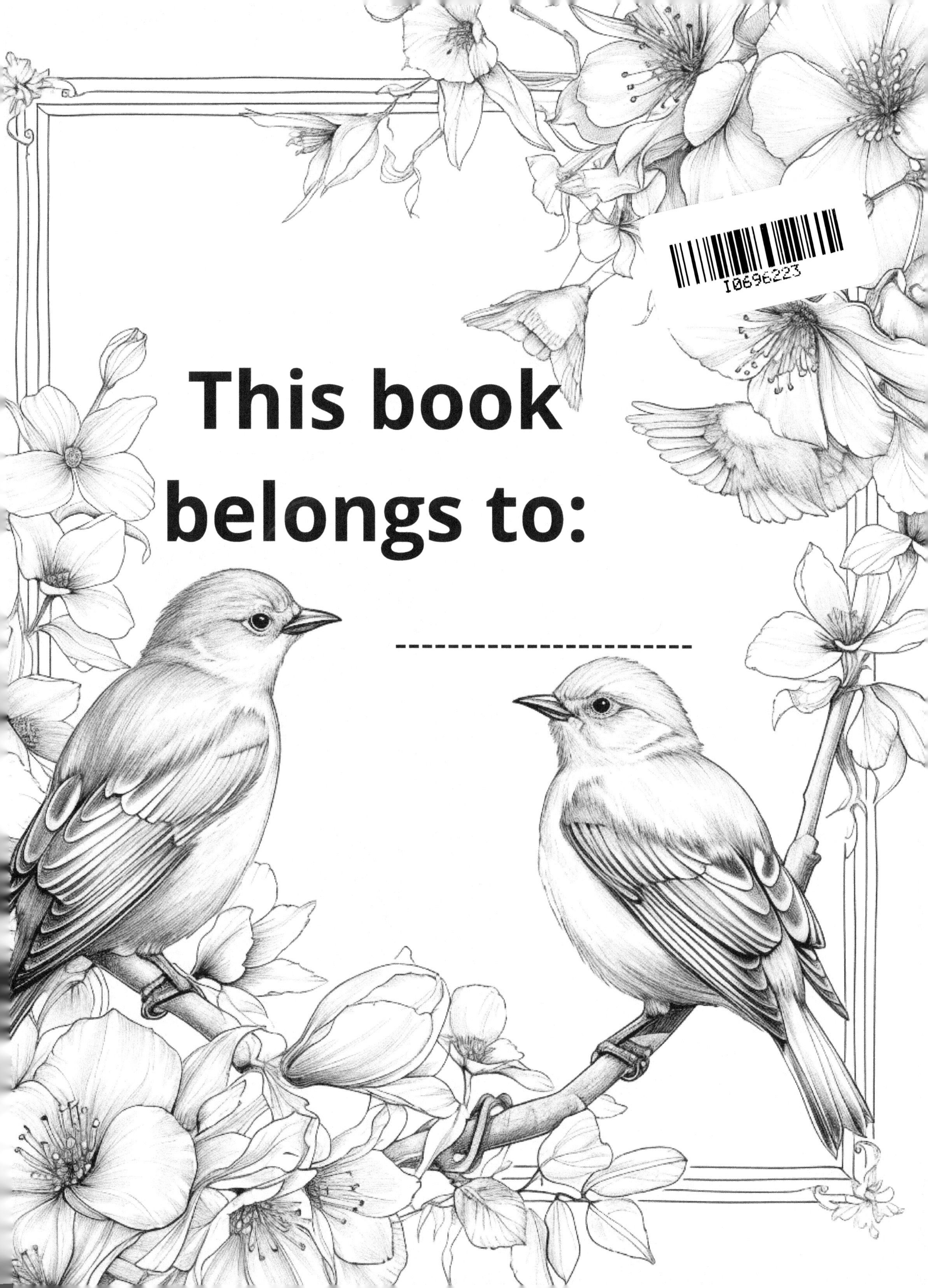
This book
belongs to:
____

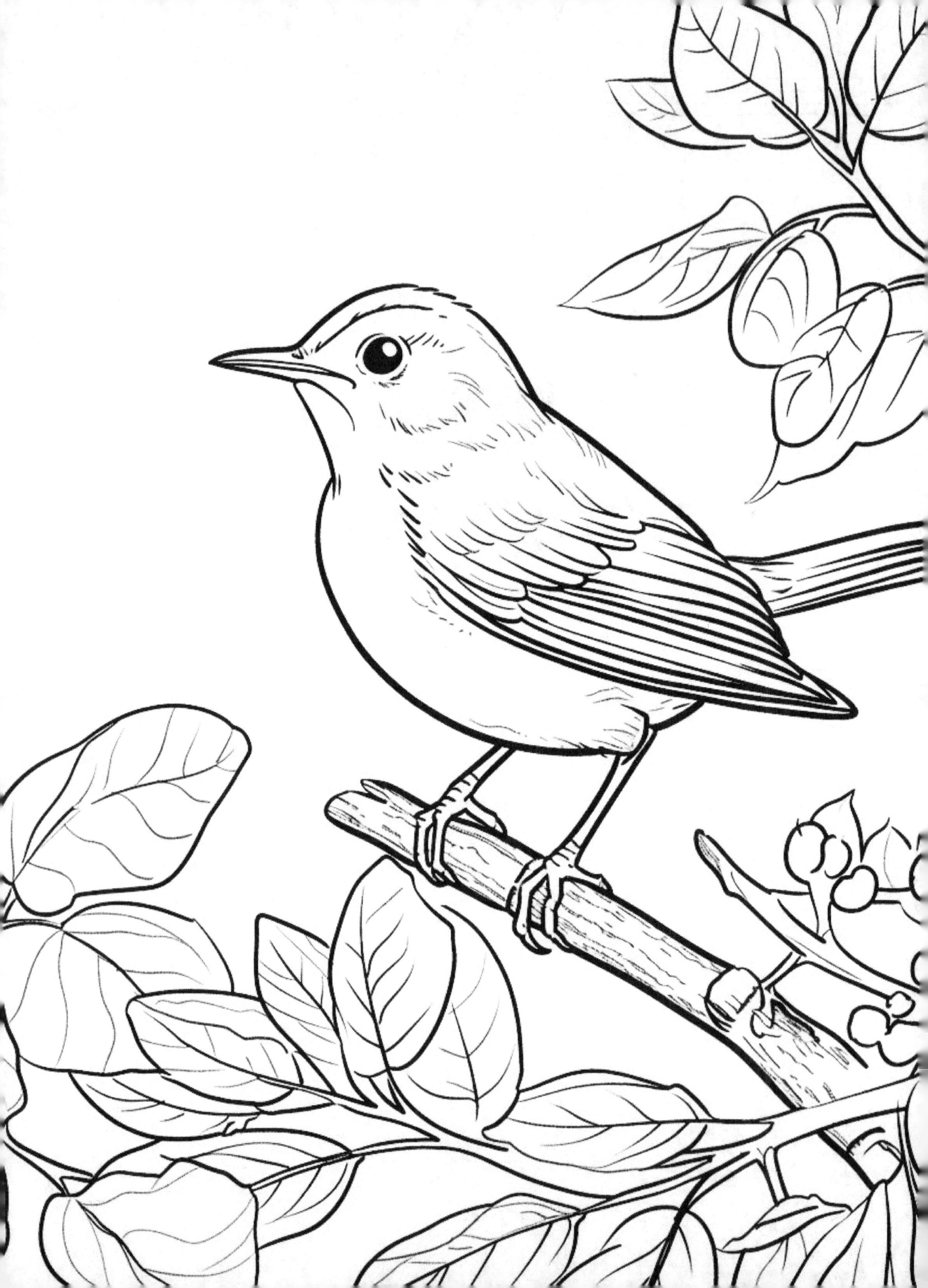

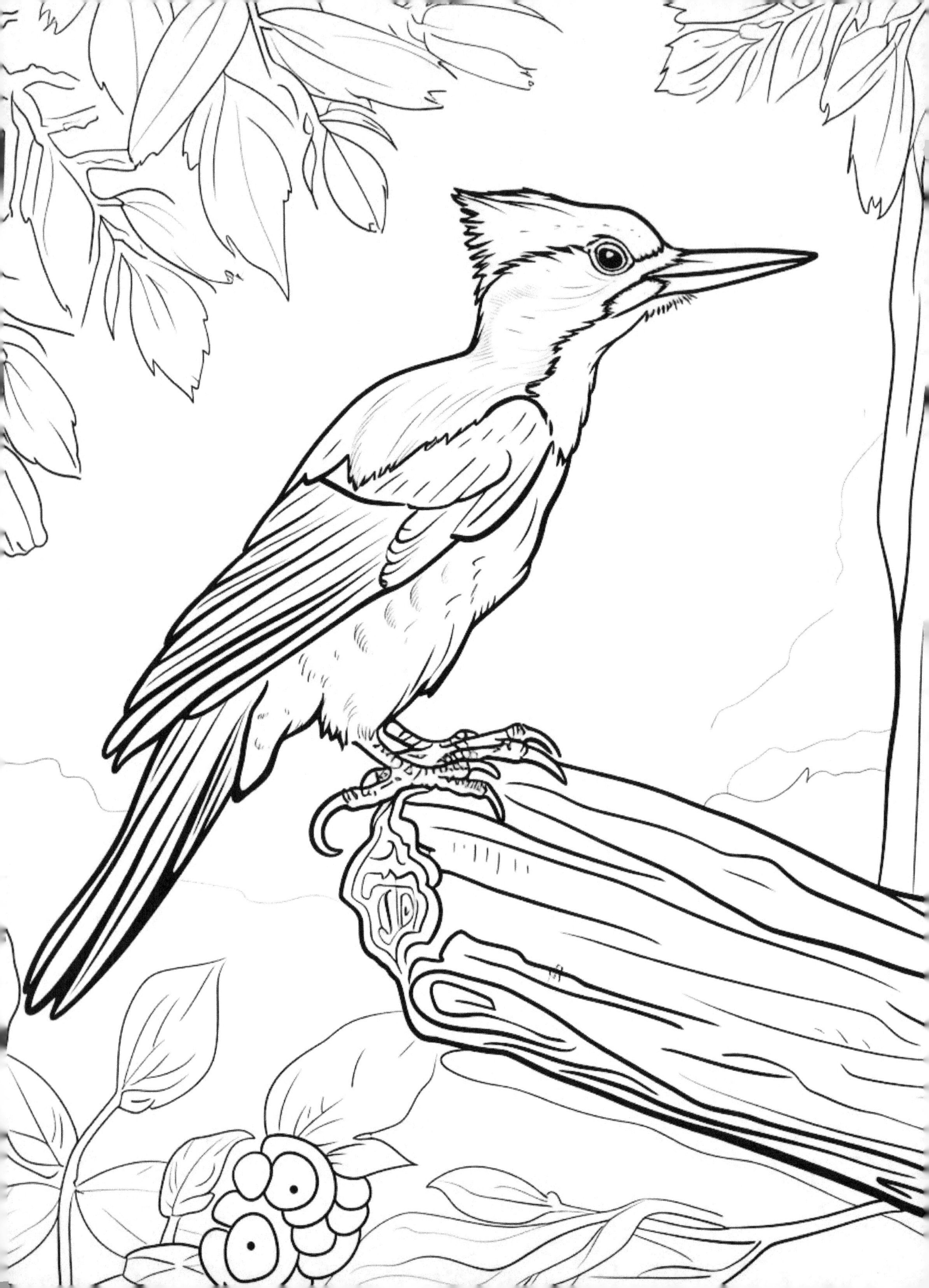

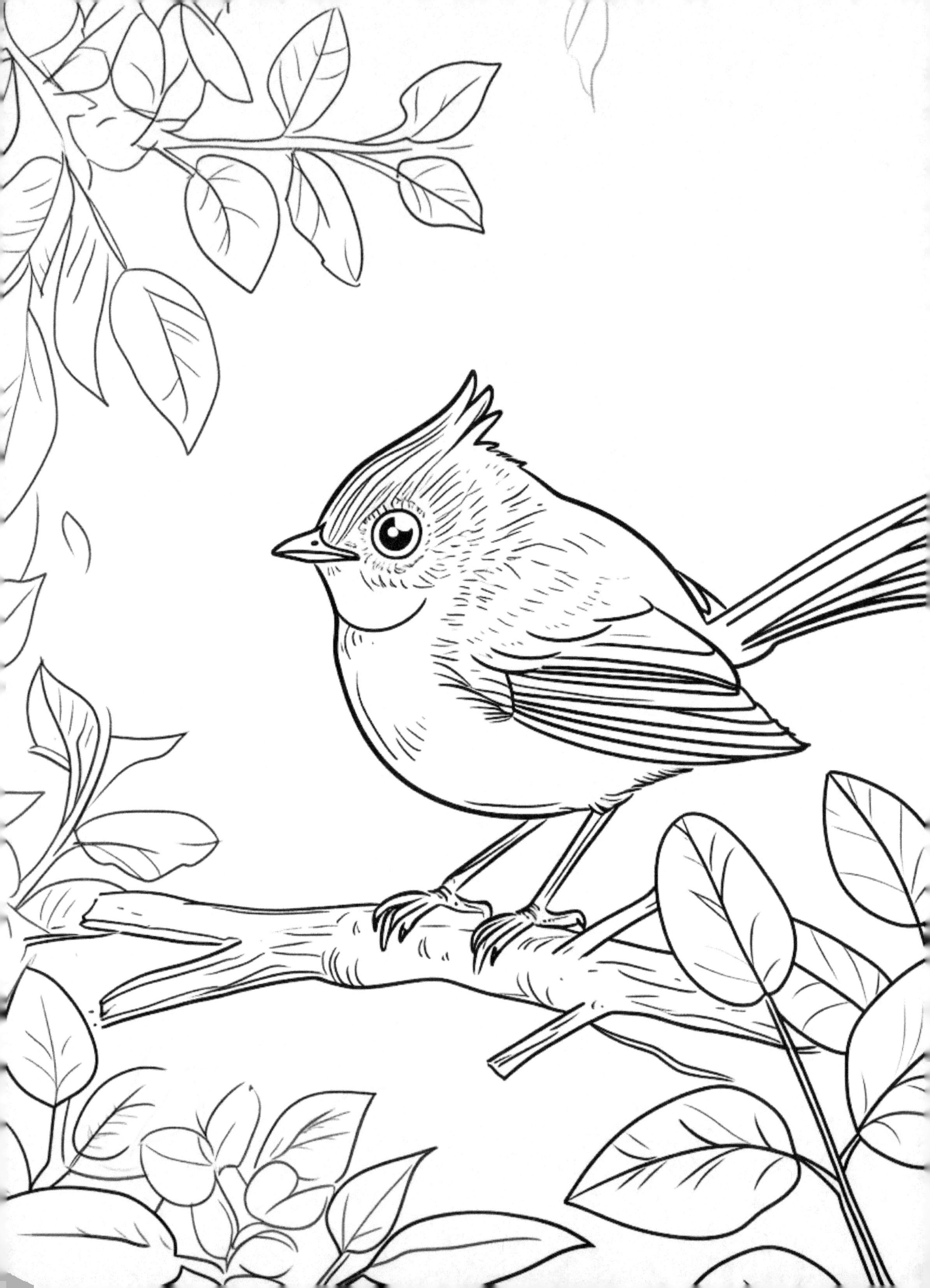

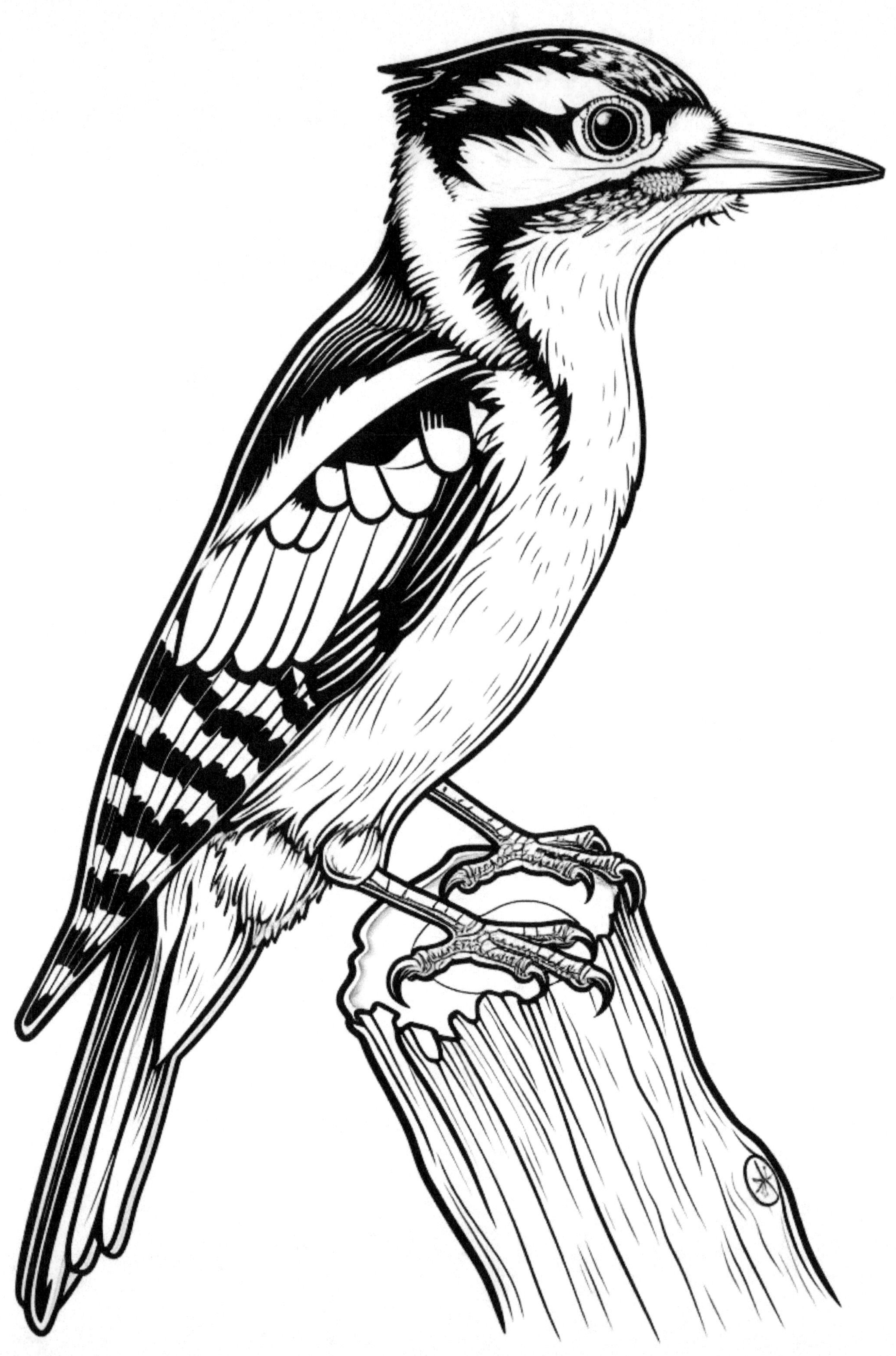

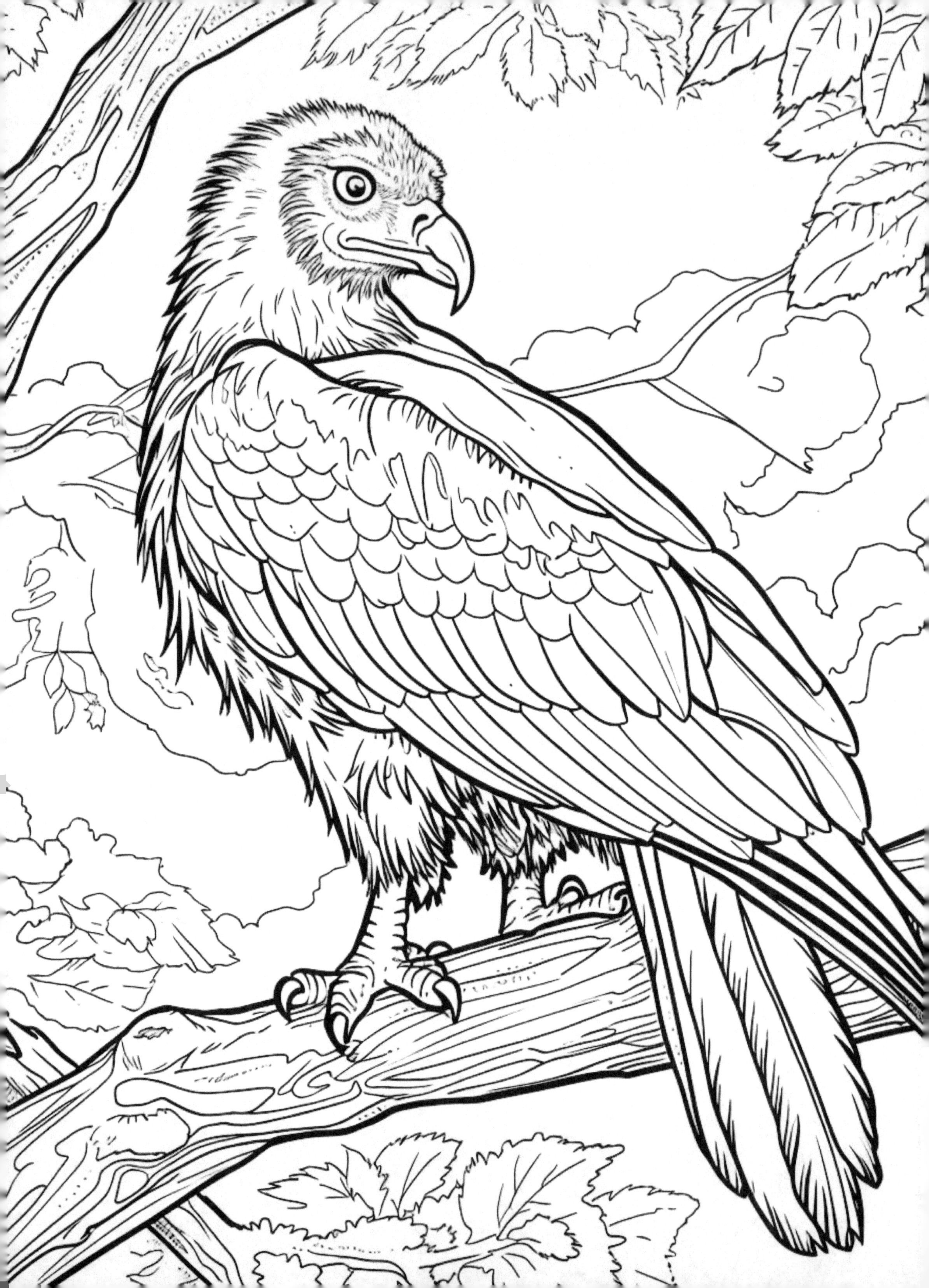

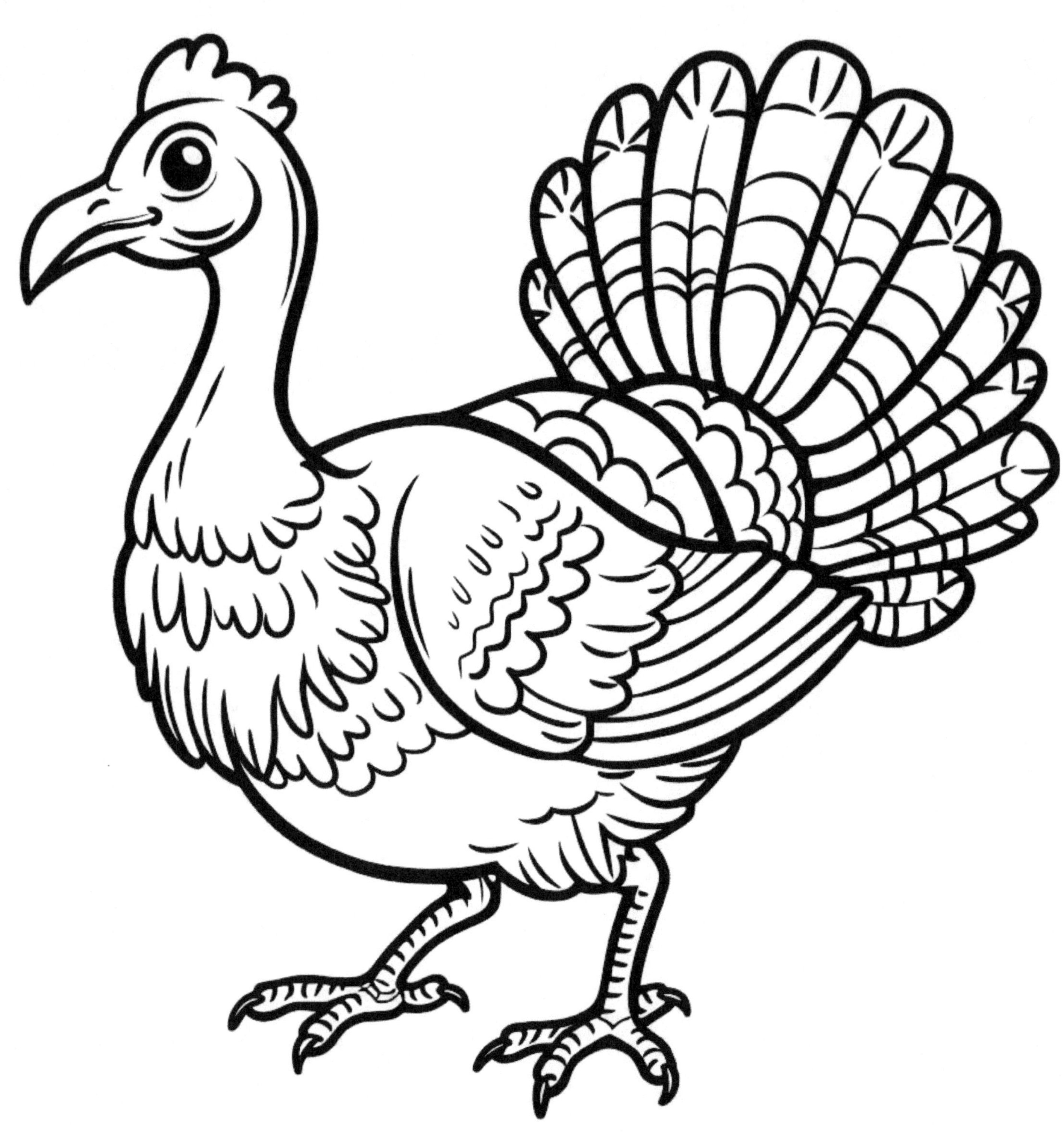

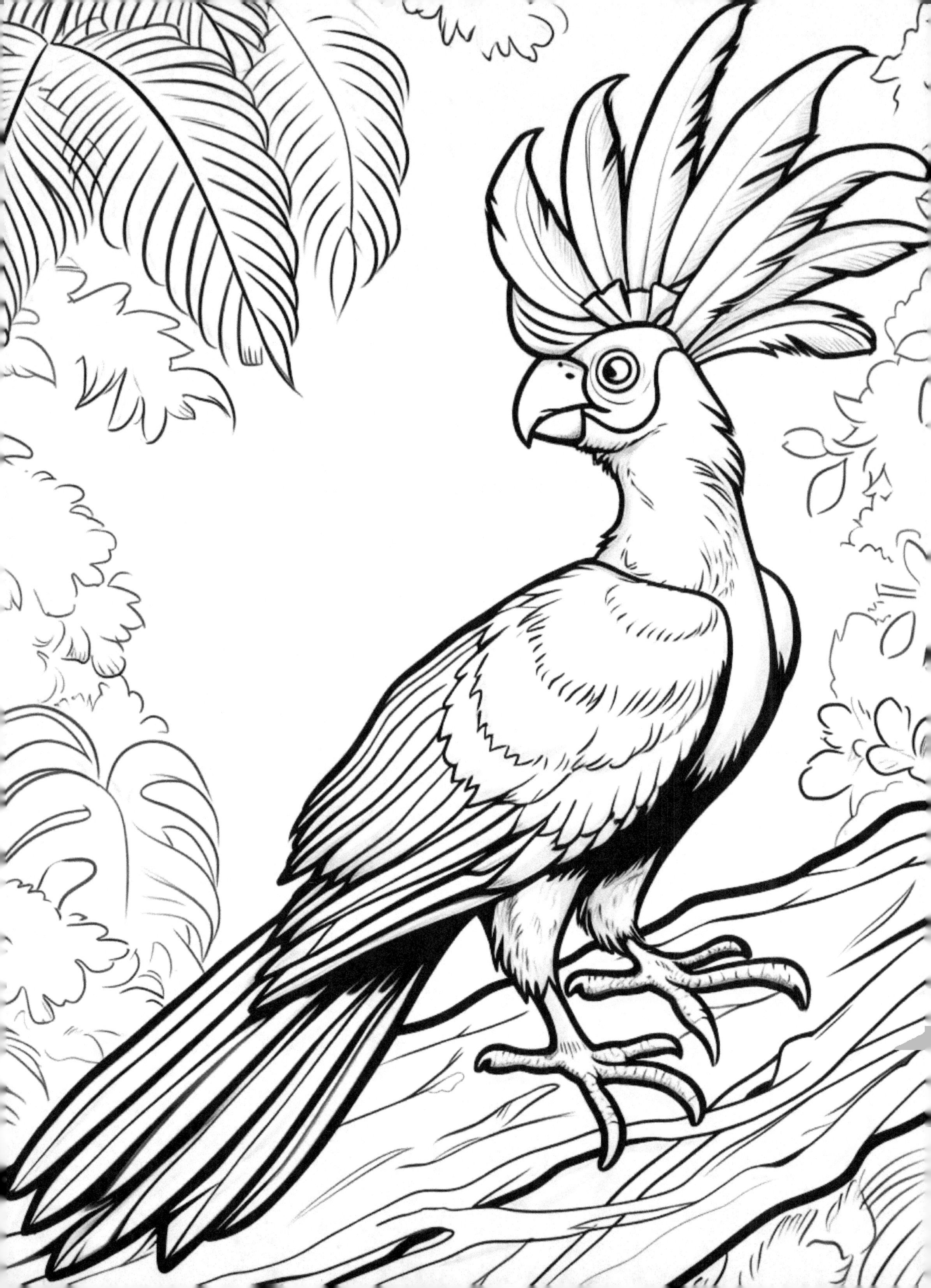

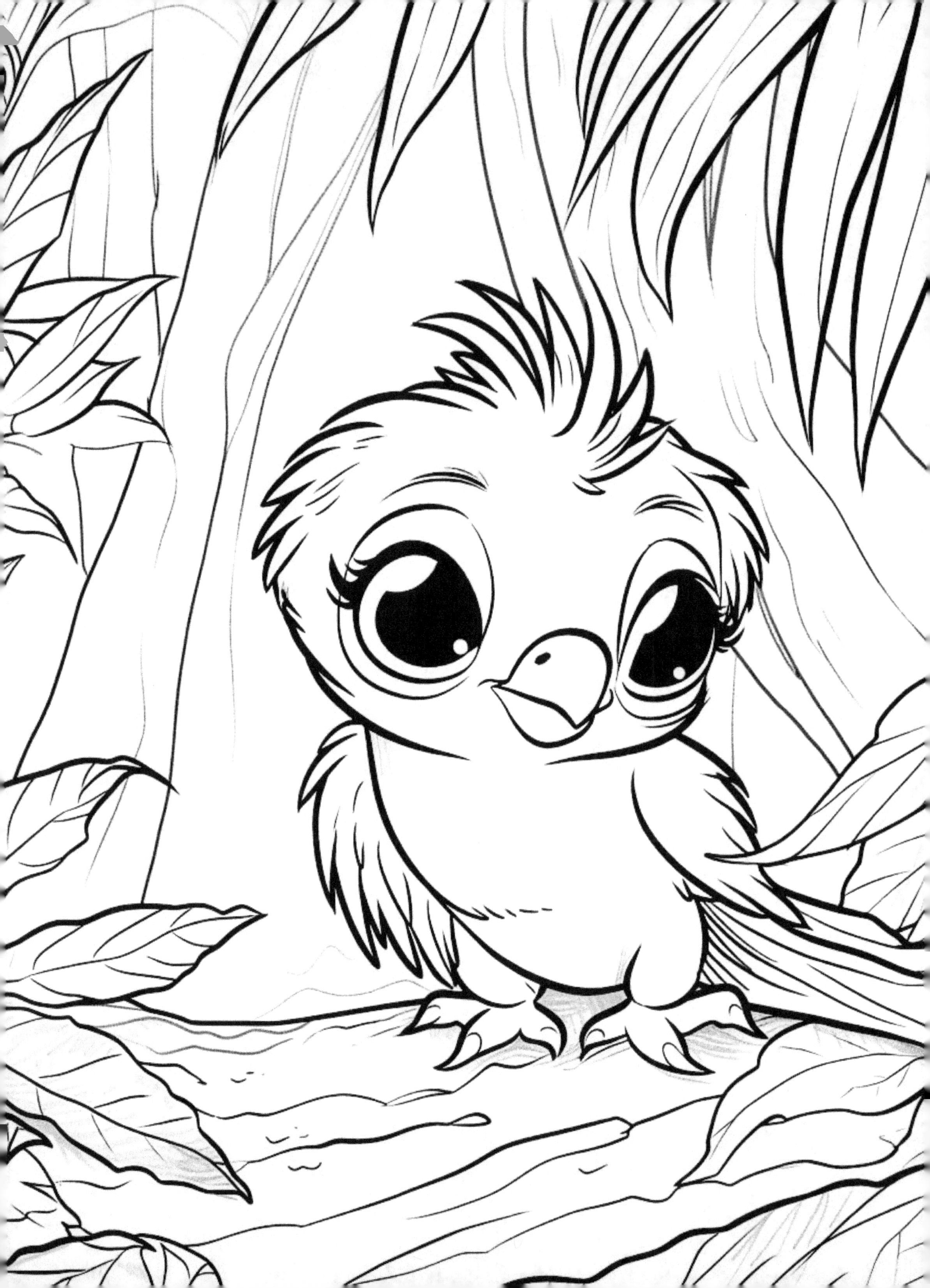

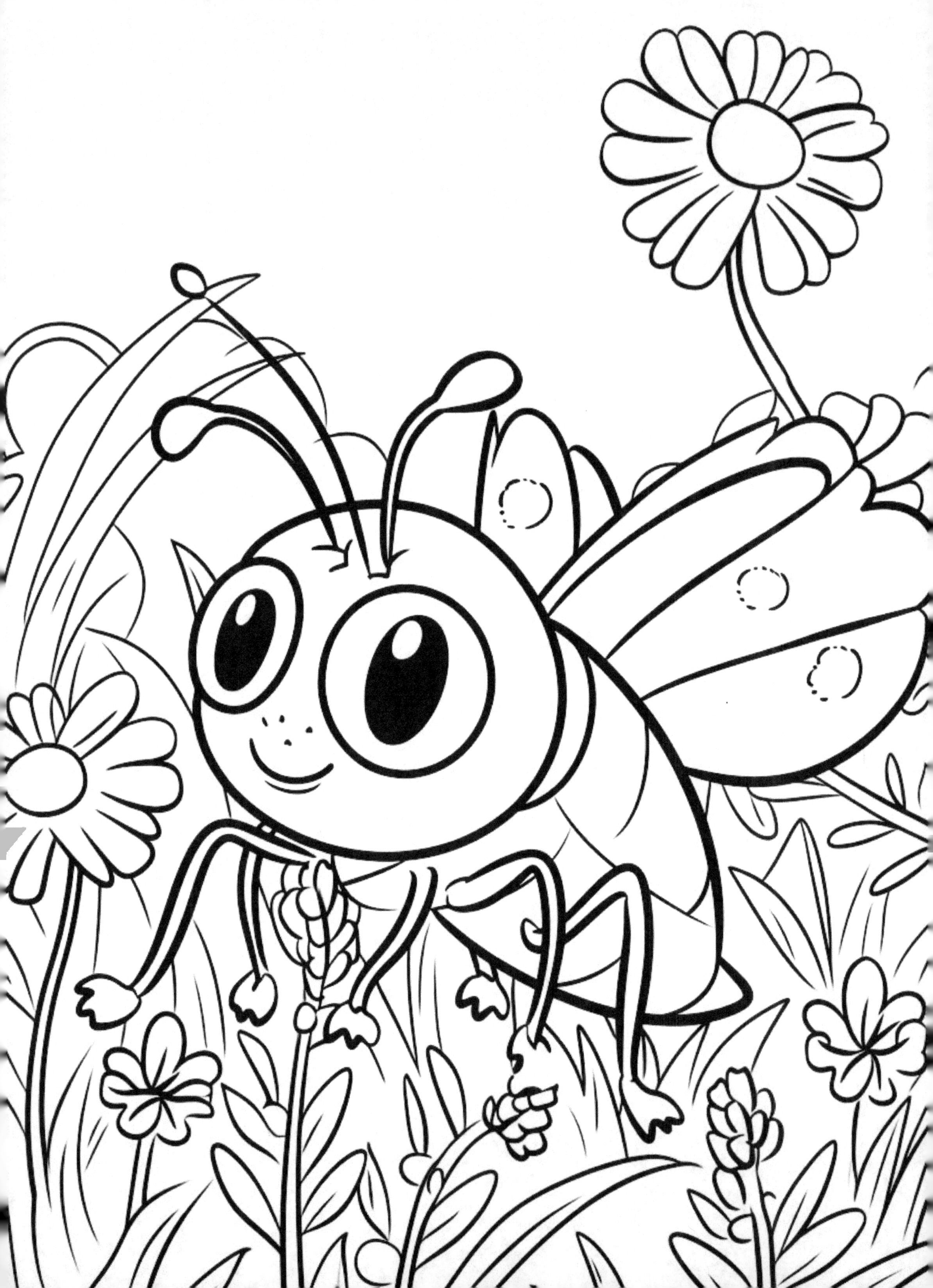

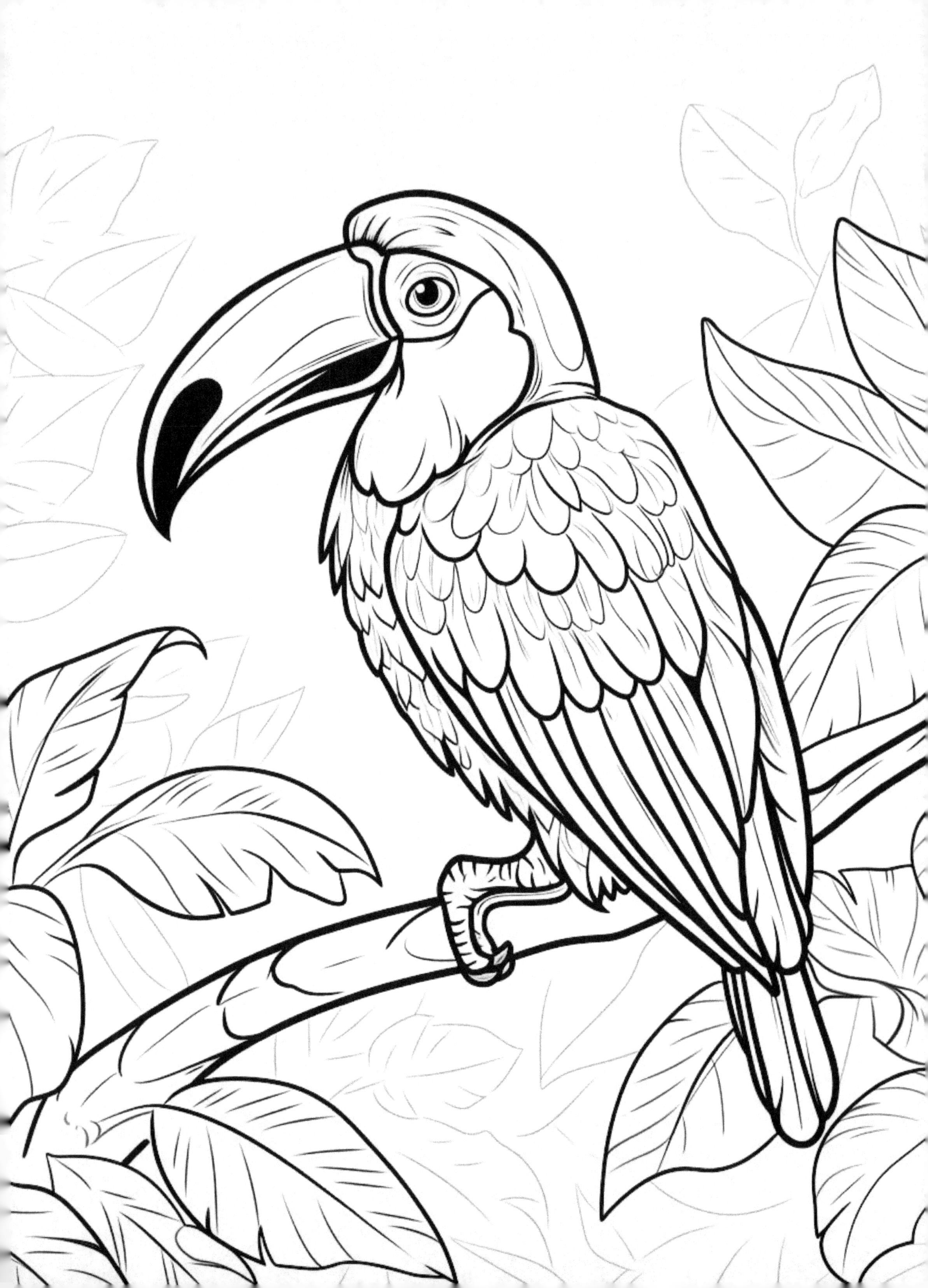

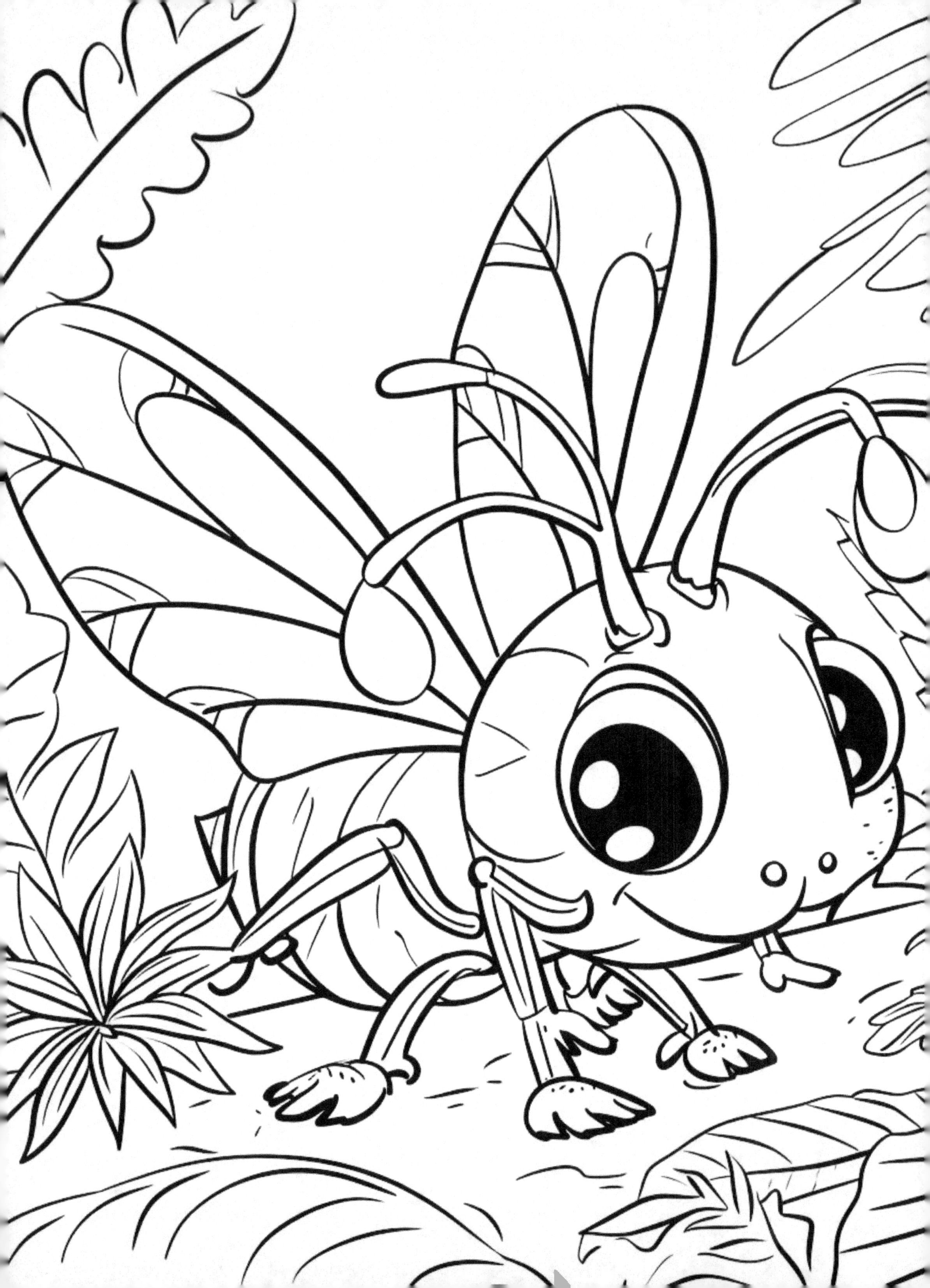

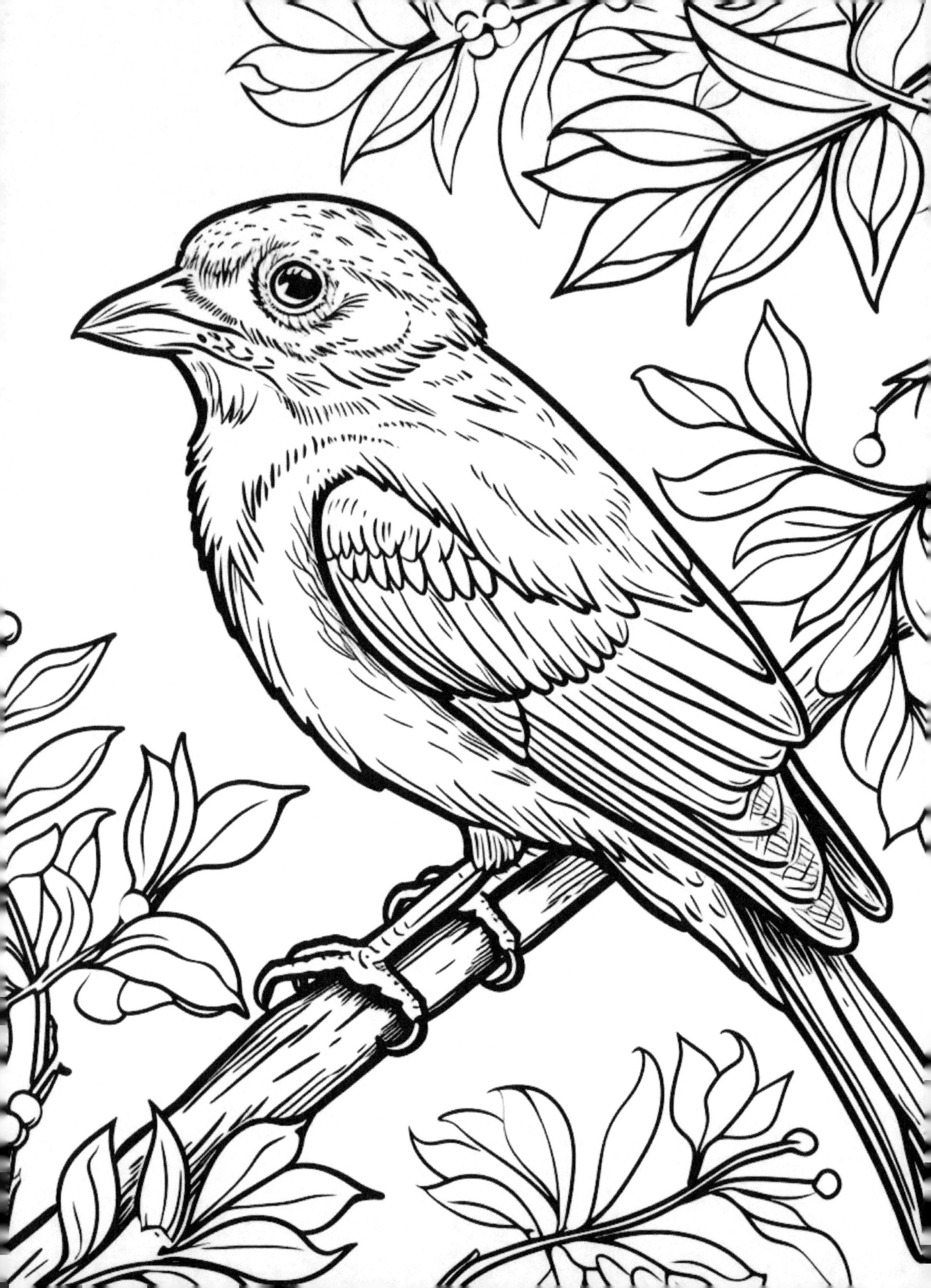

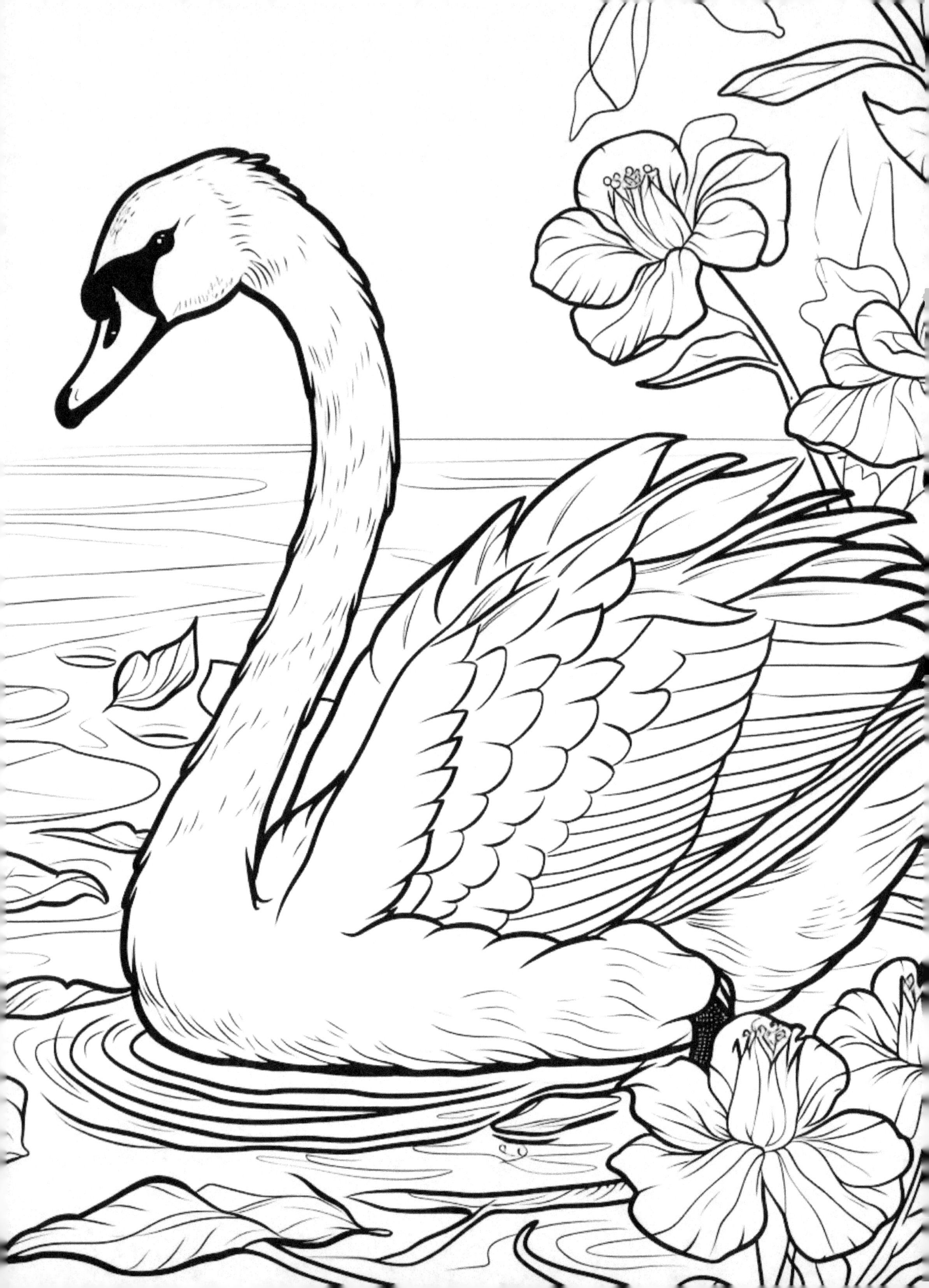

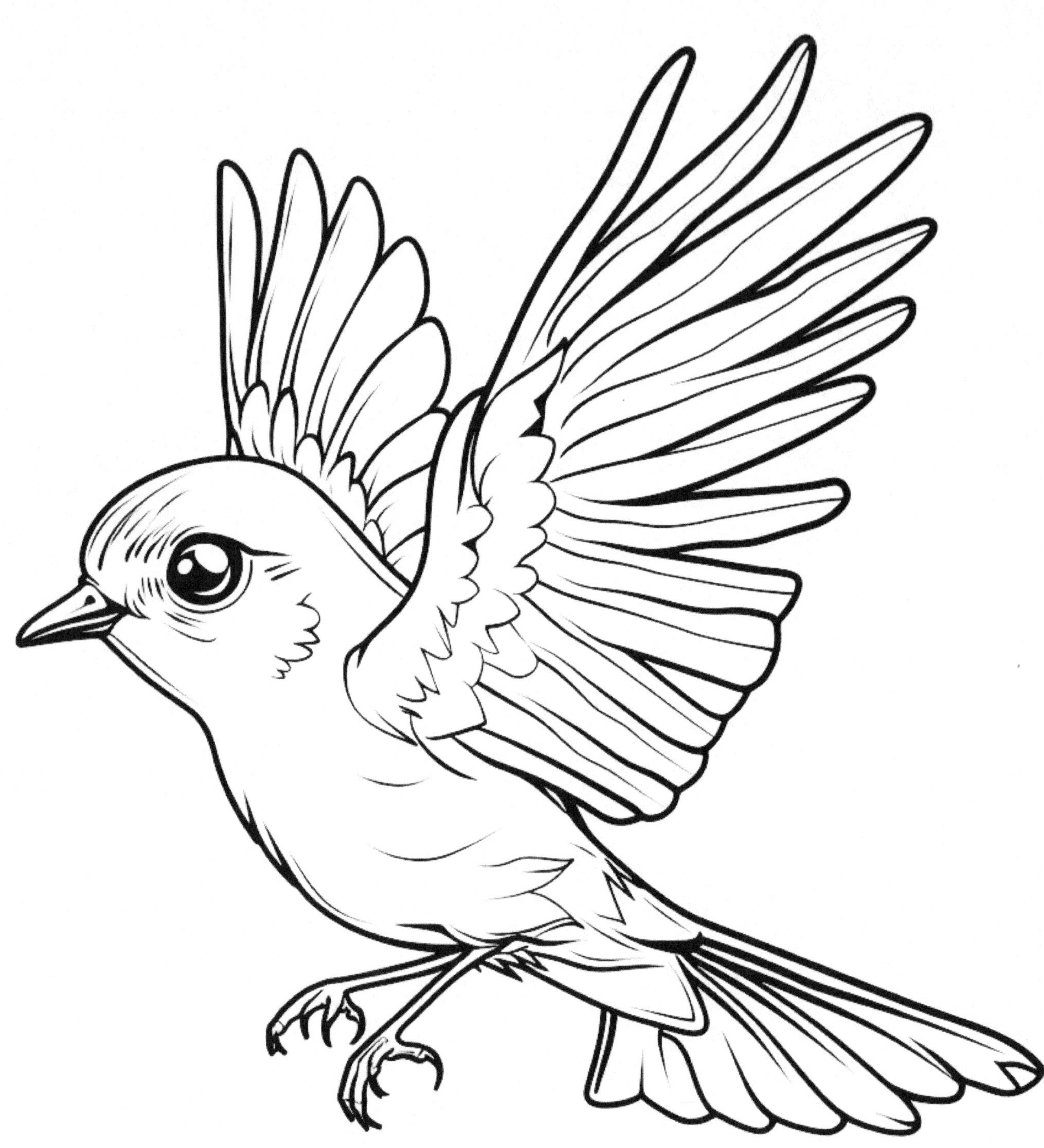

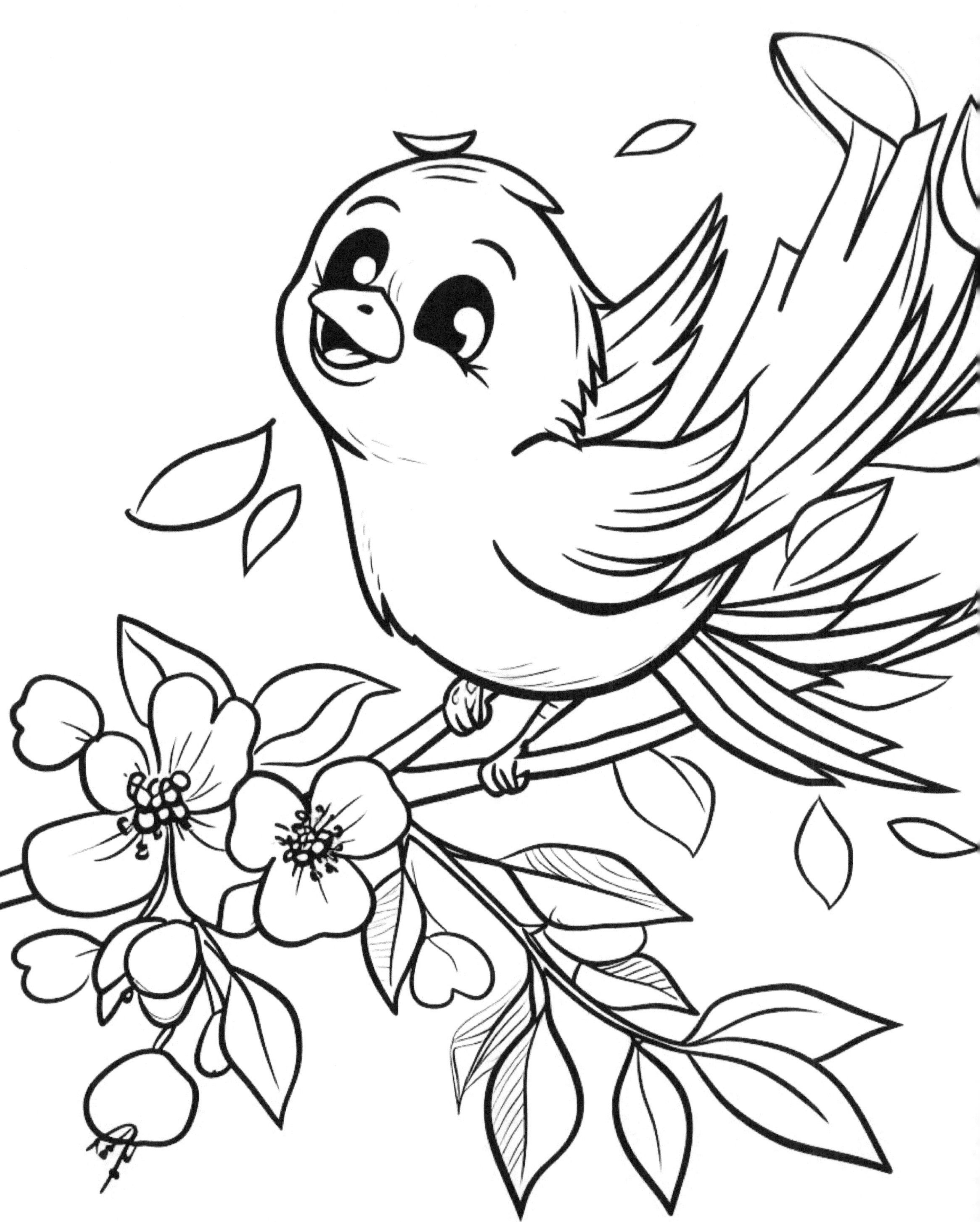

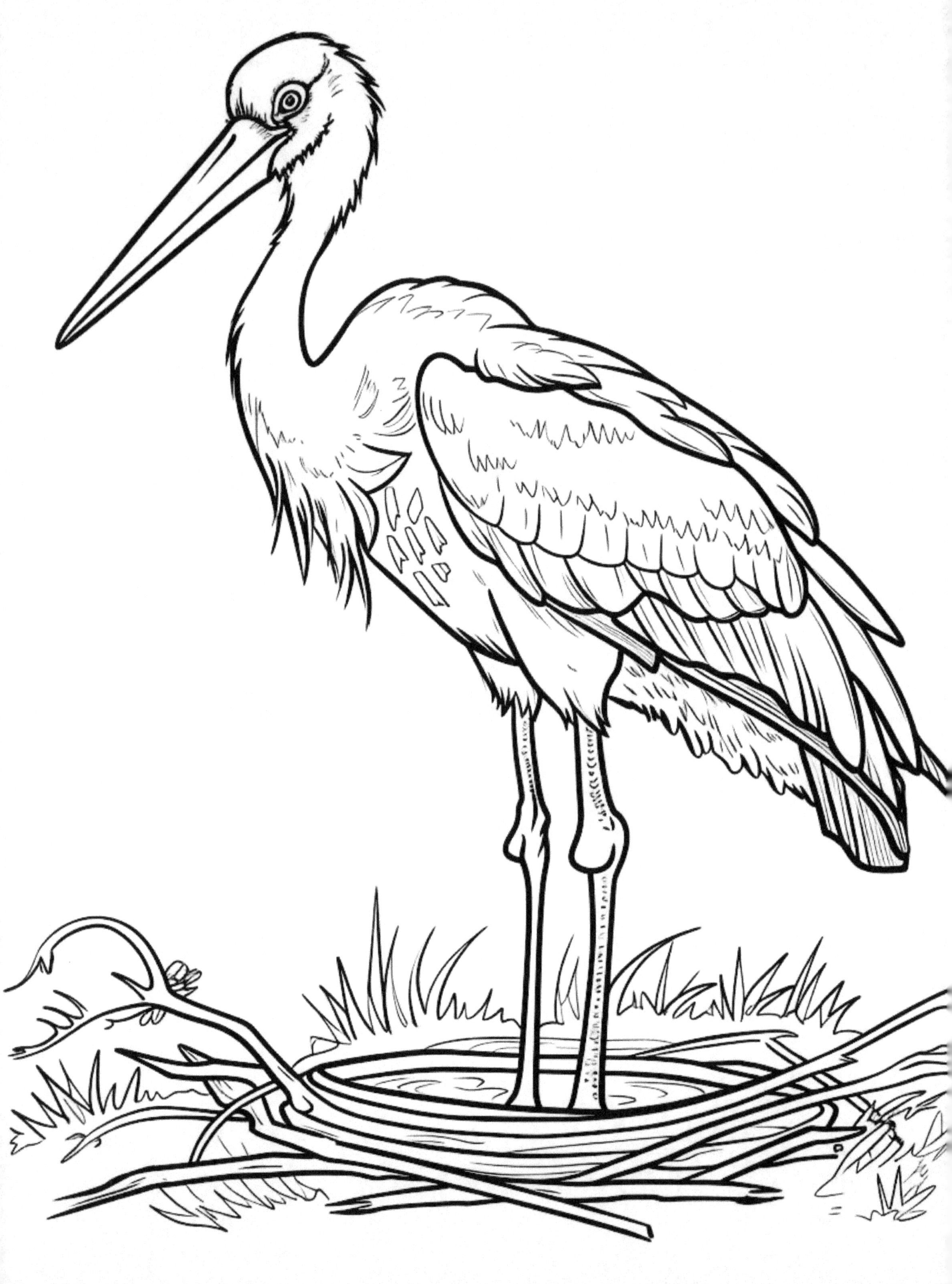

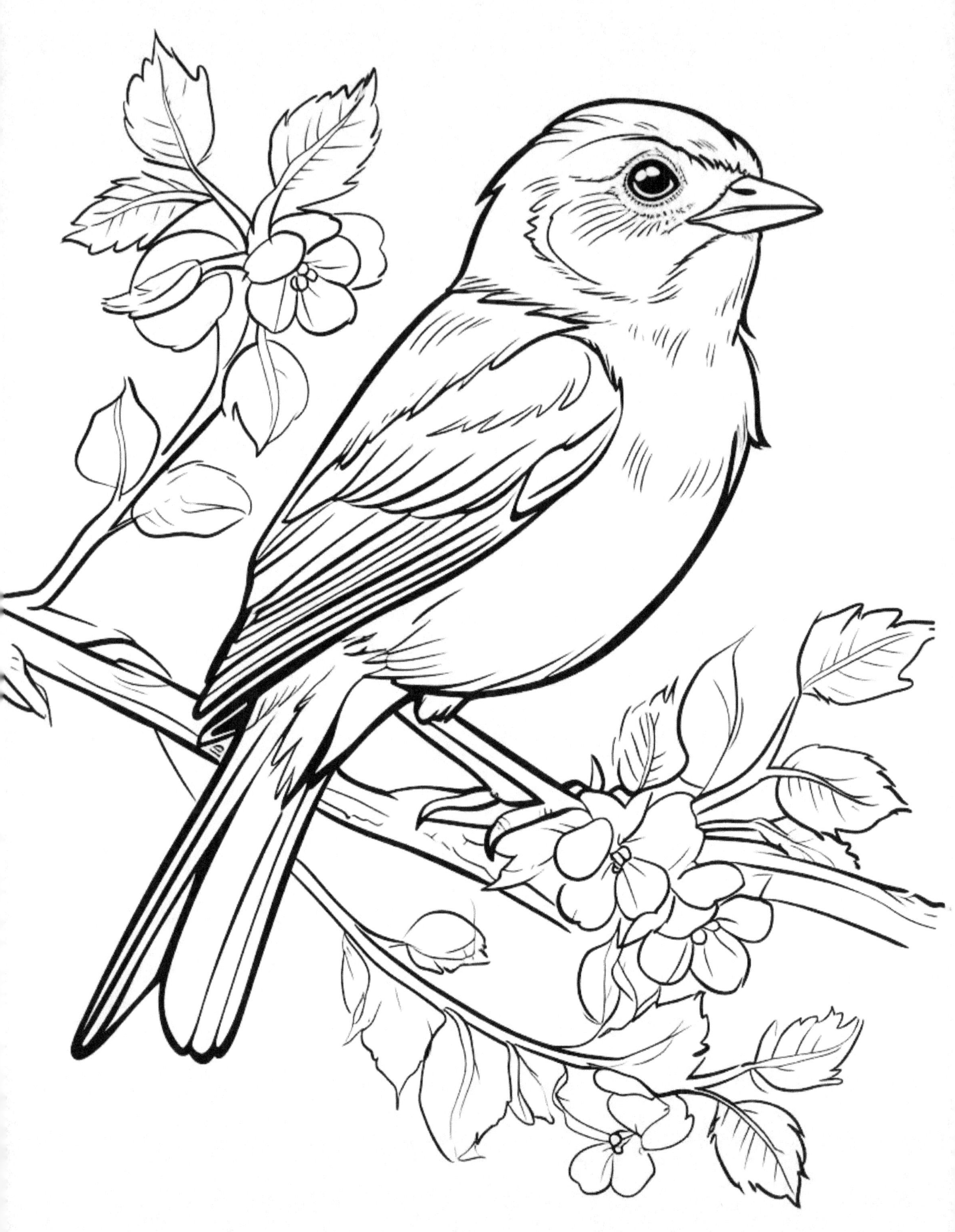

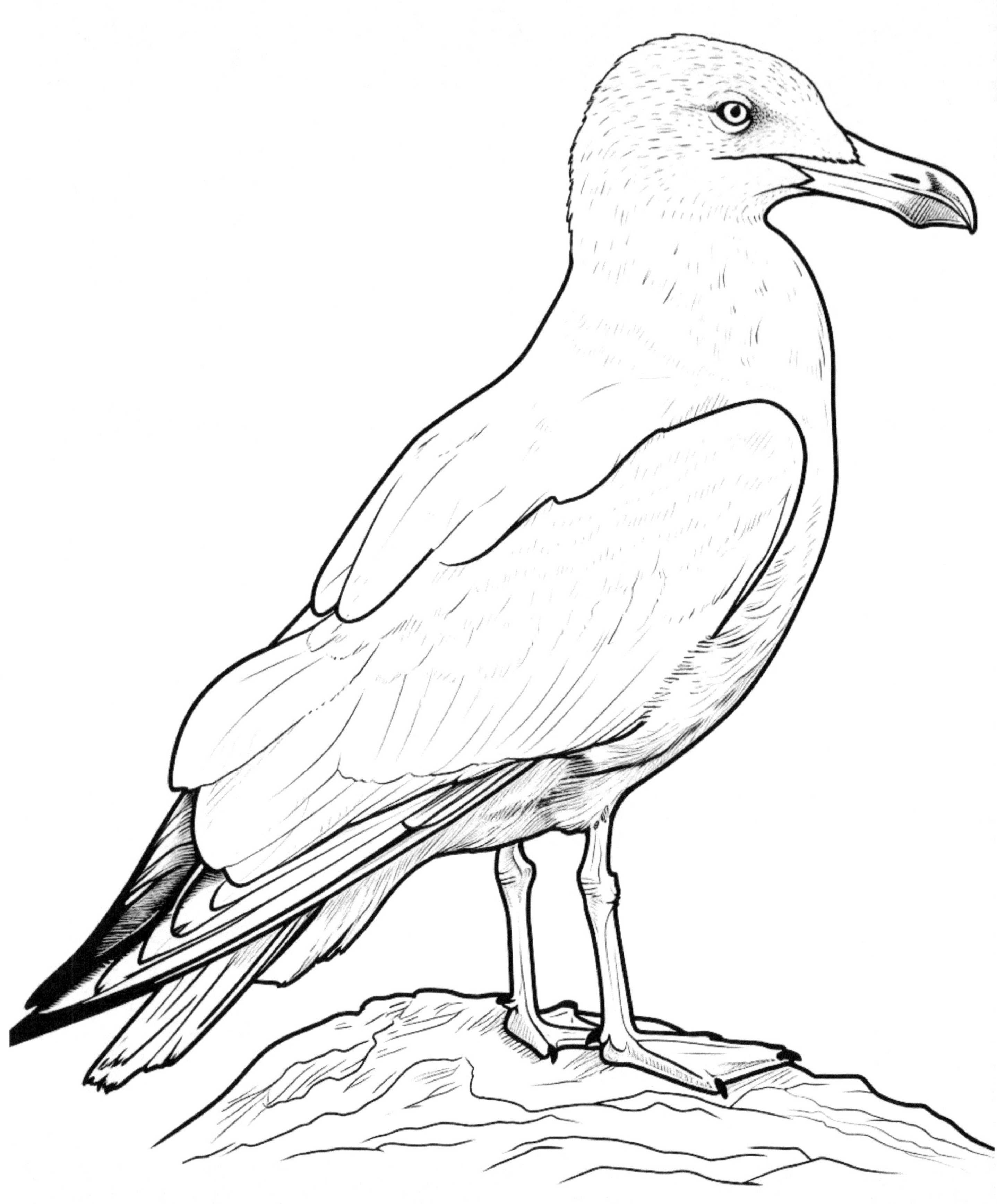

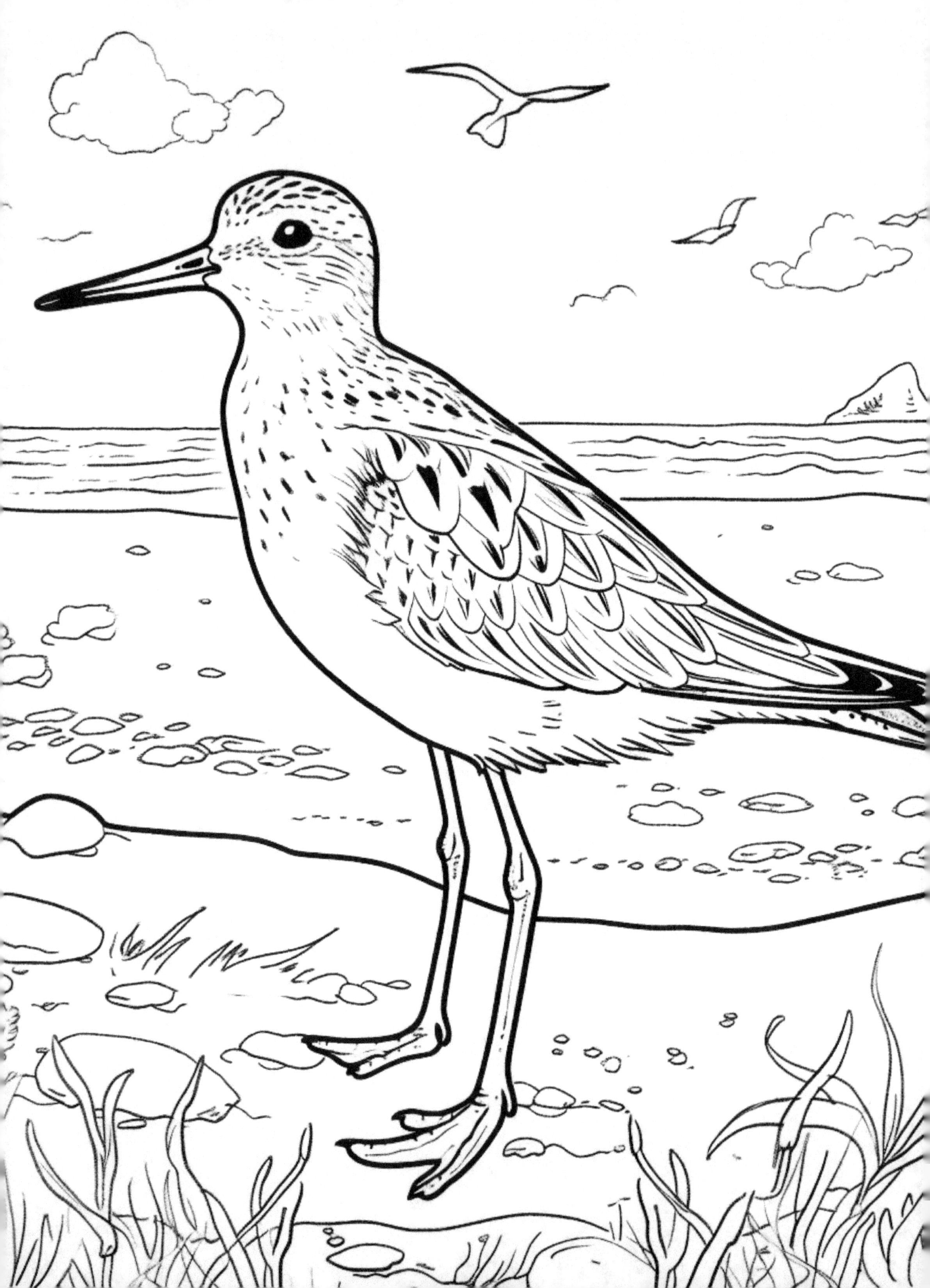

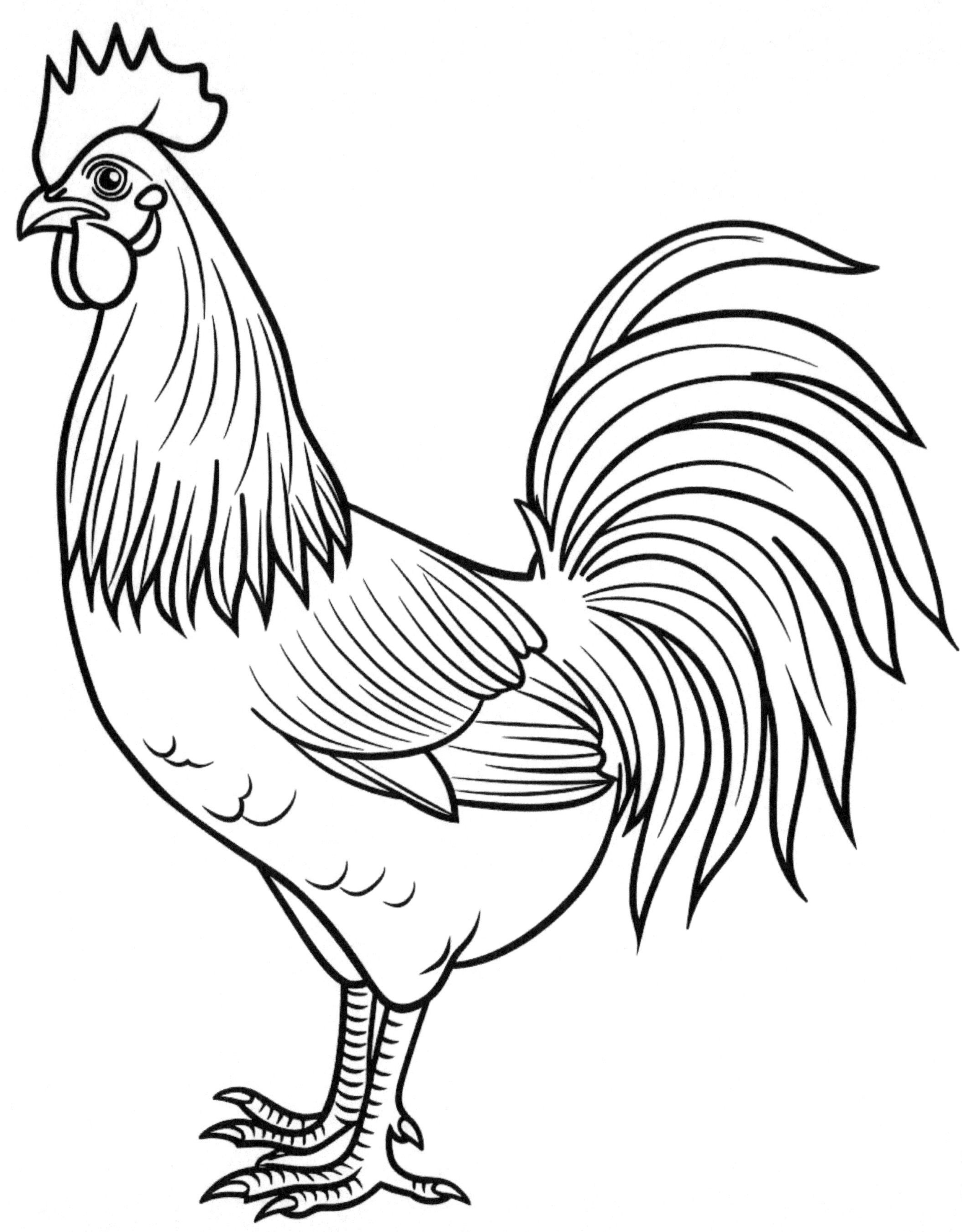

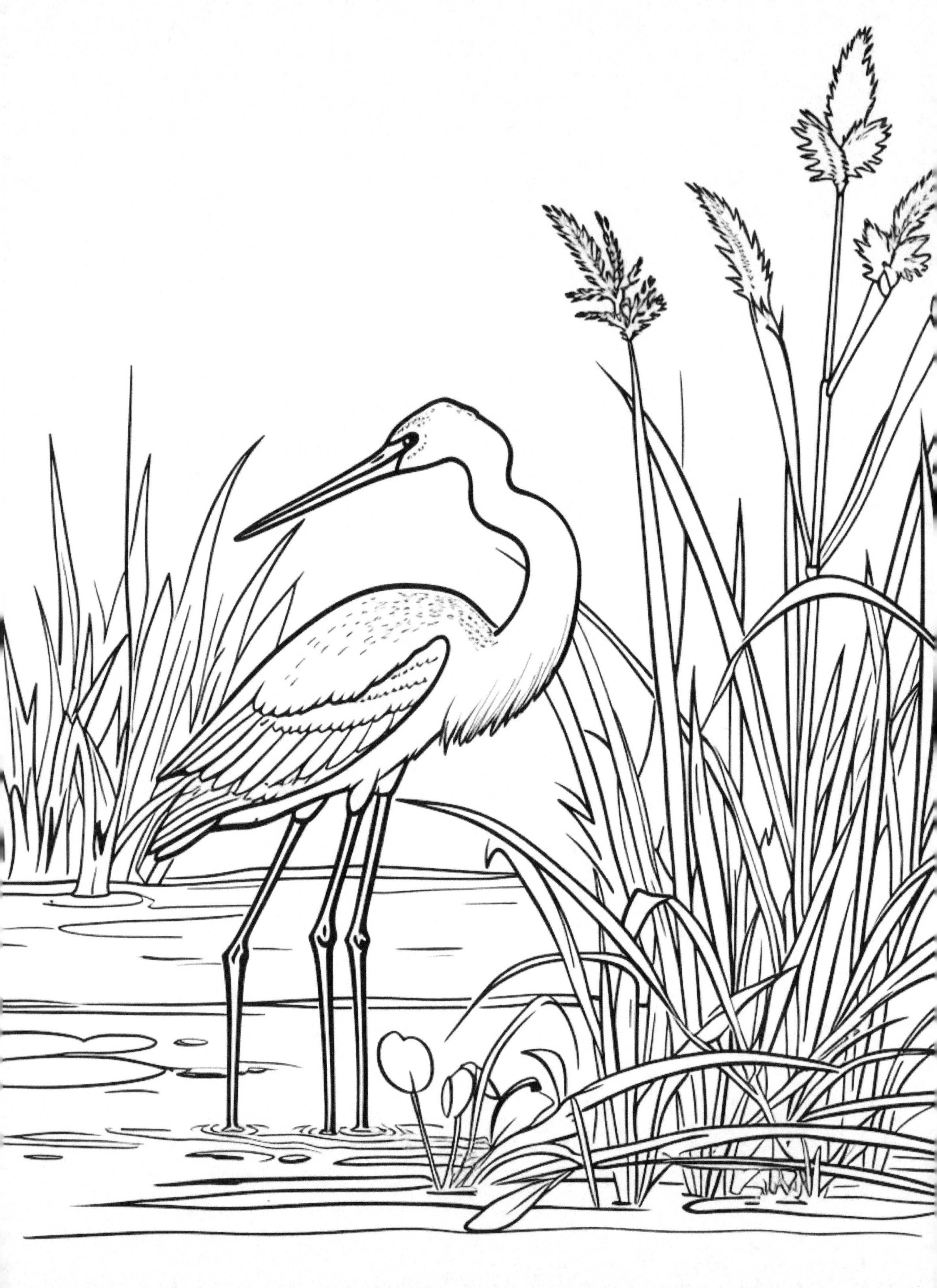

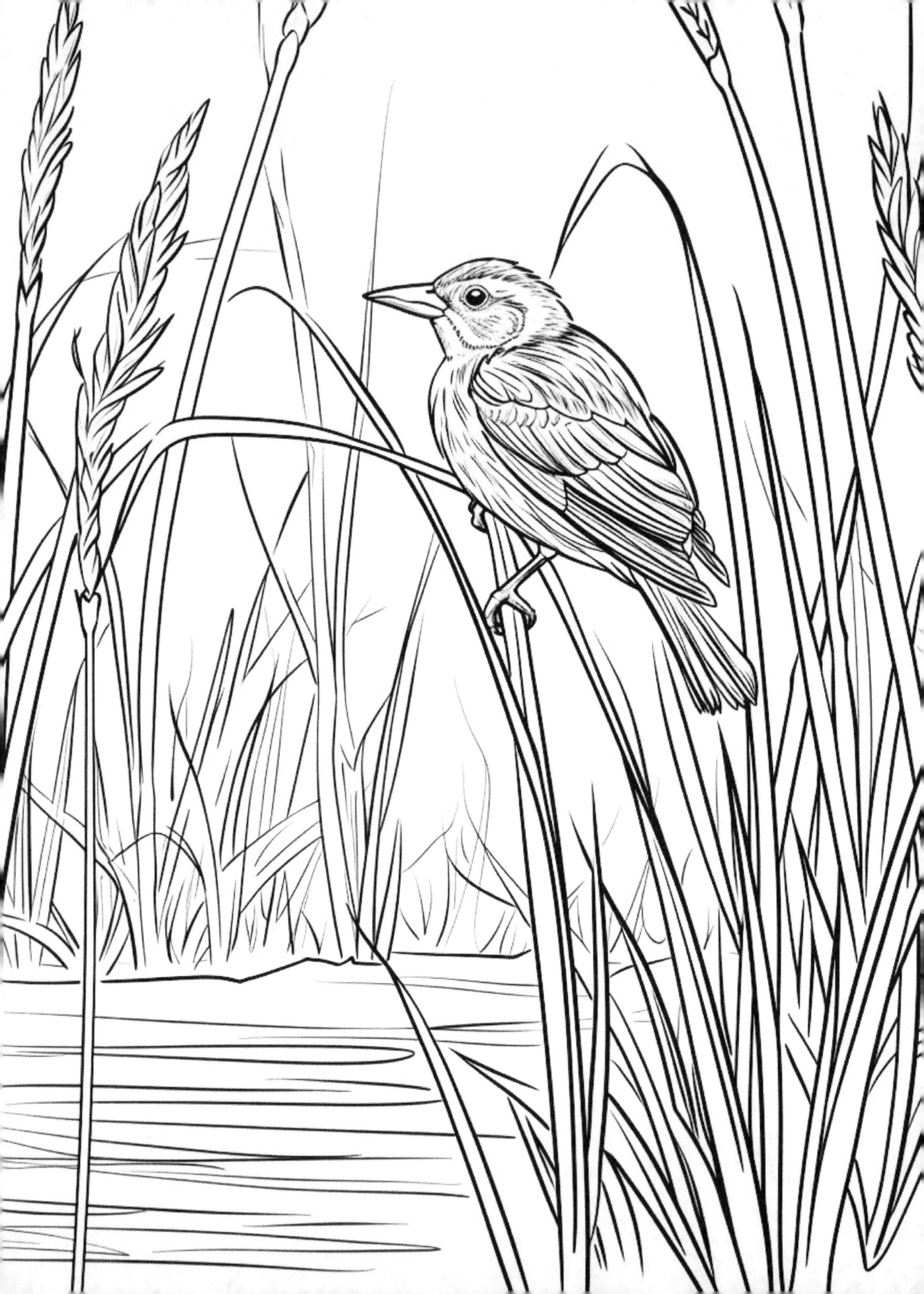

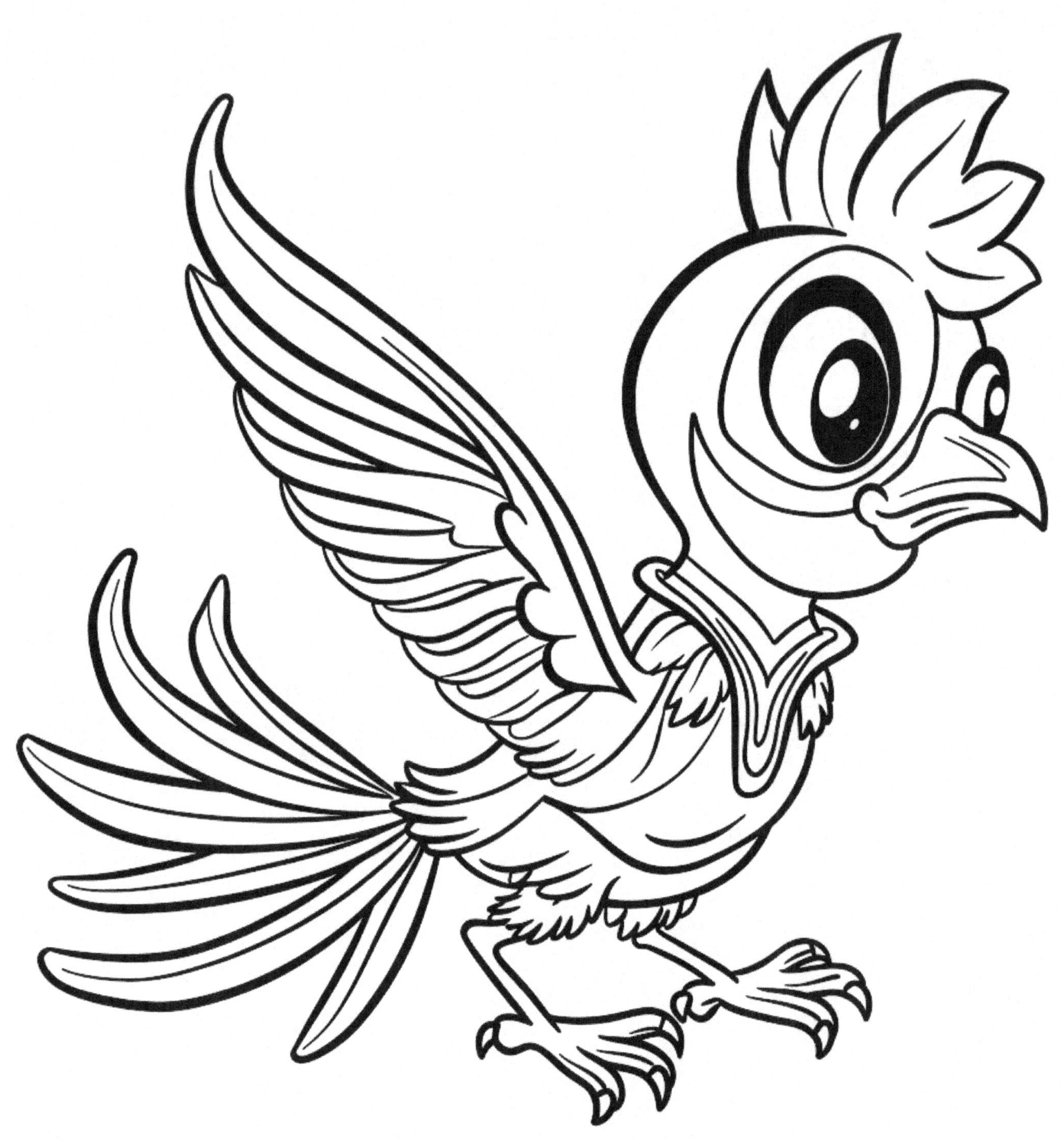

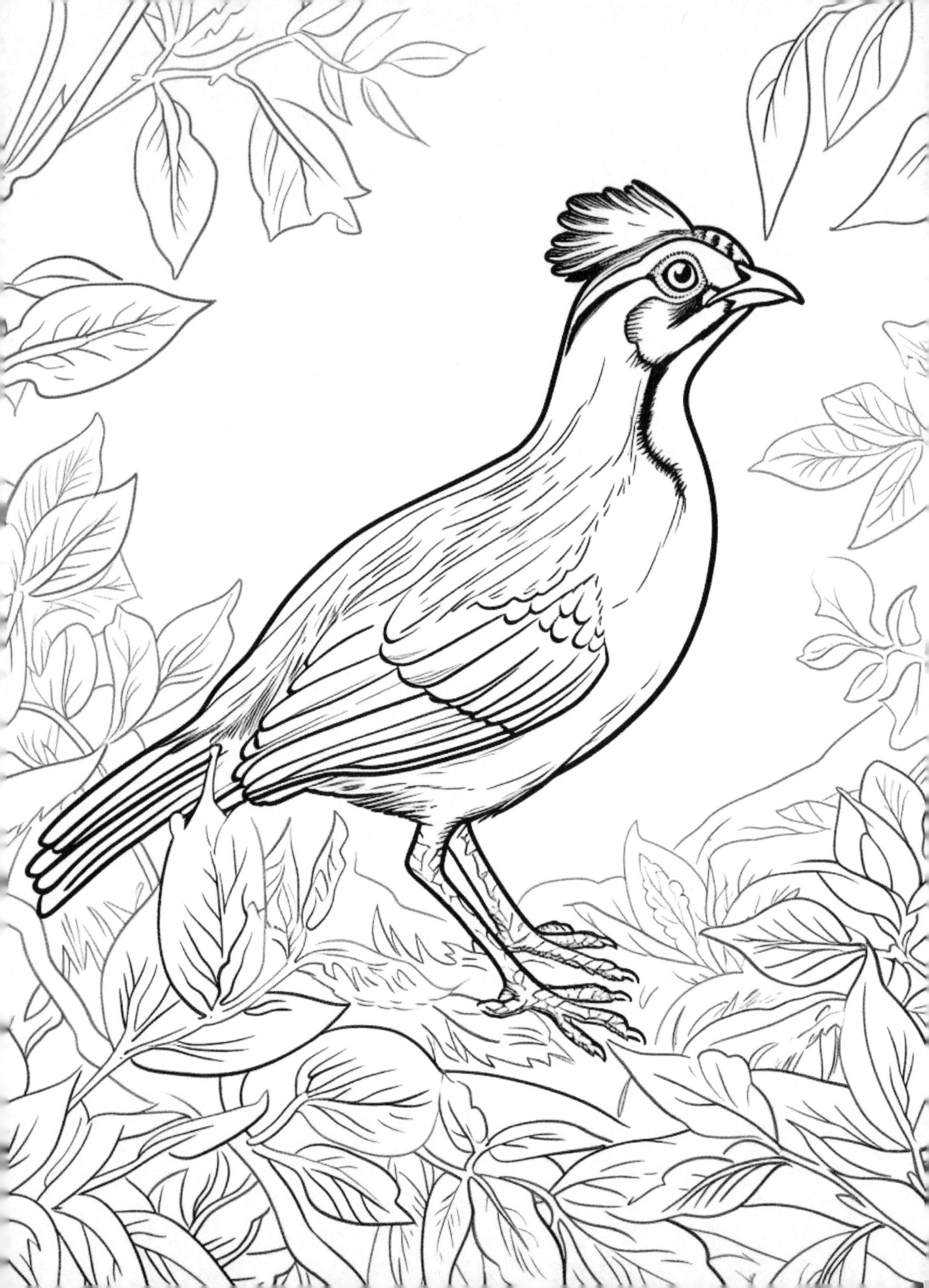

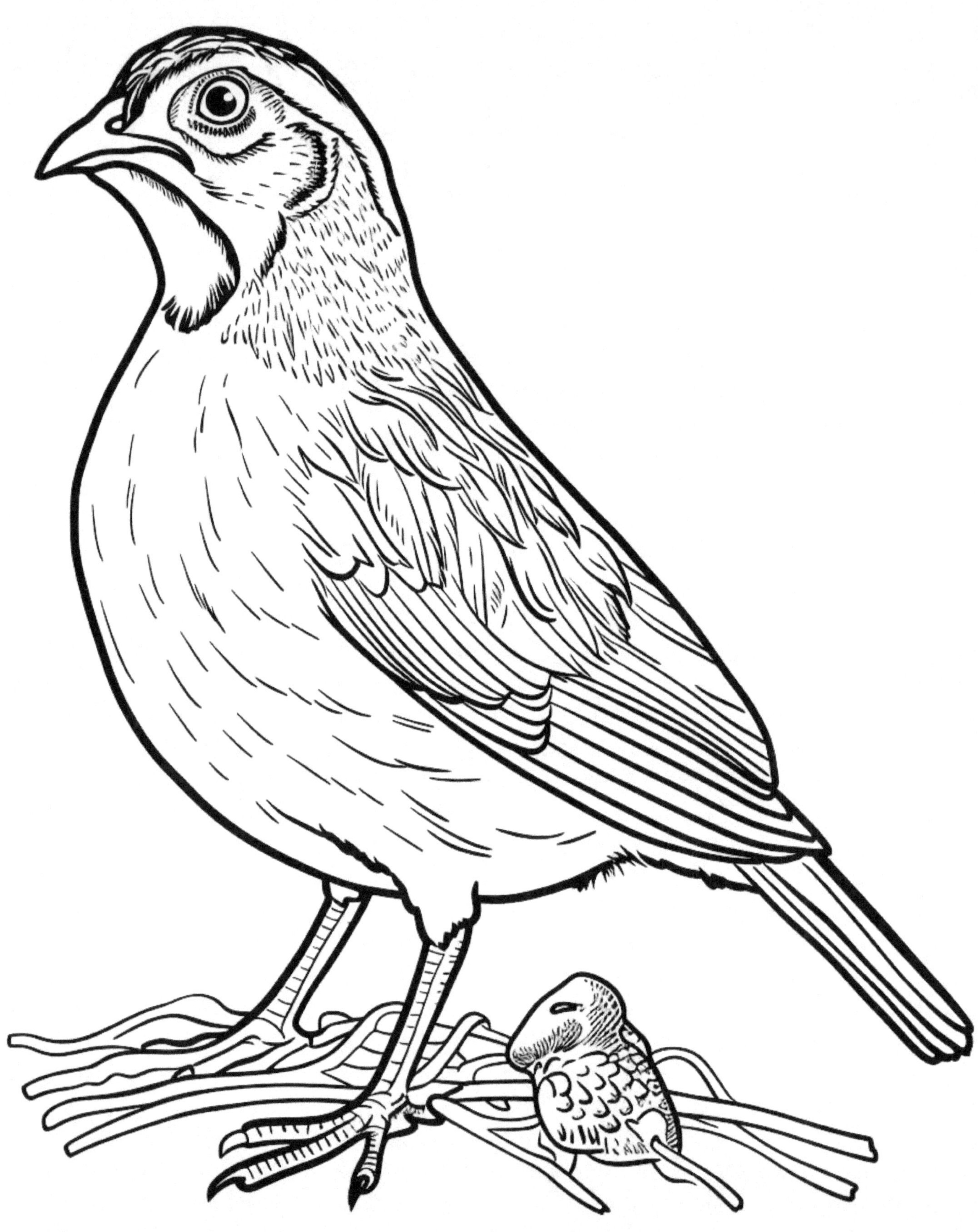

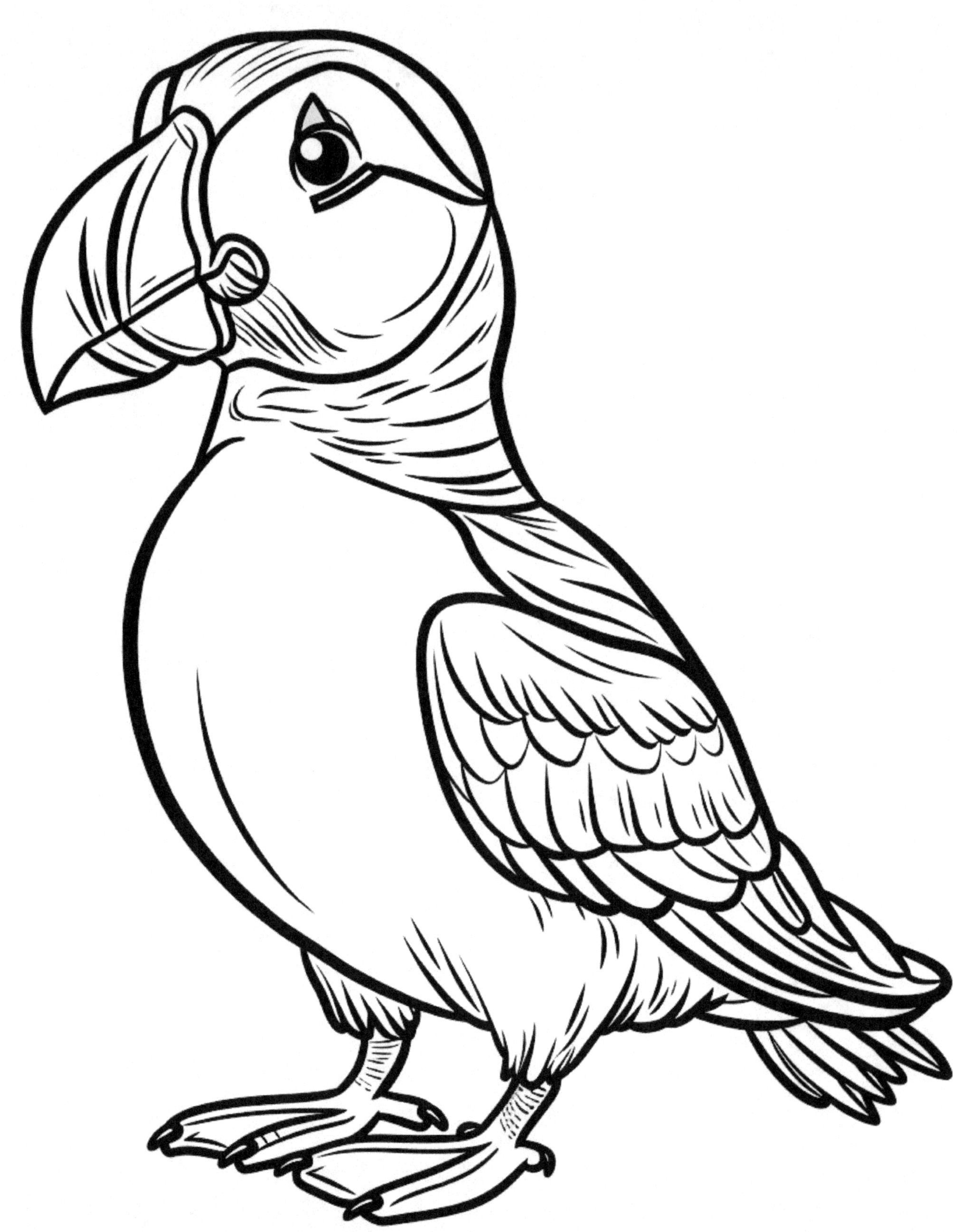

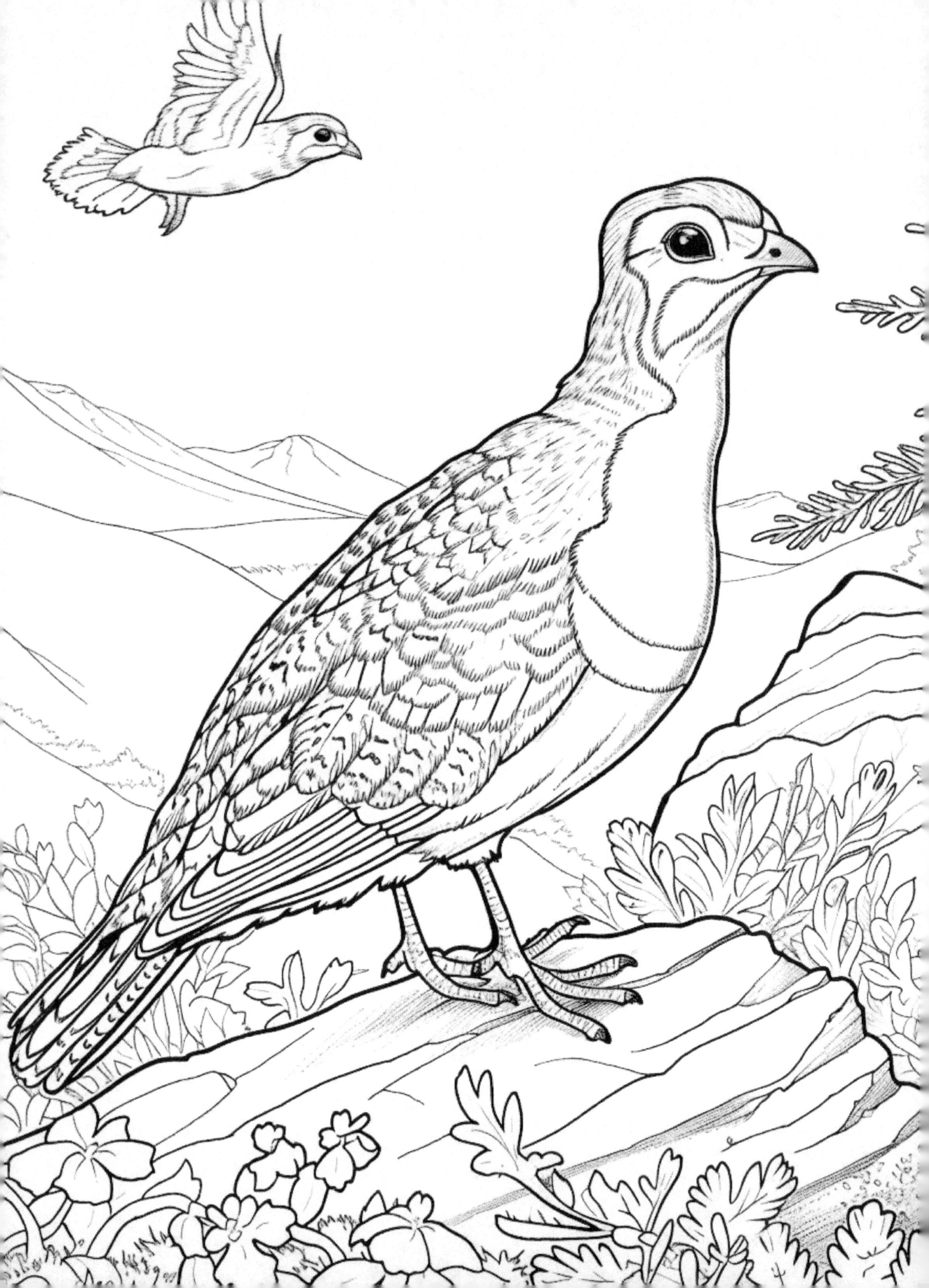

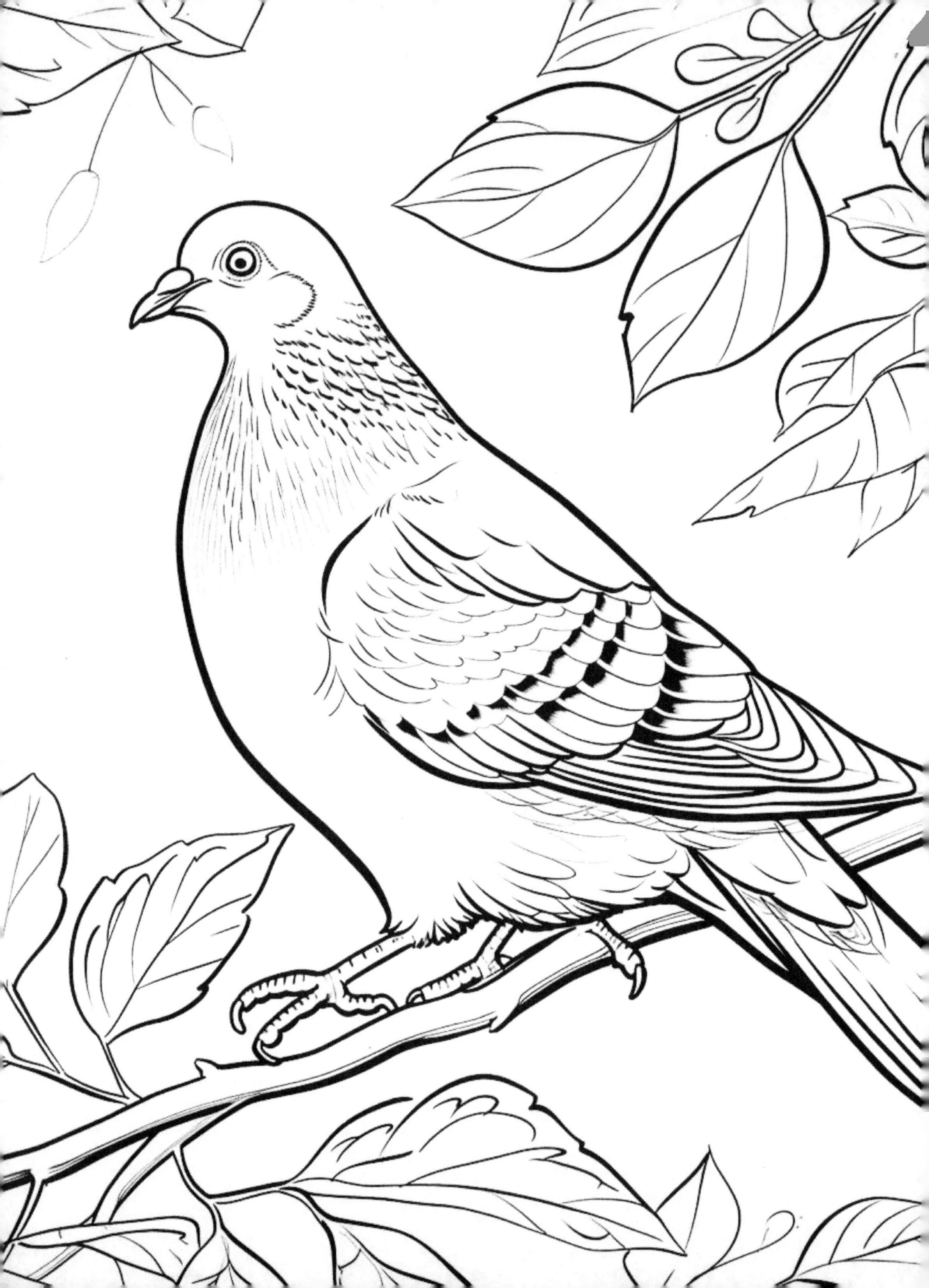

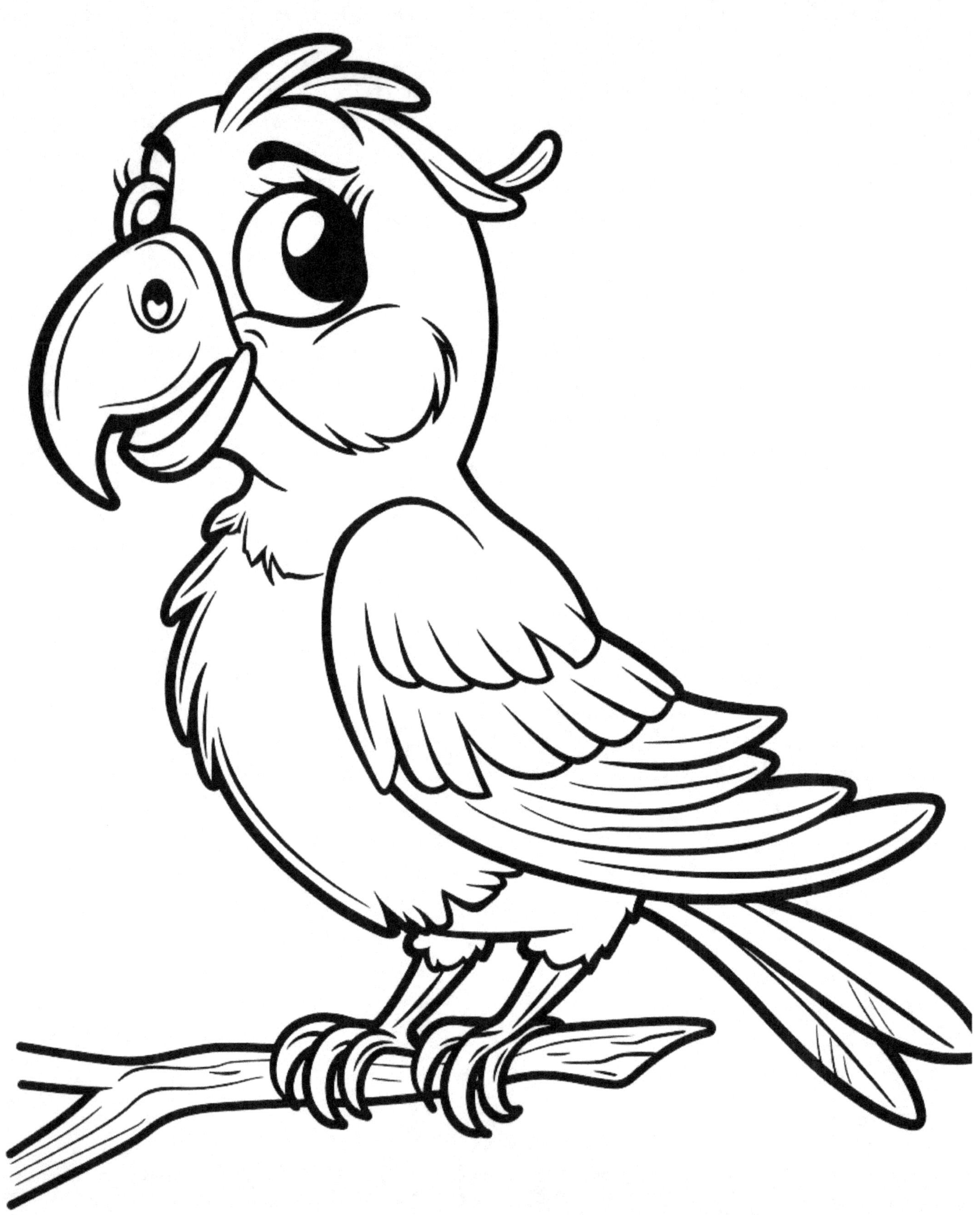

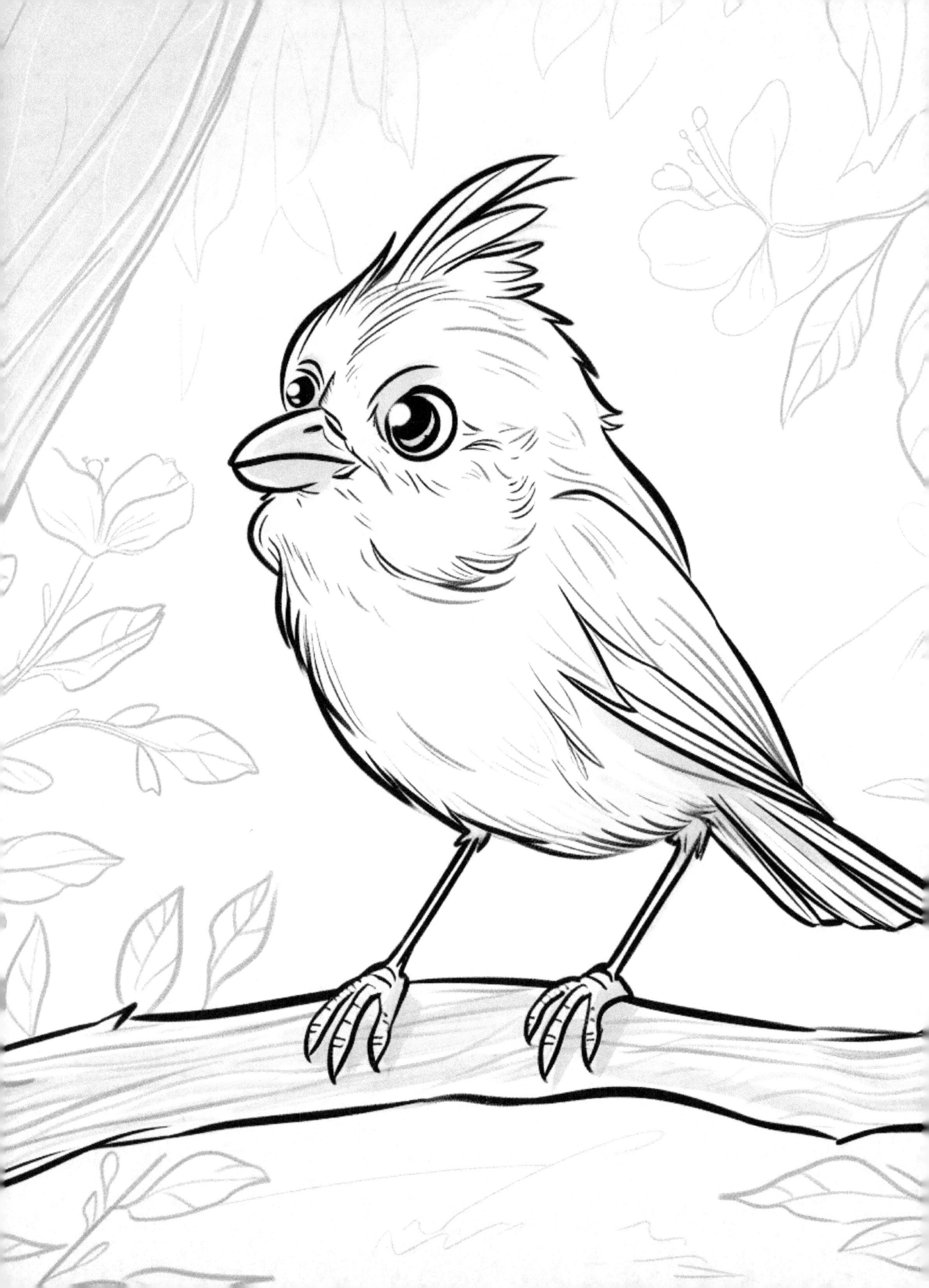

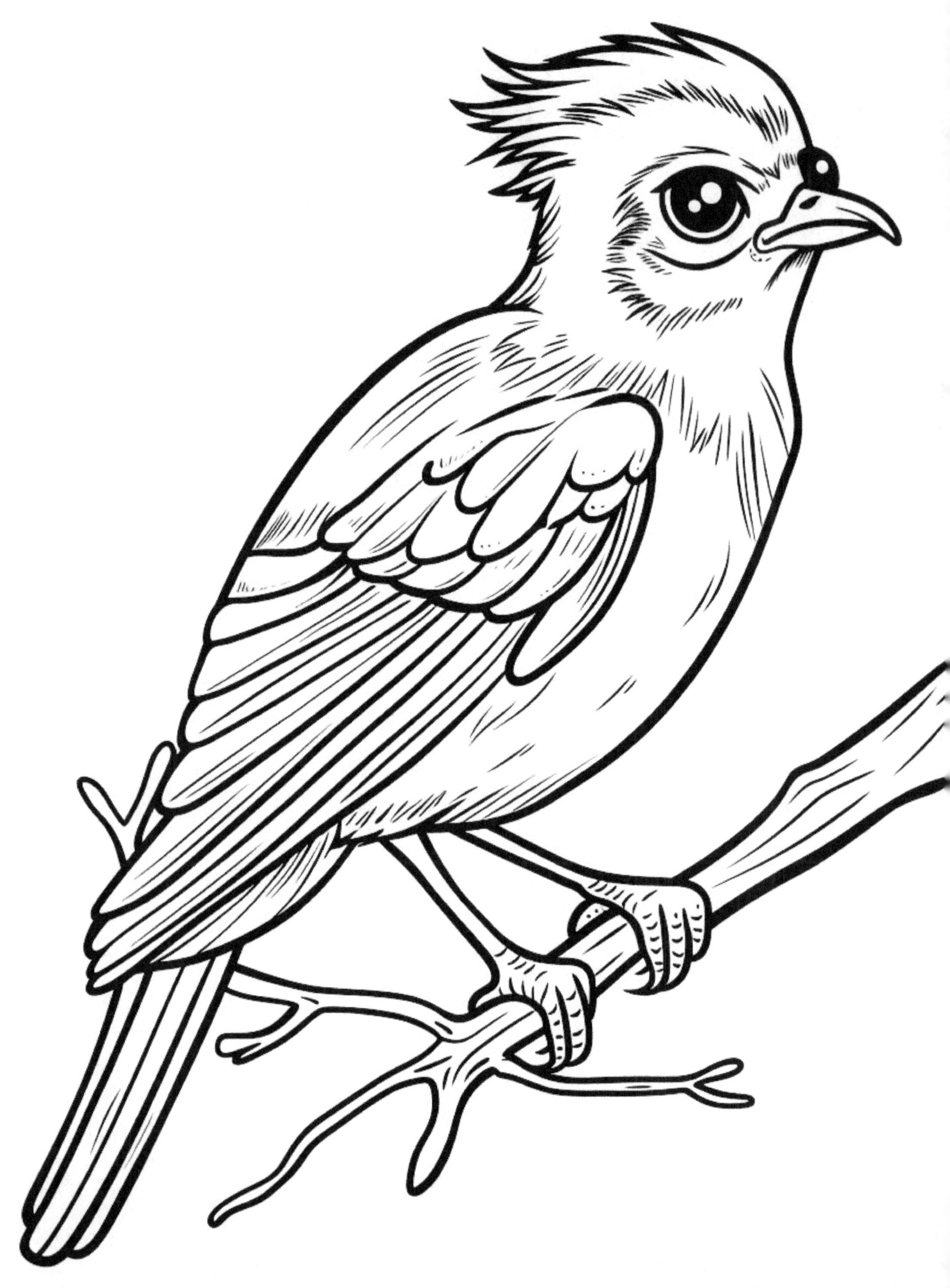

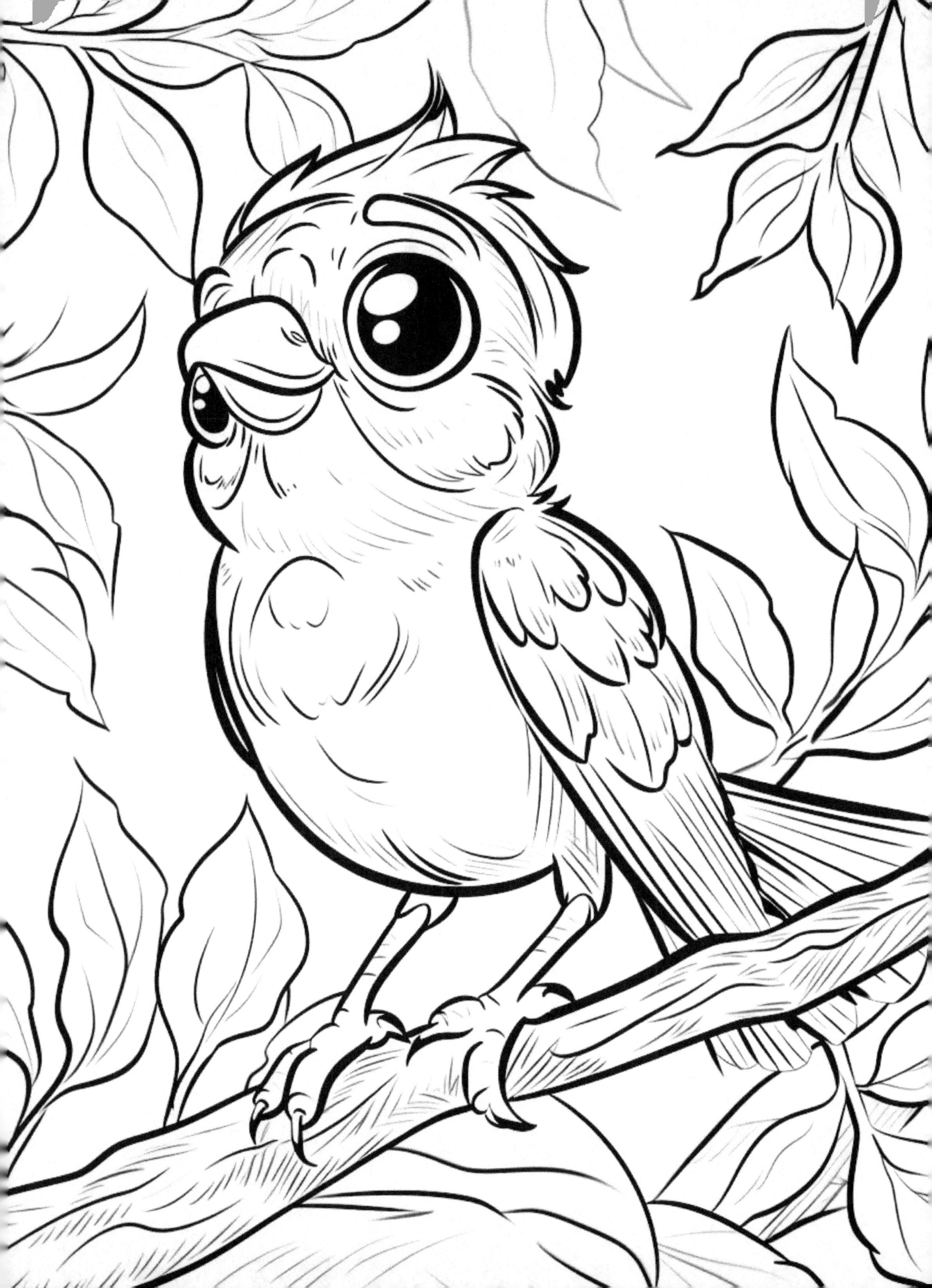

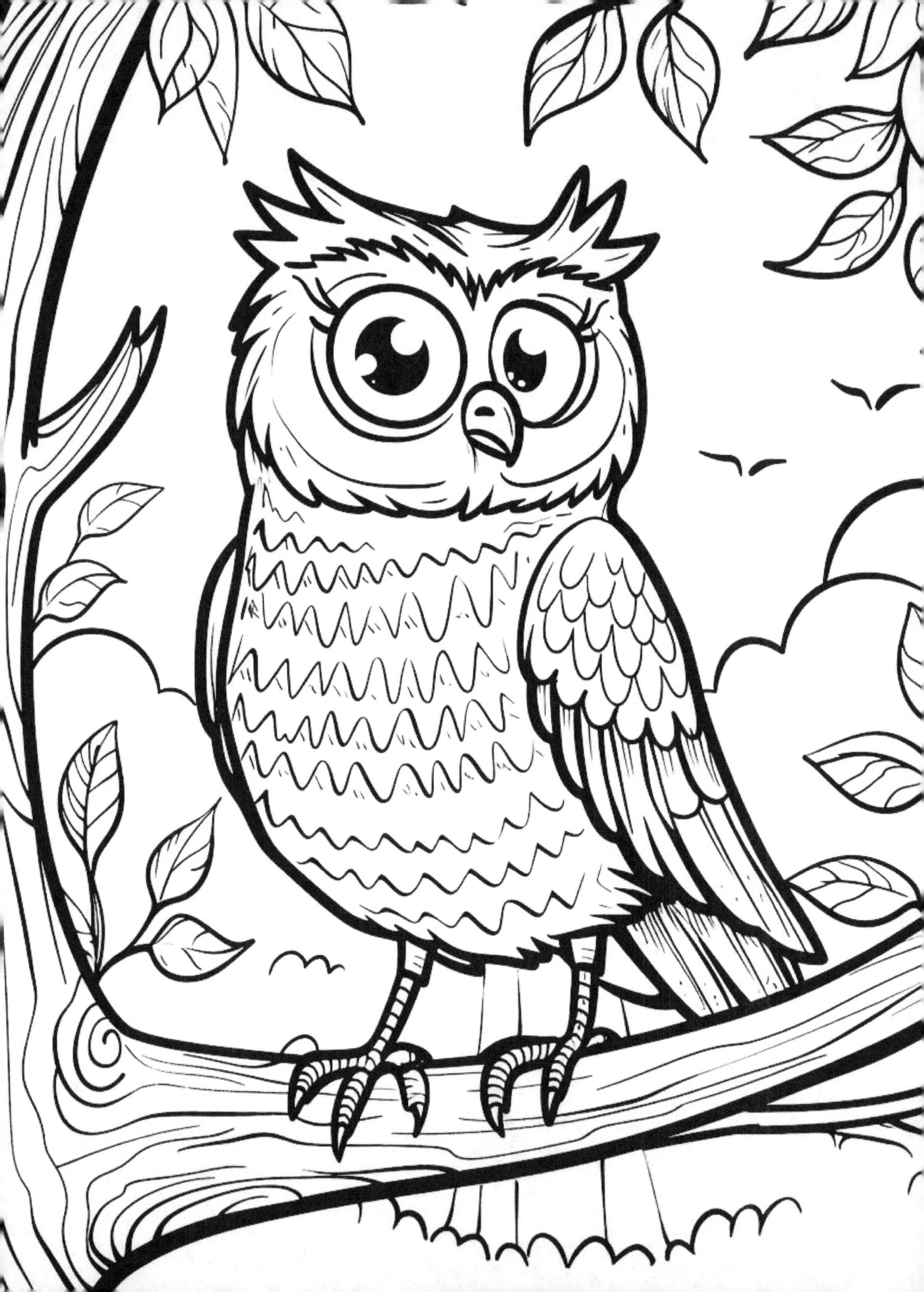

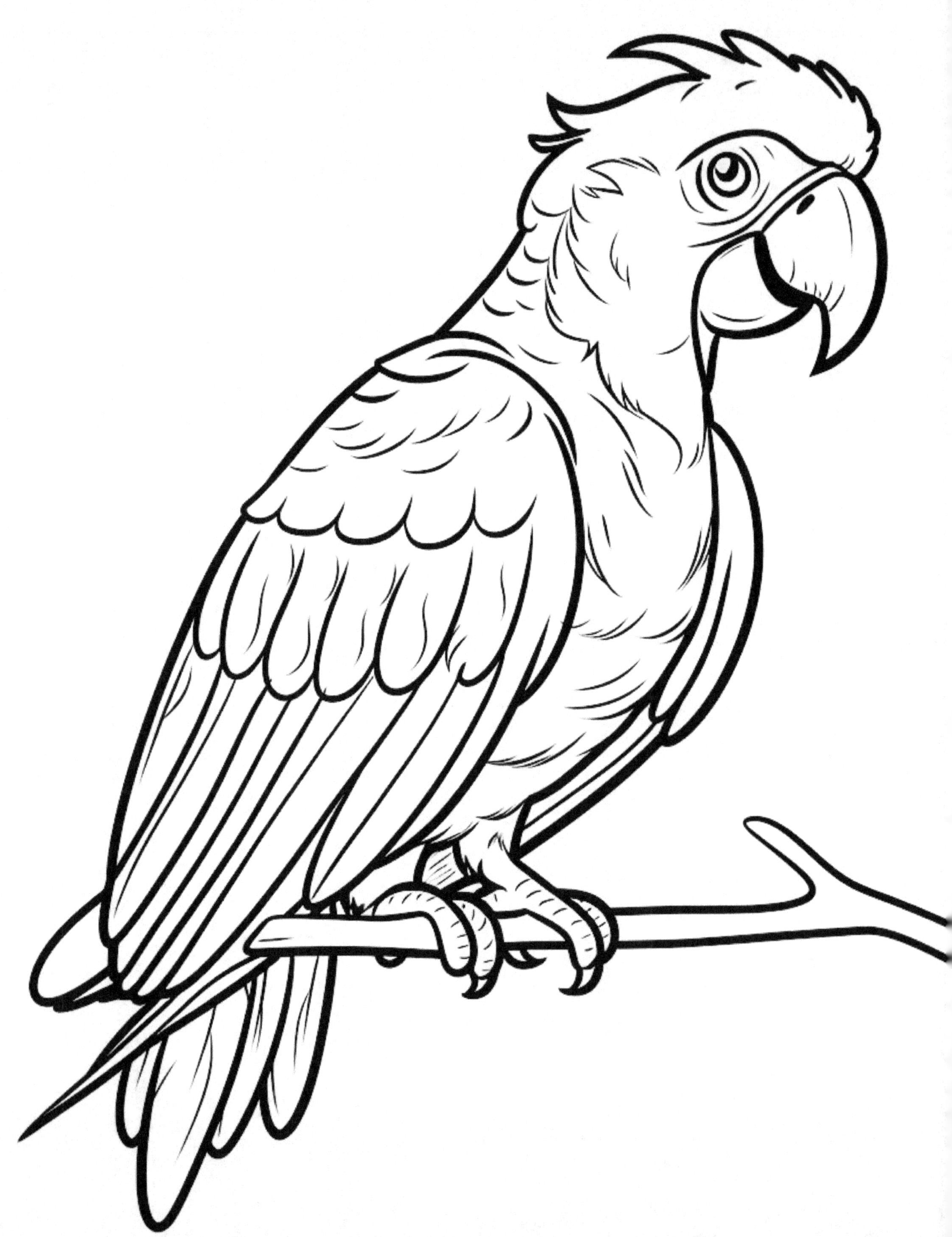

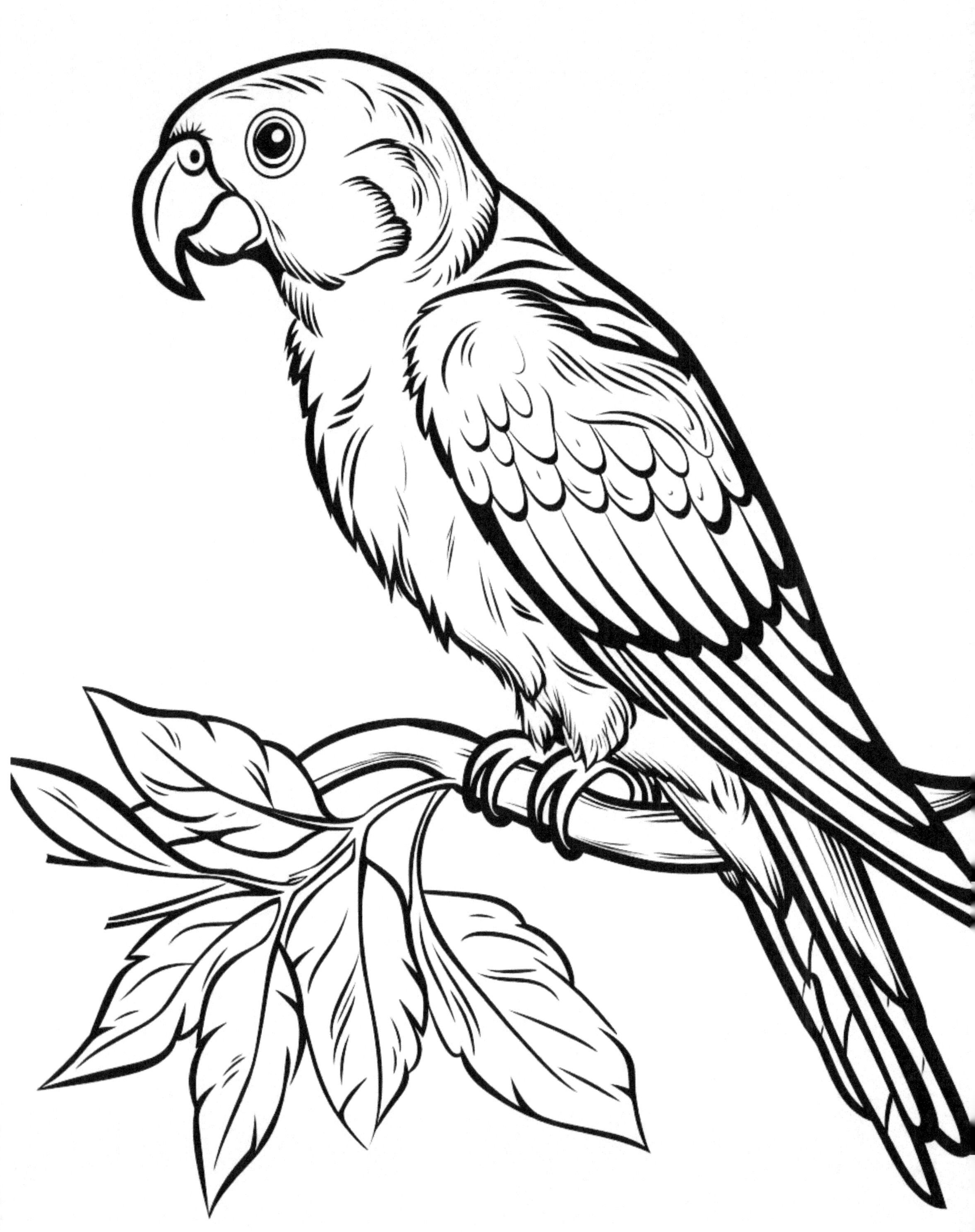

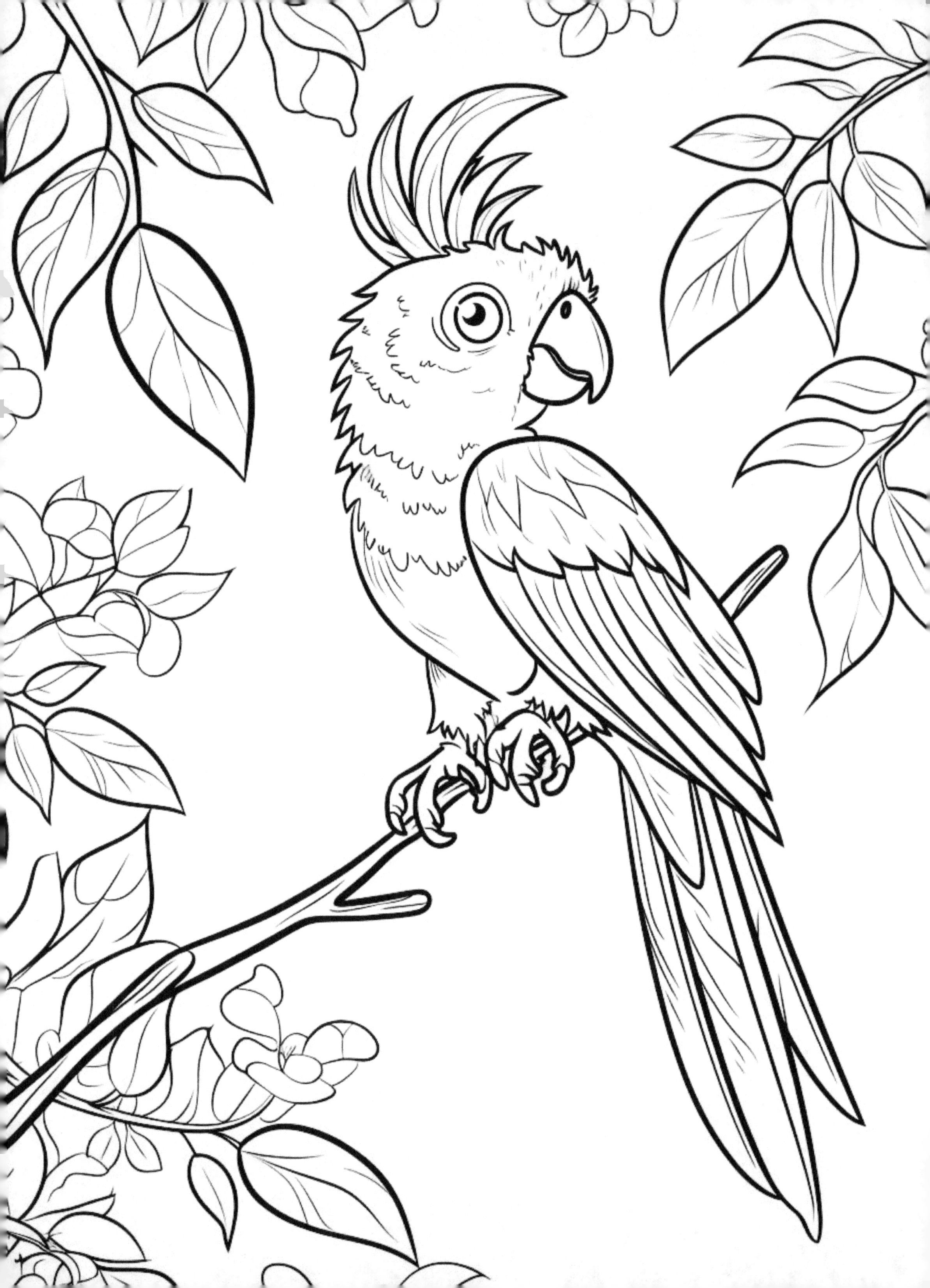

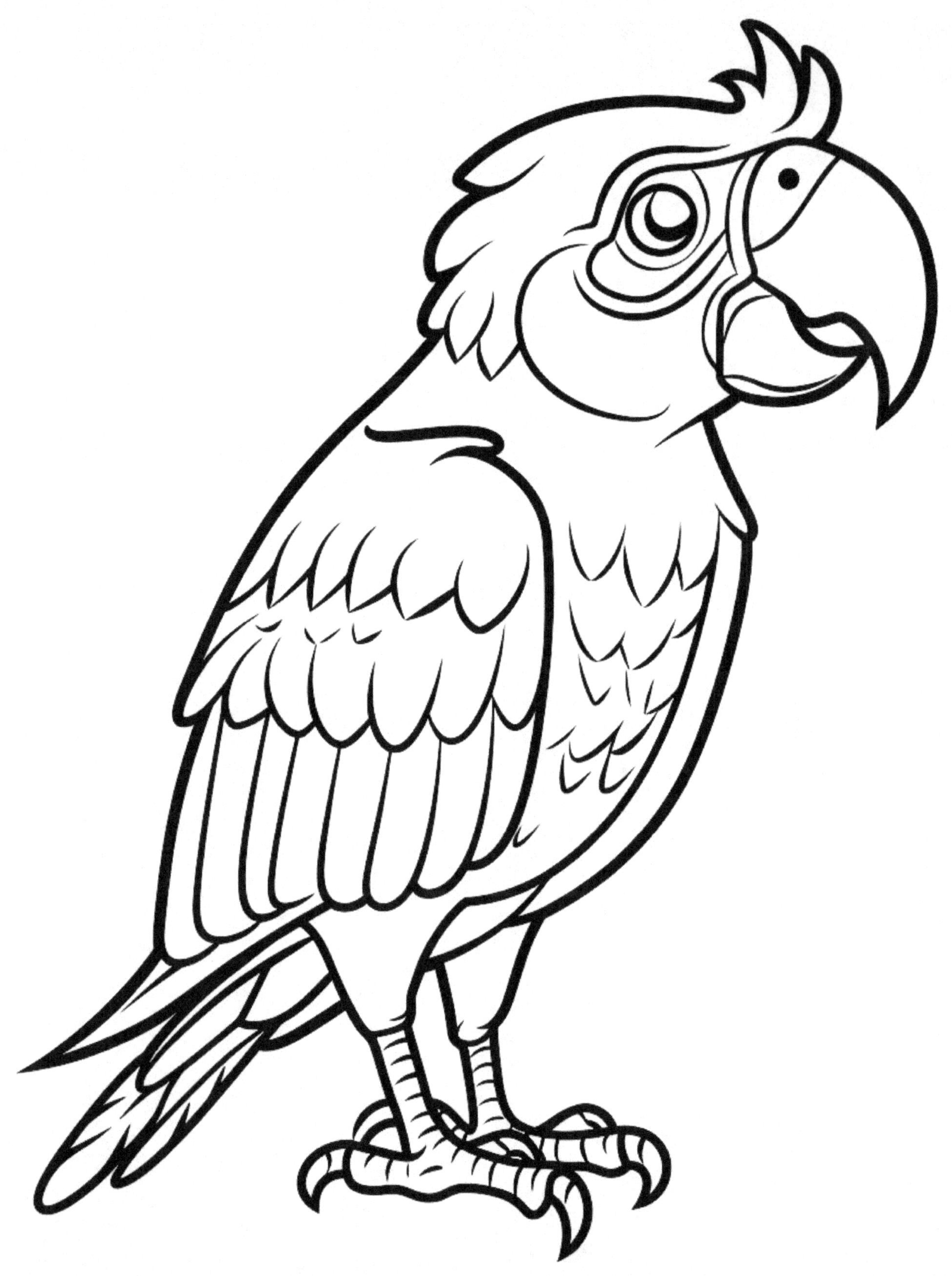

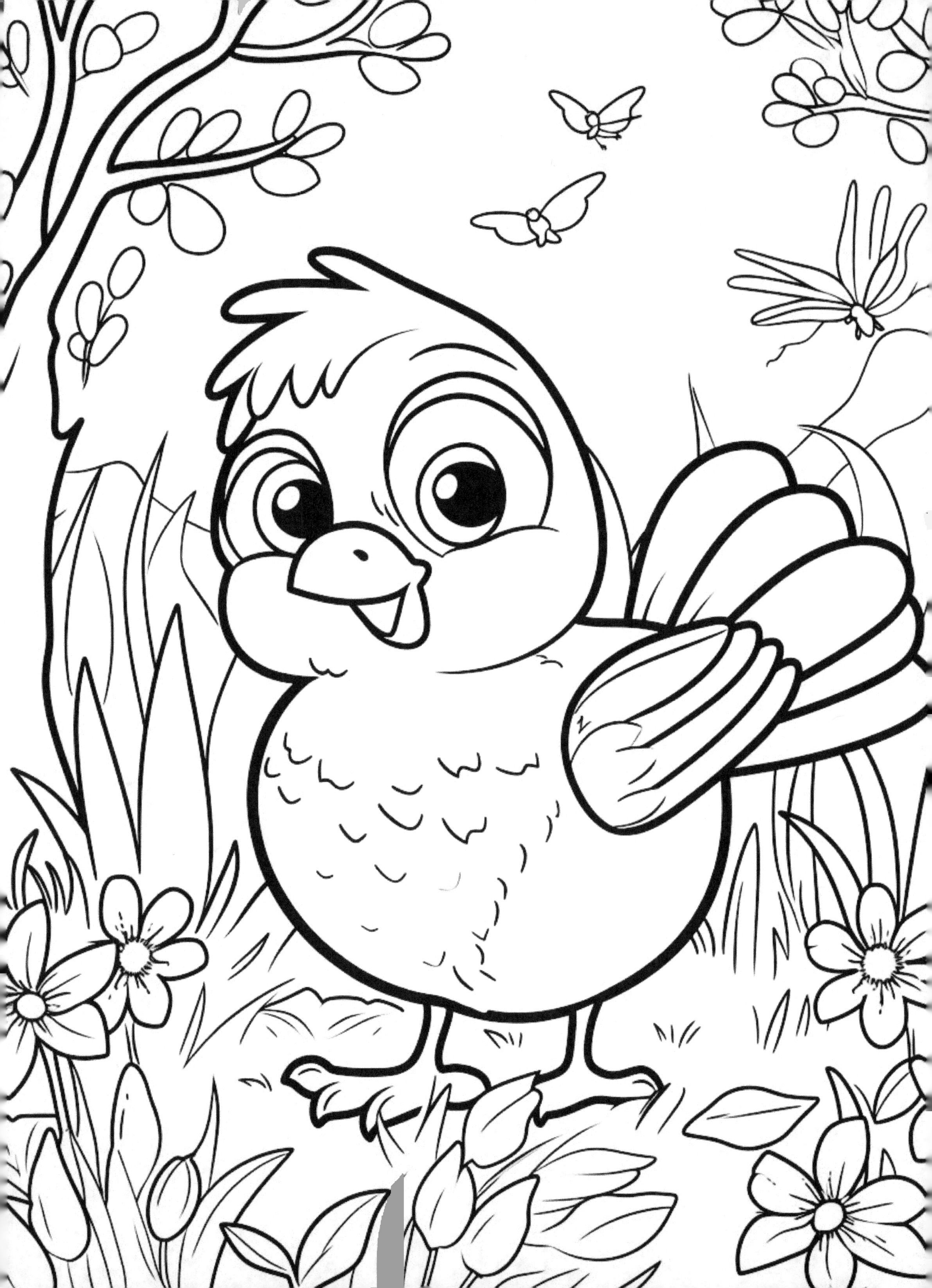

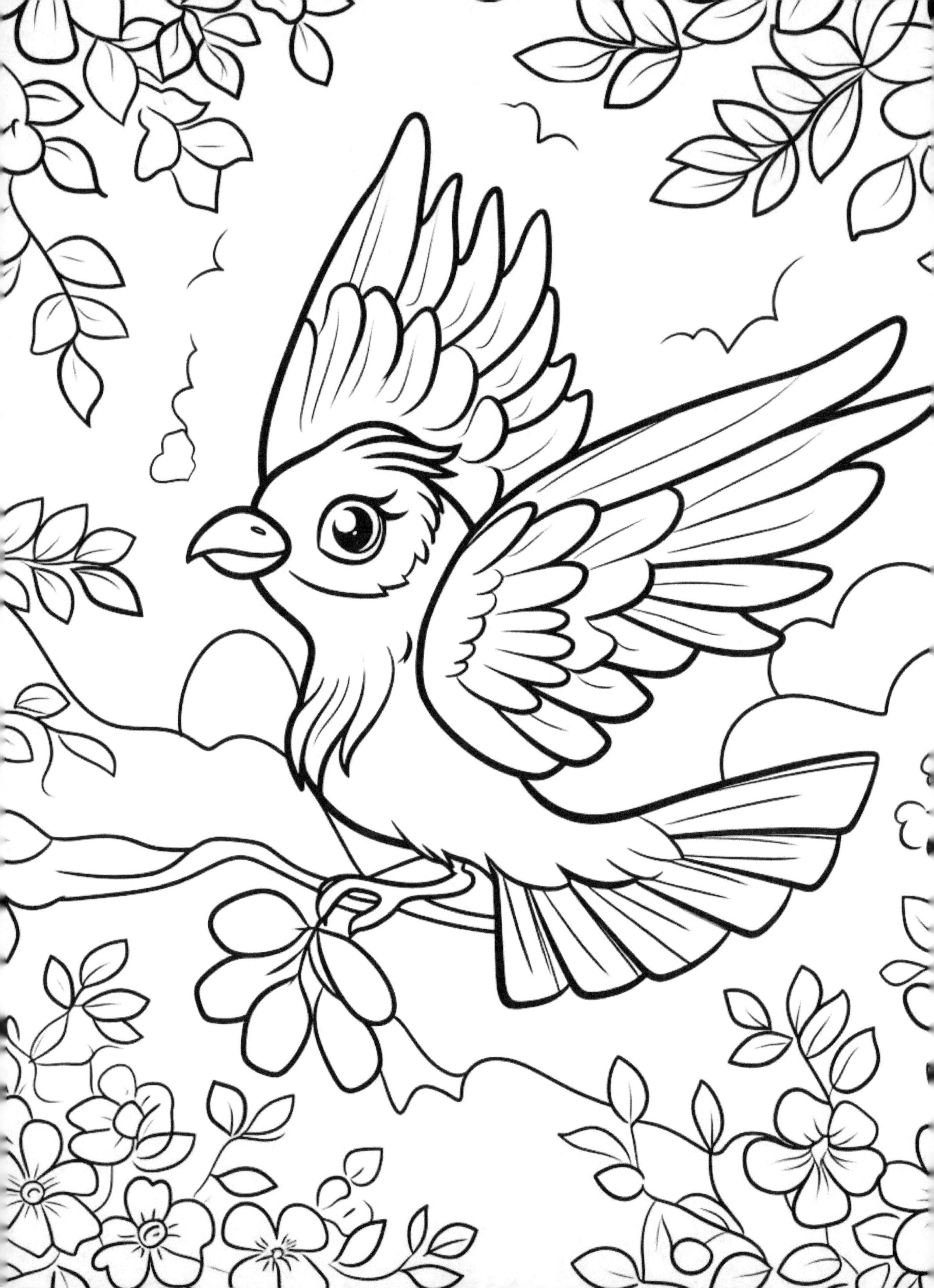

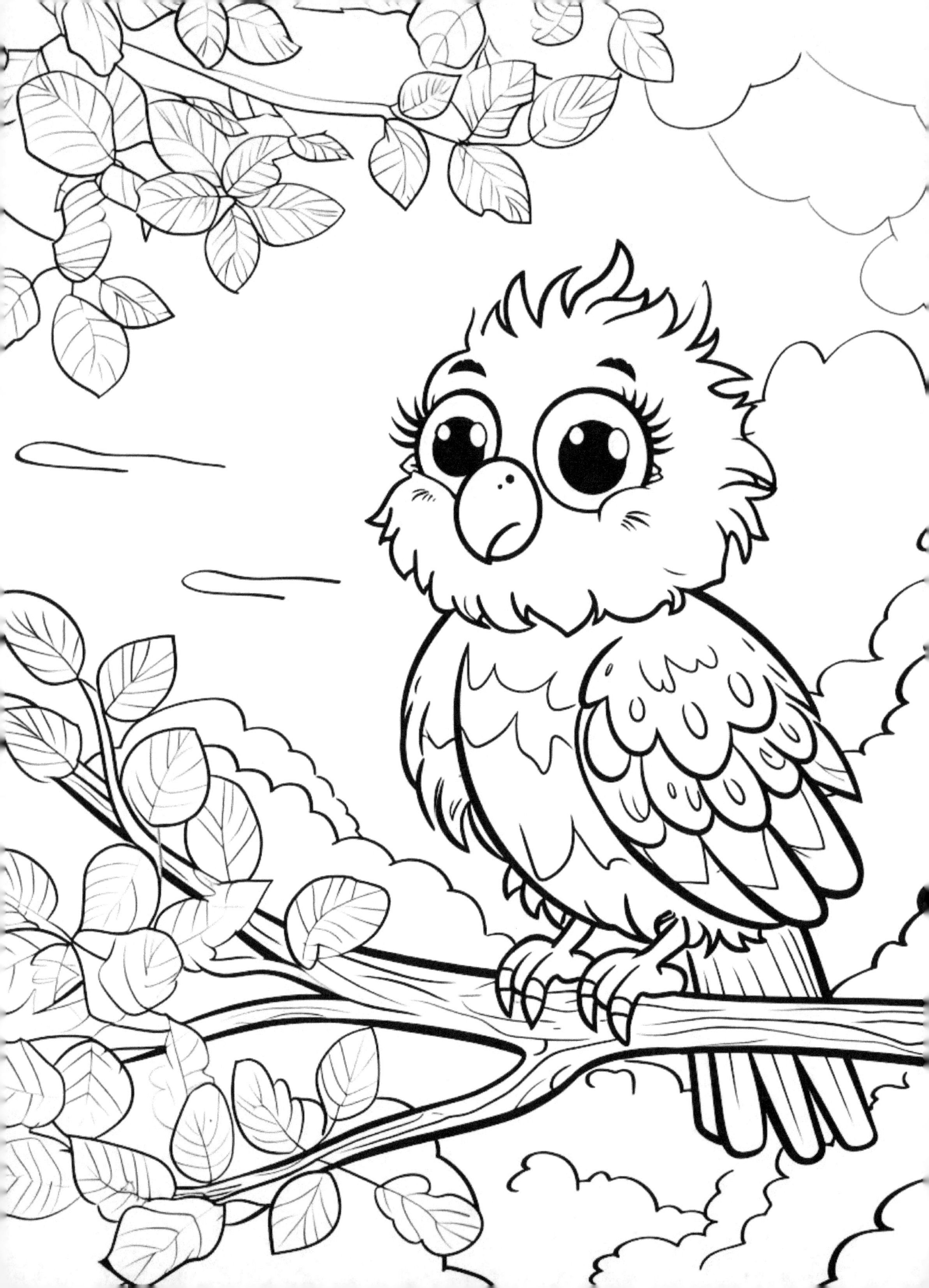

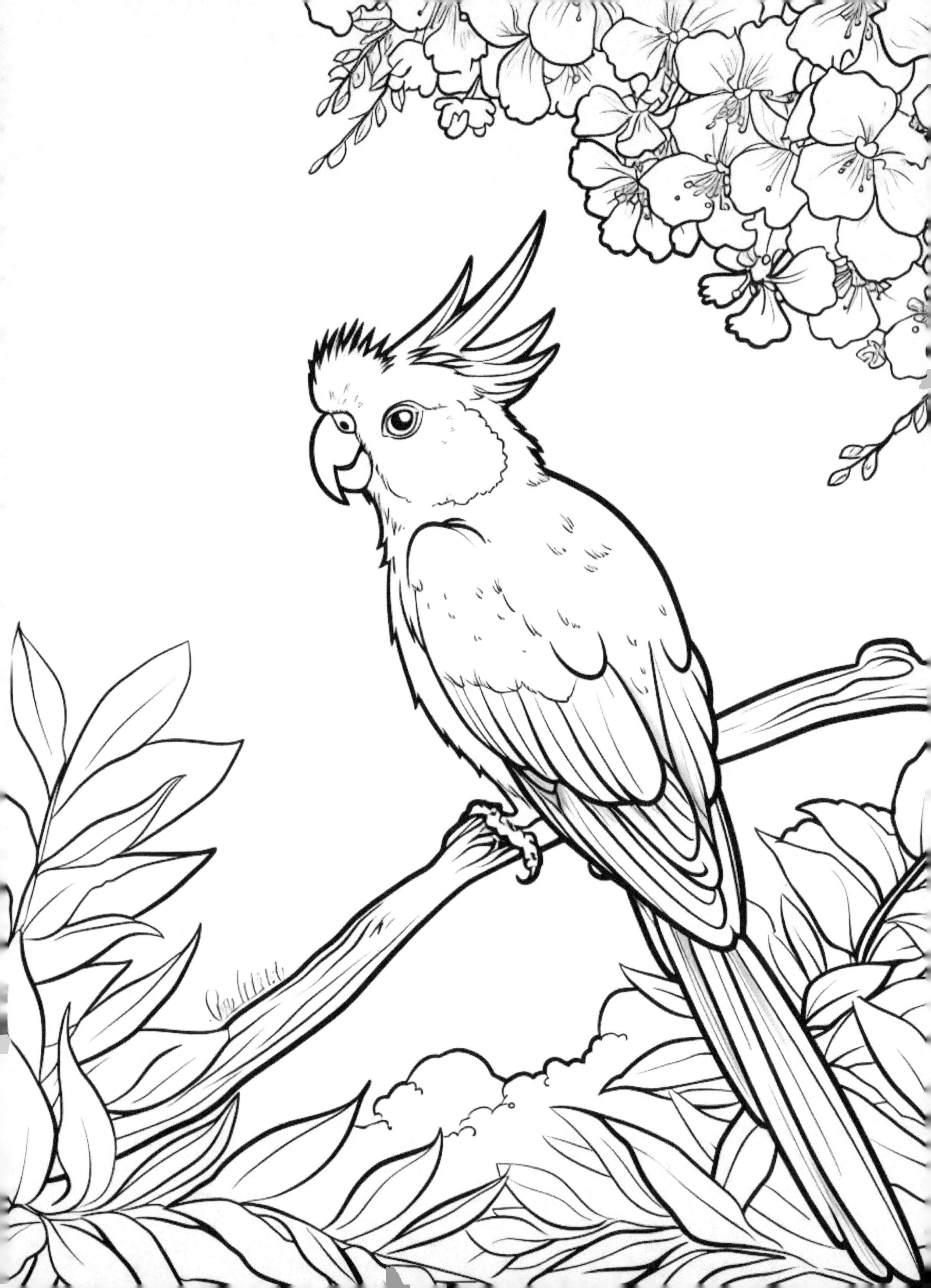

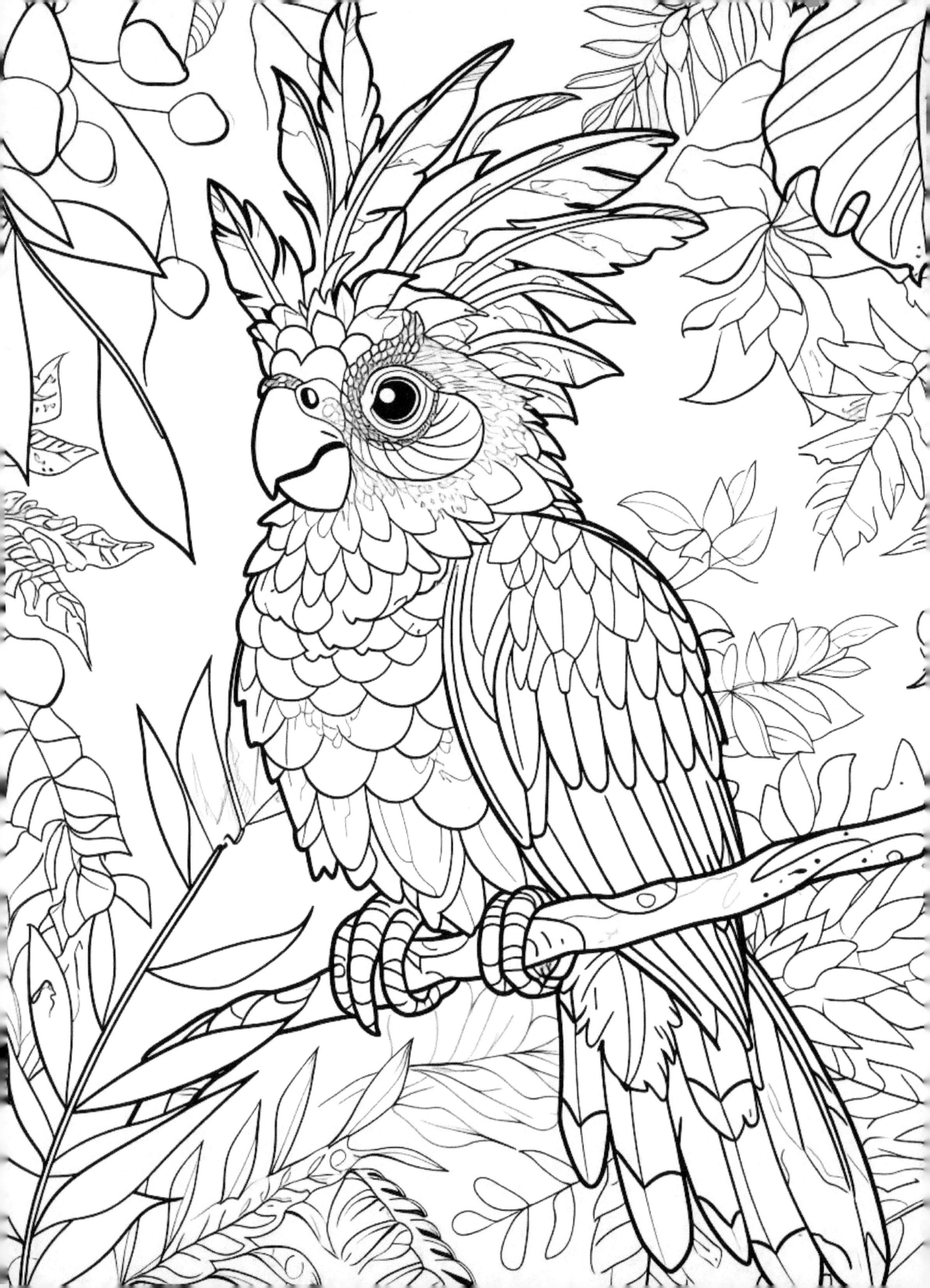

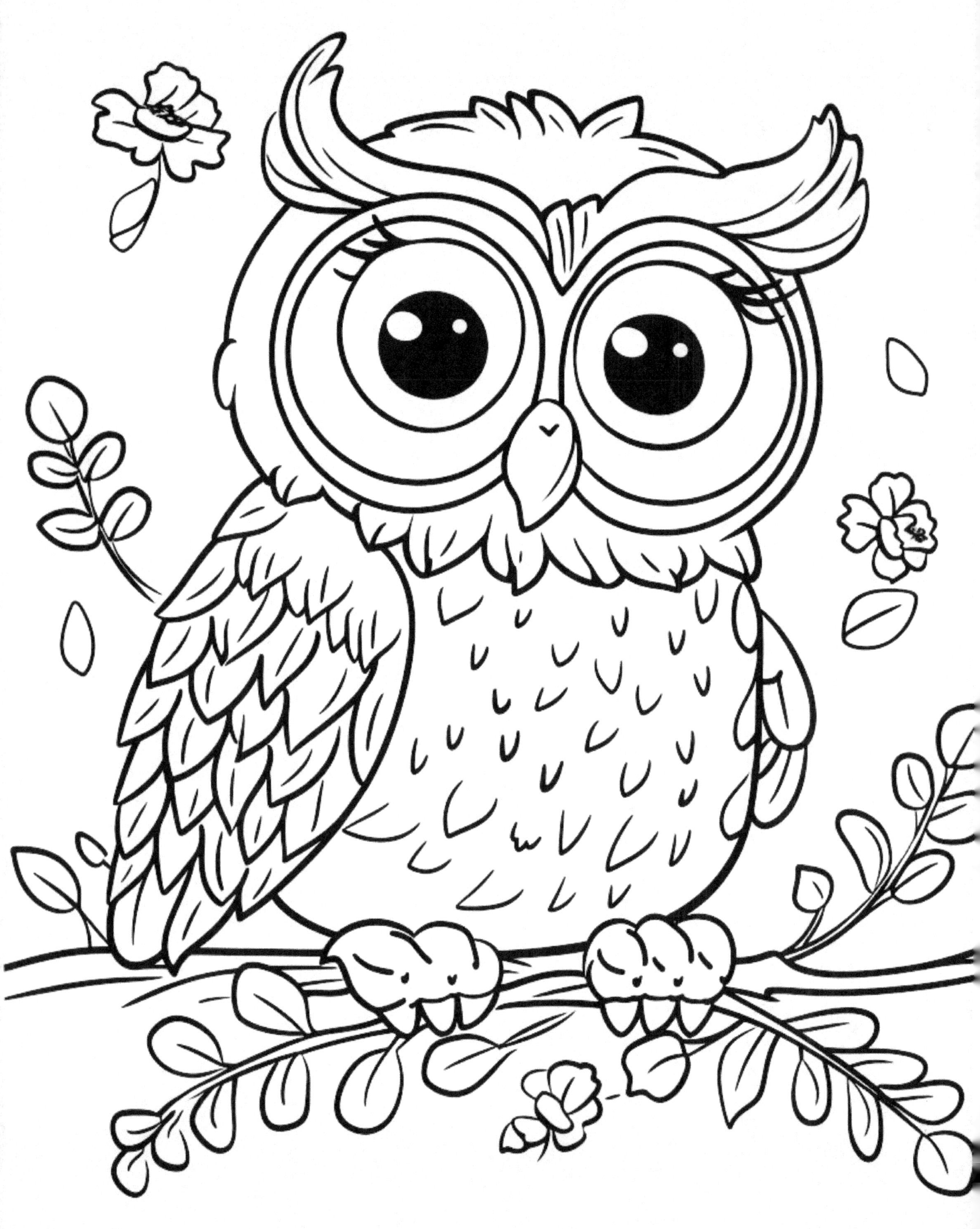

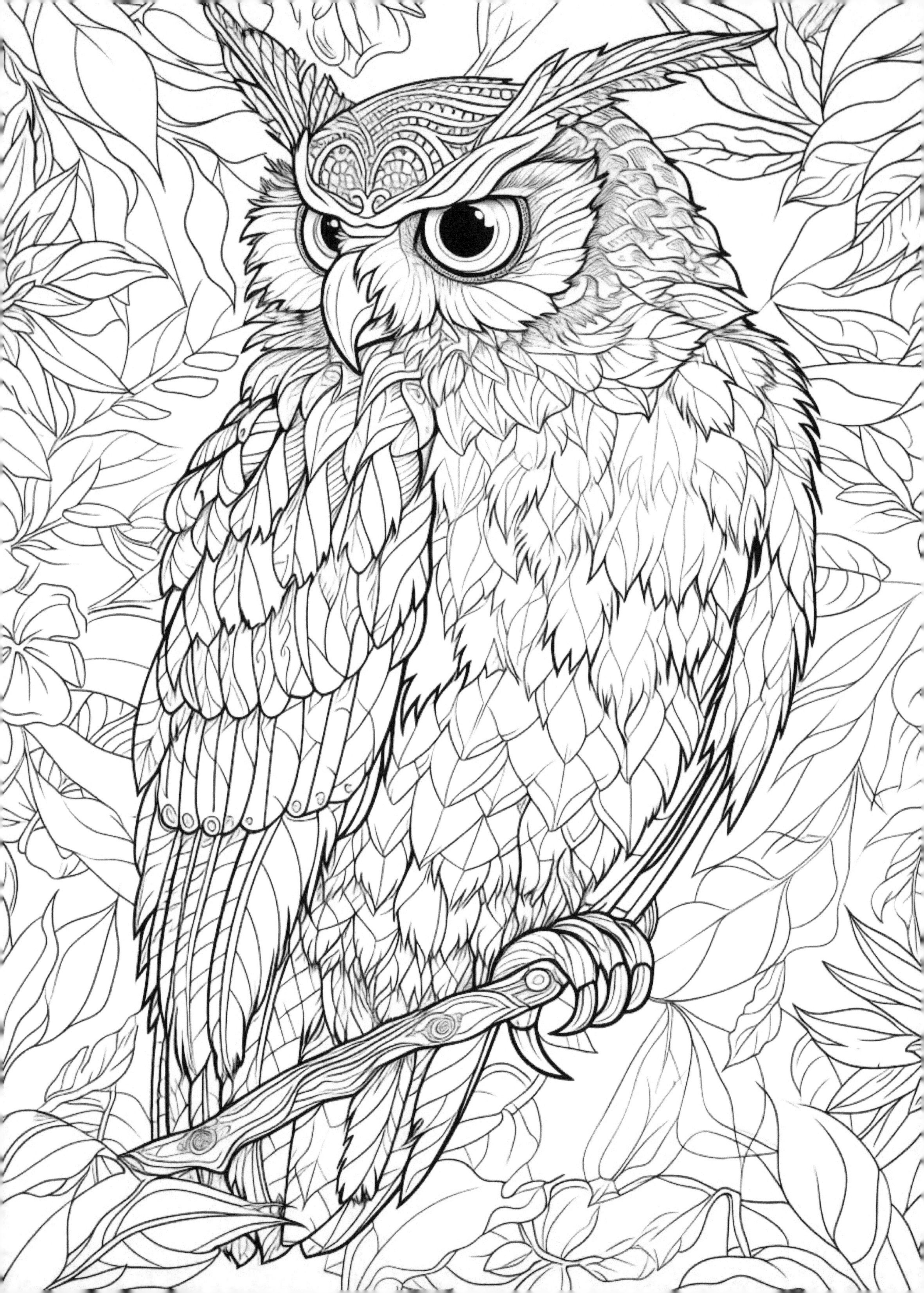

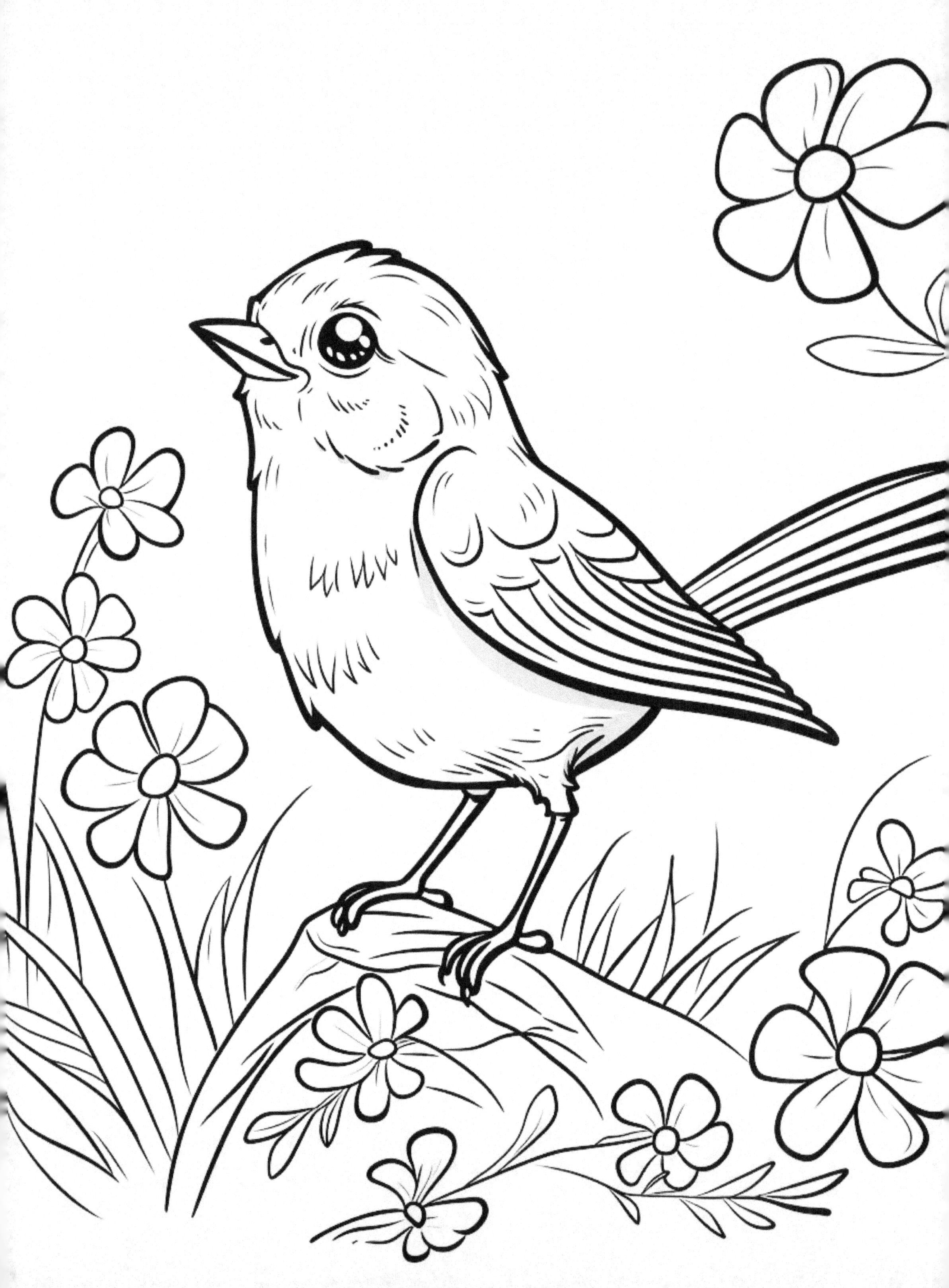

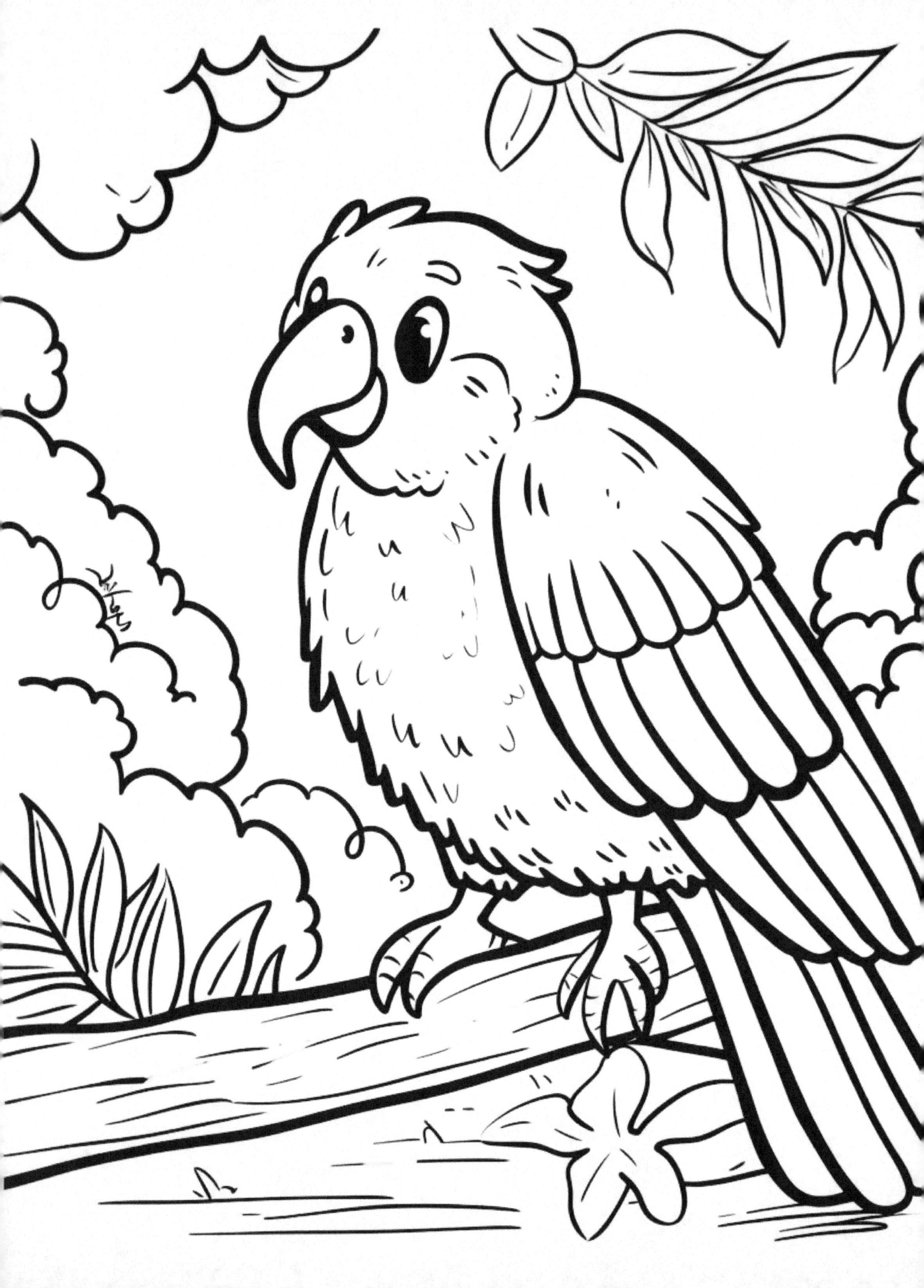

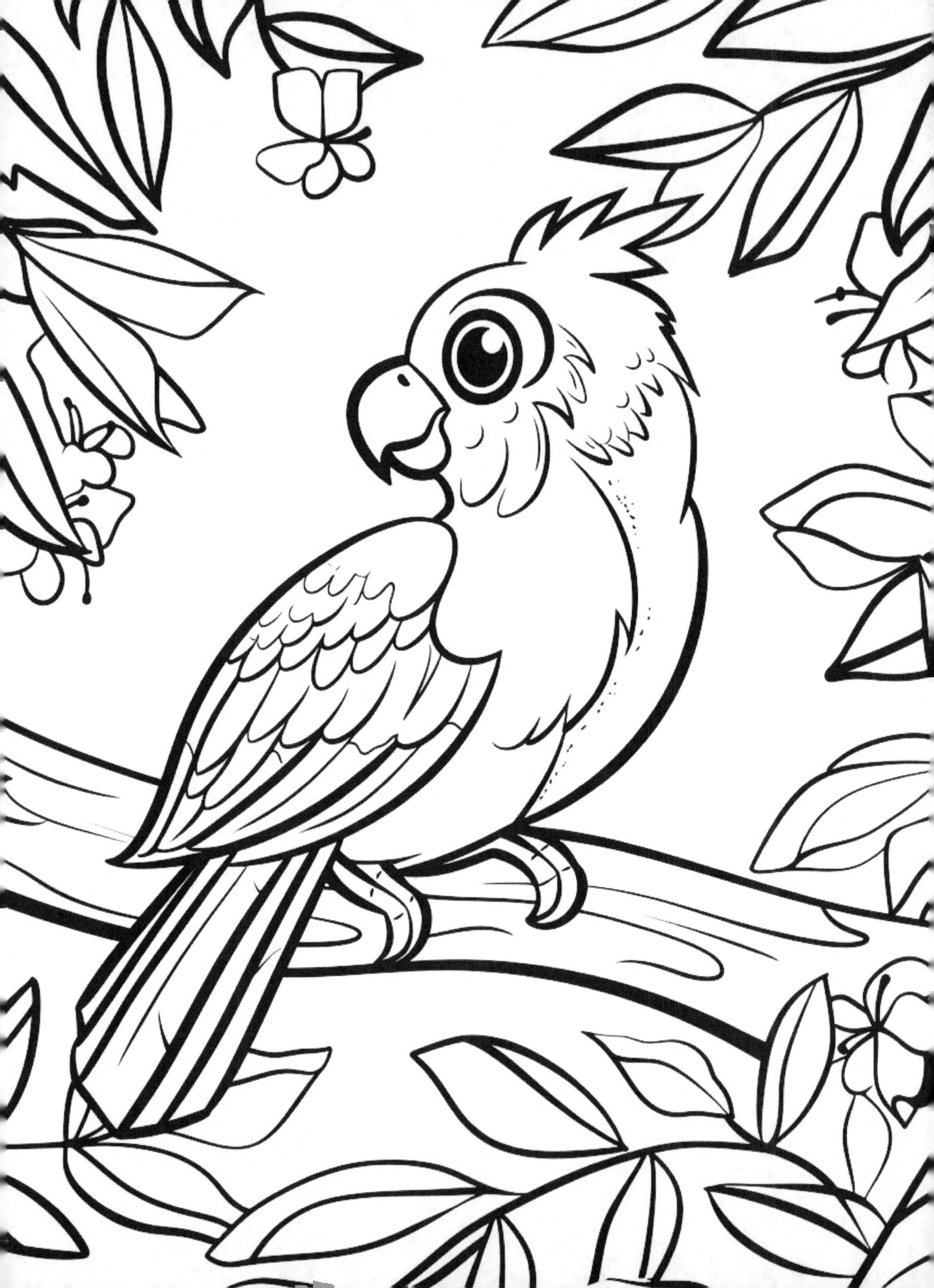

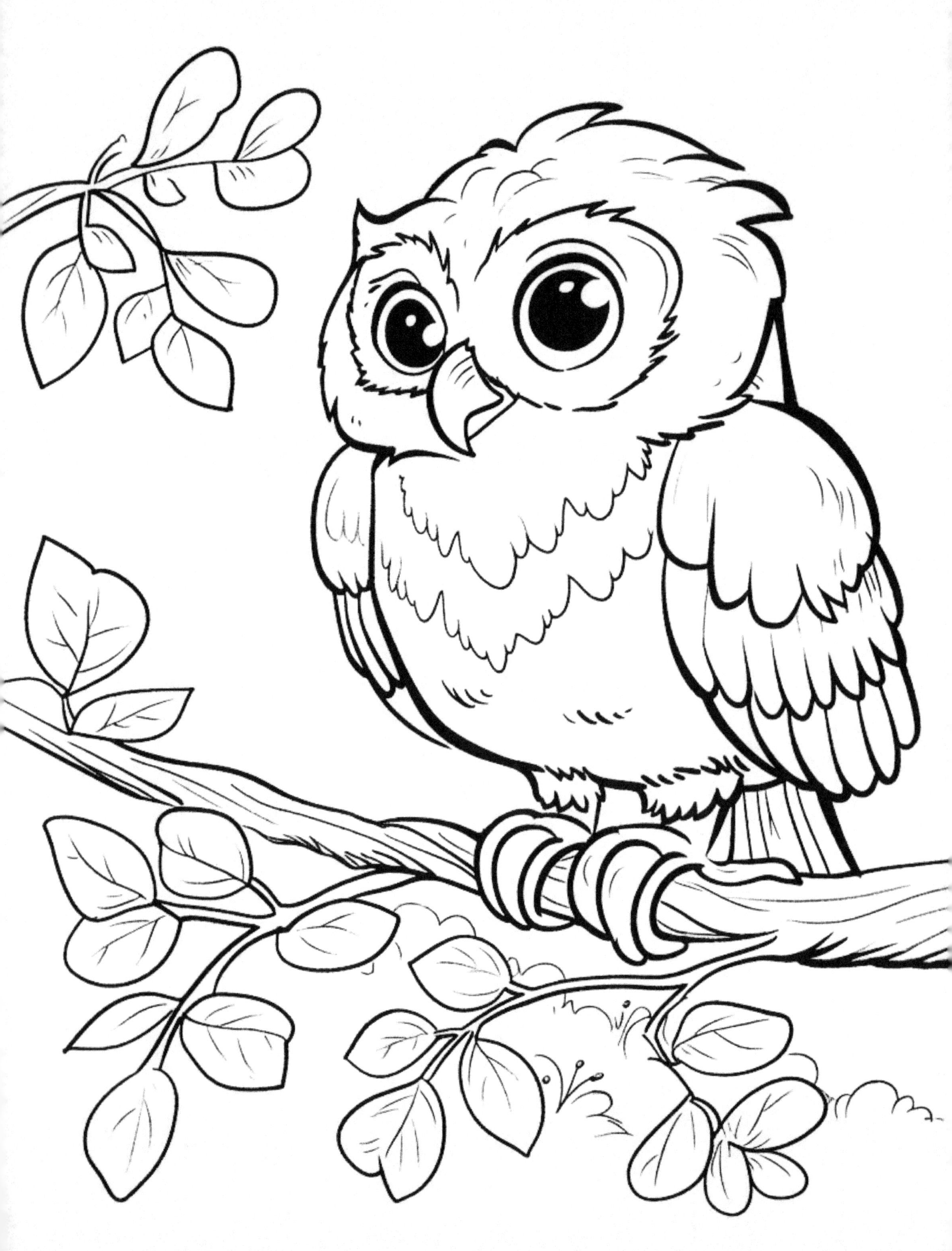

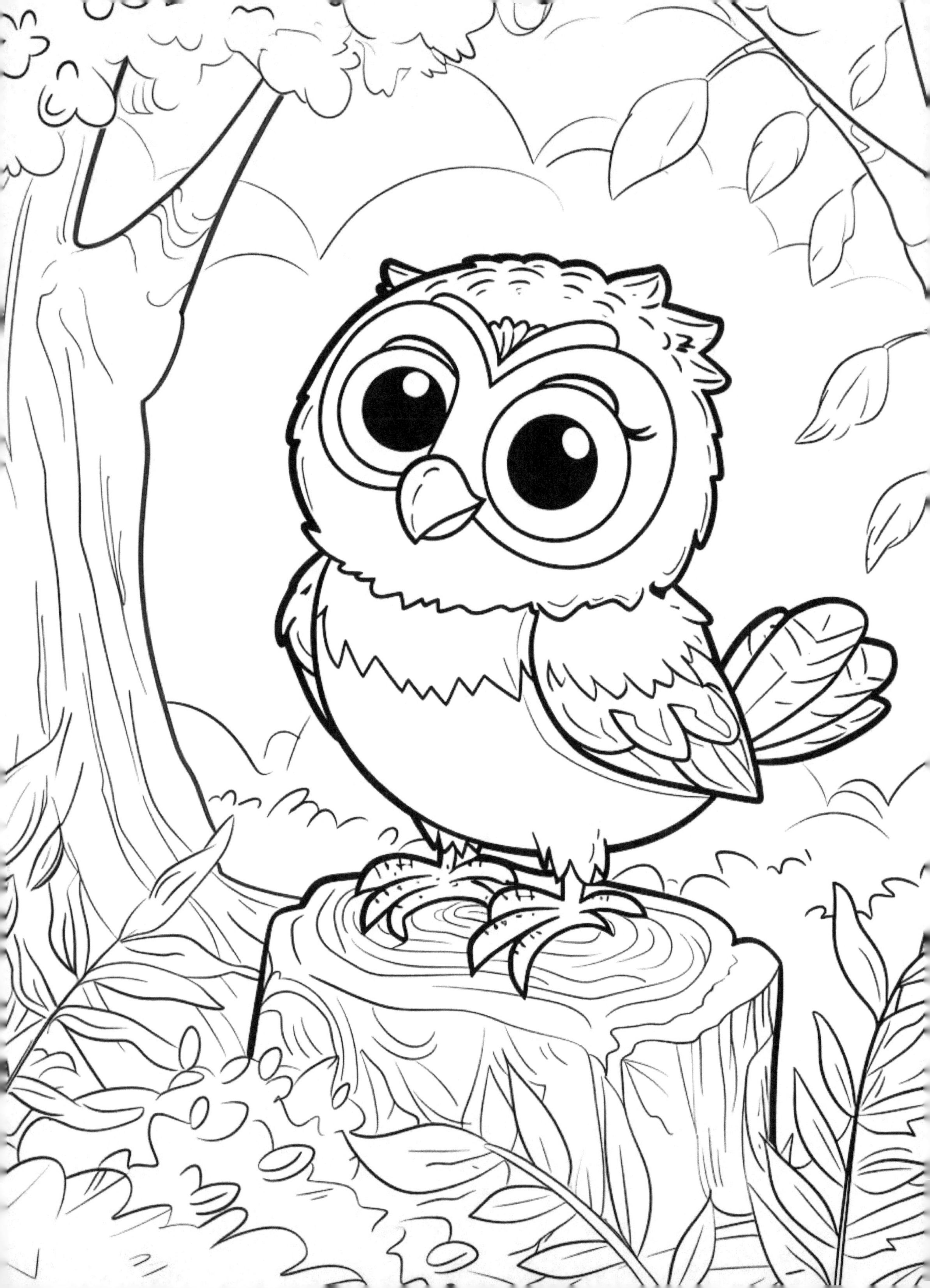

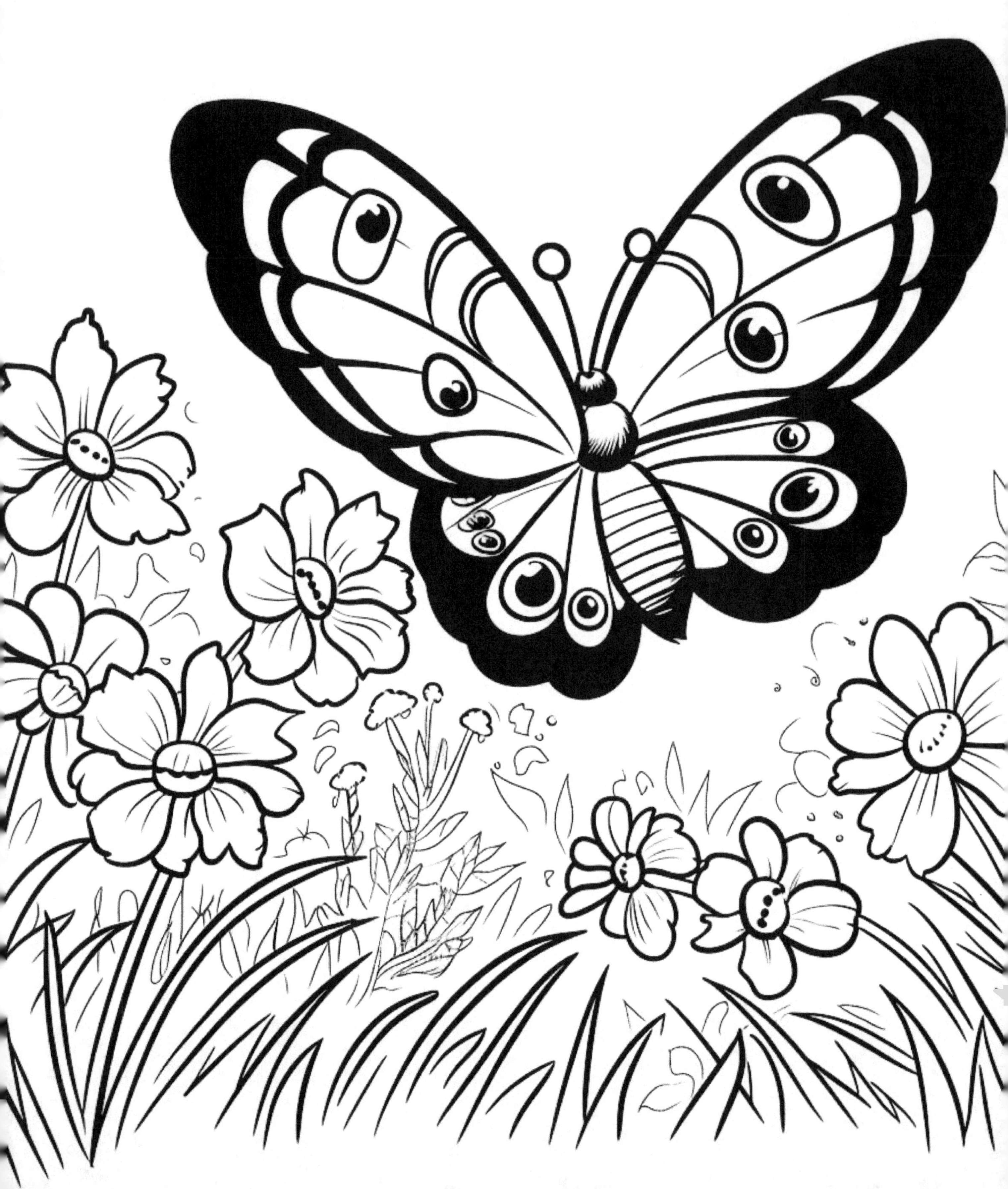

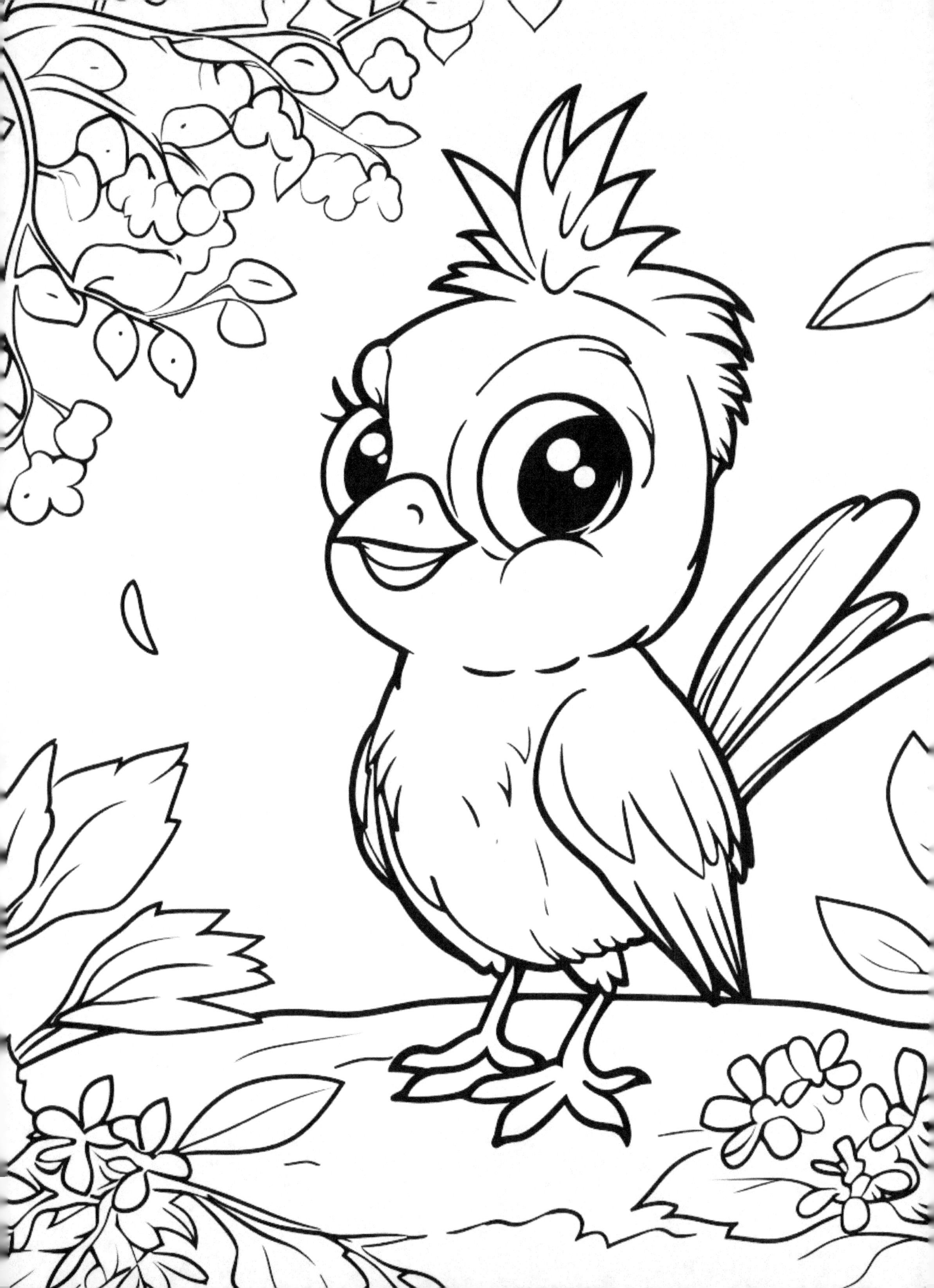

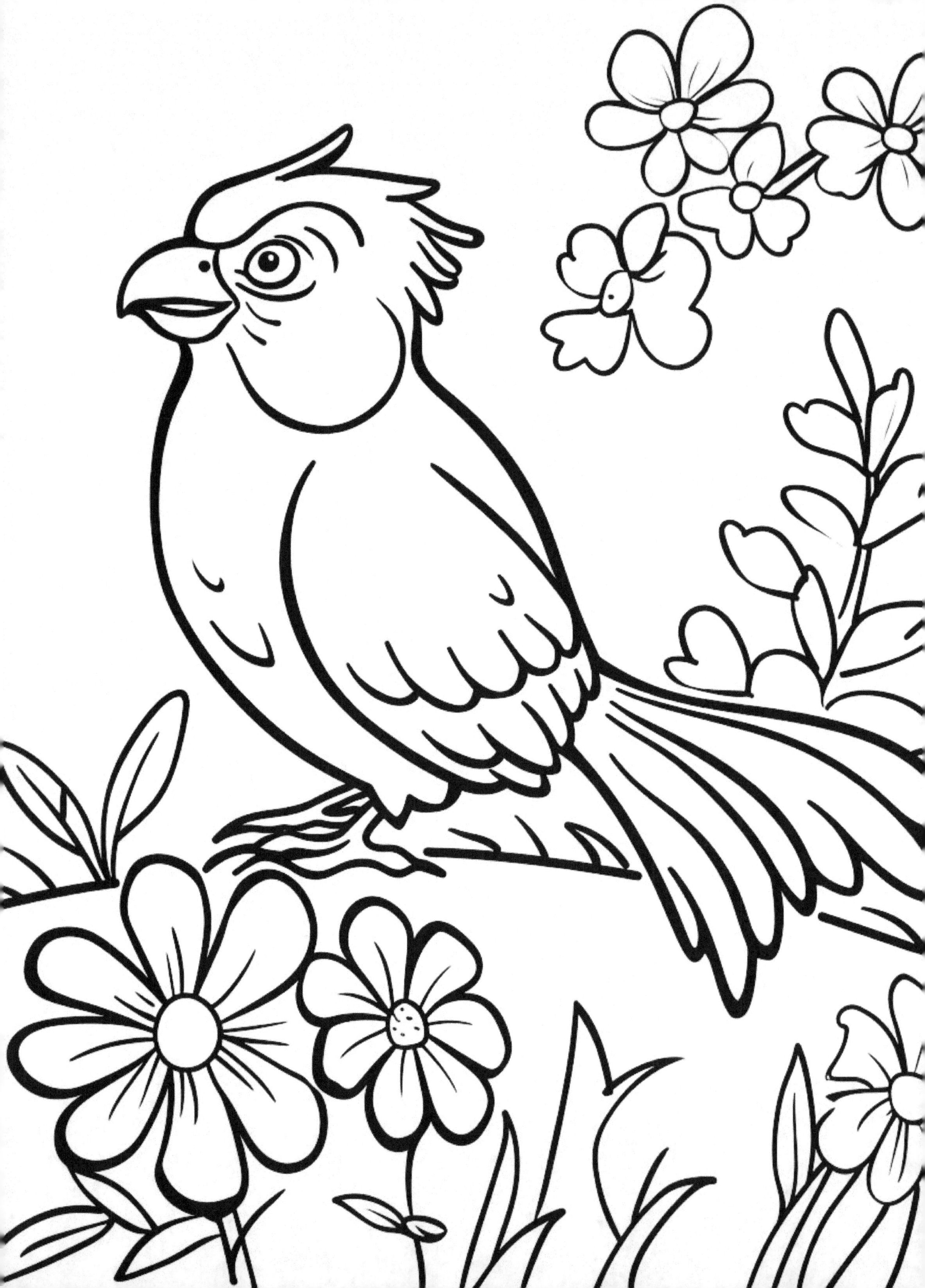

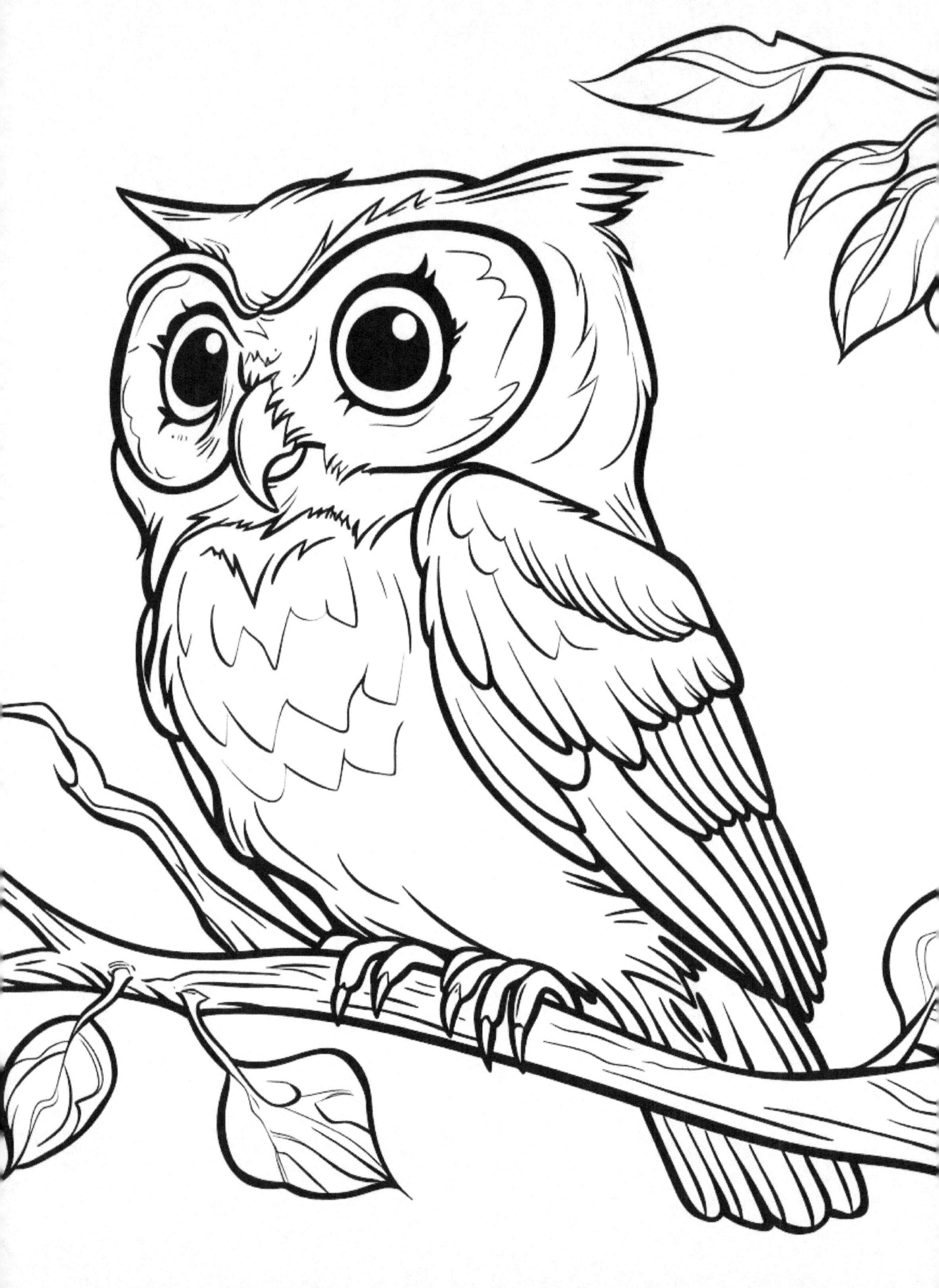

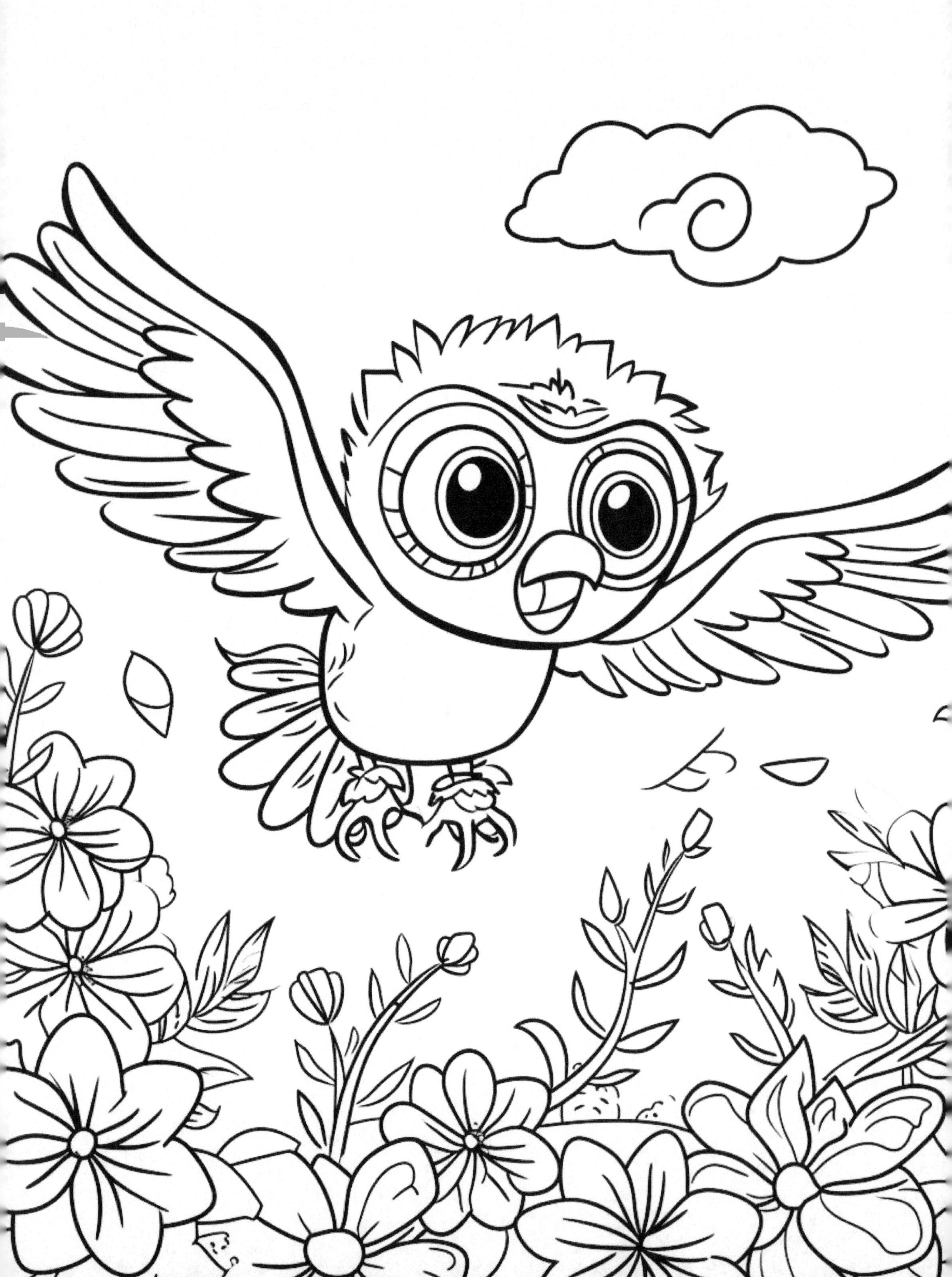

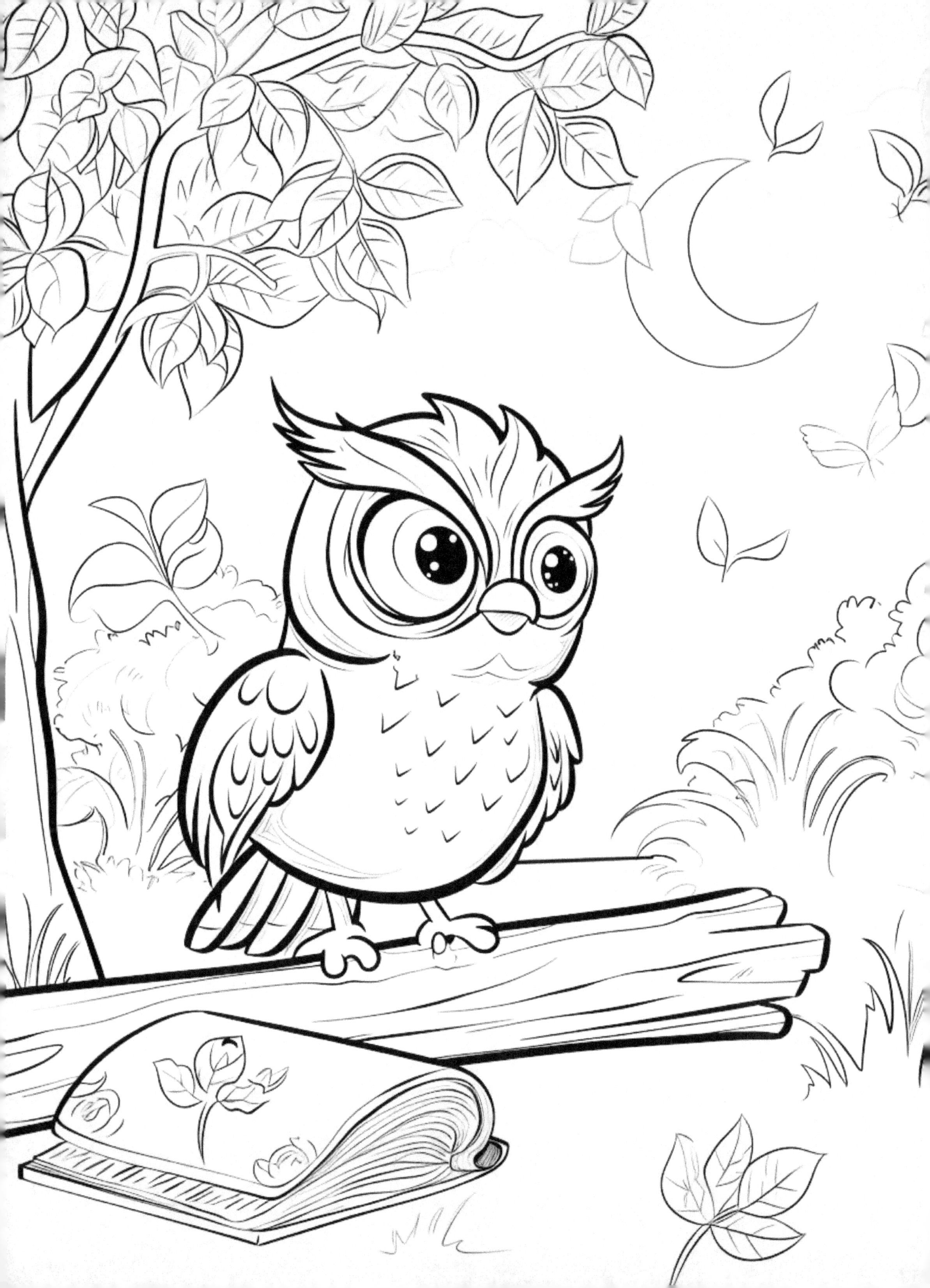

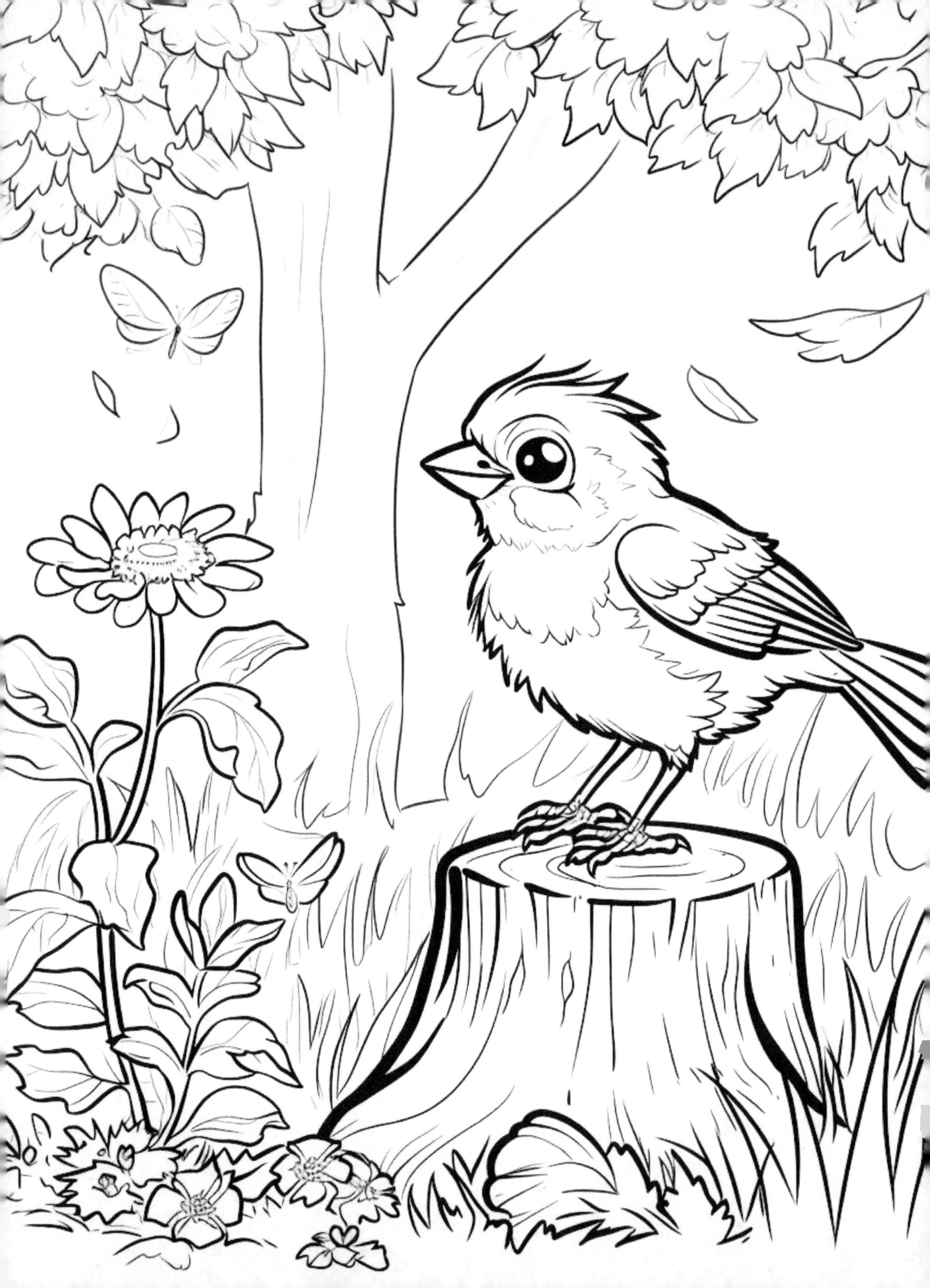

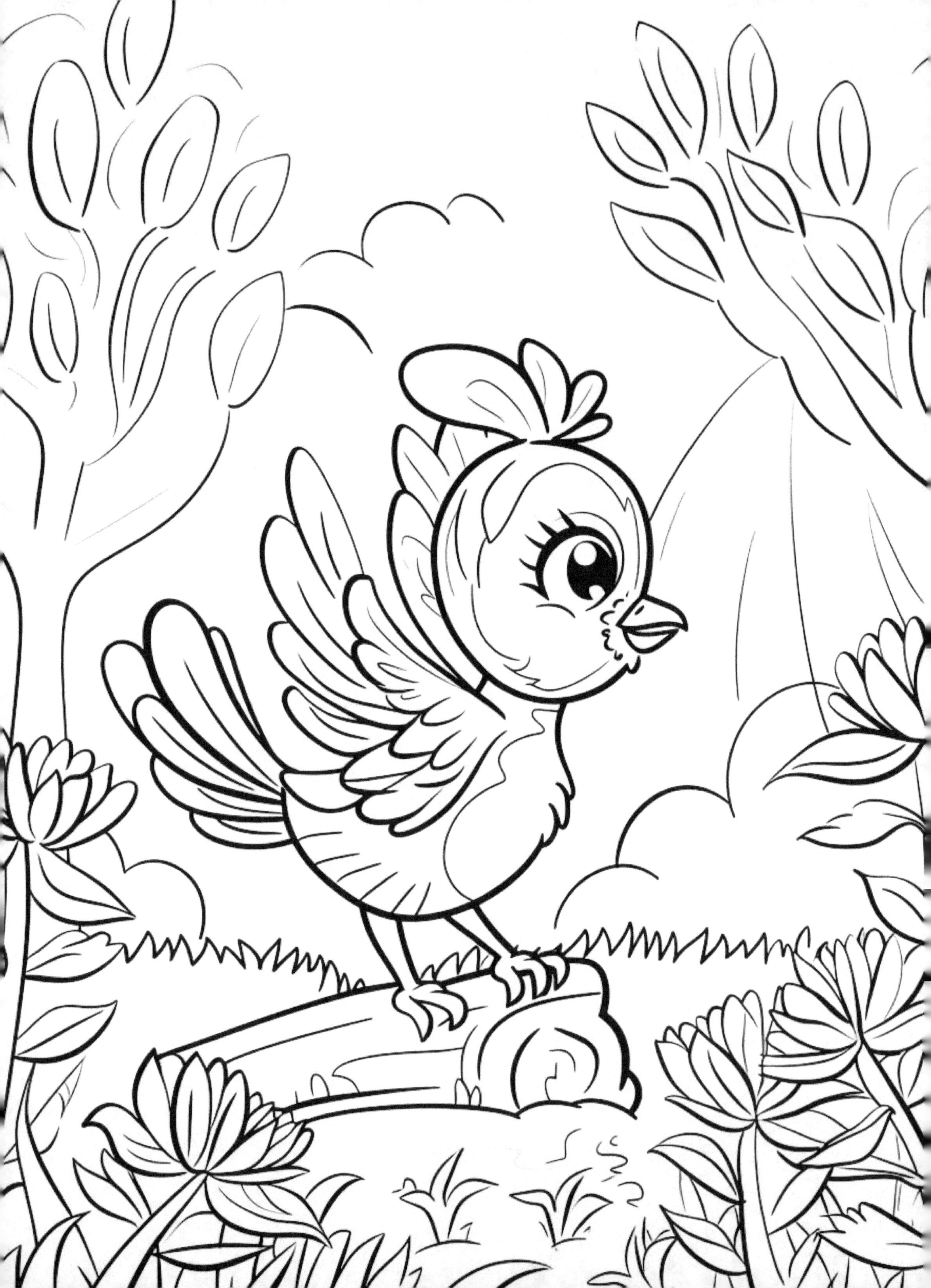

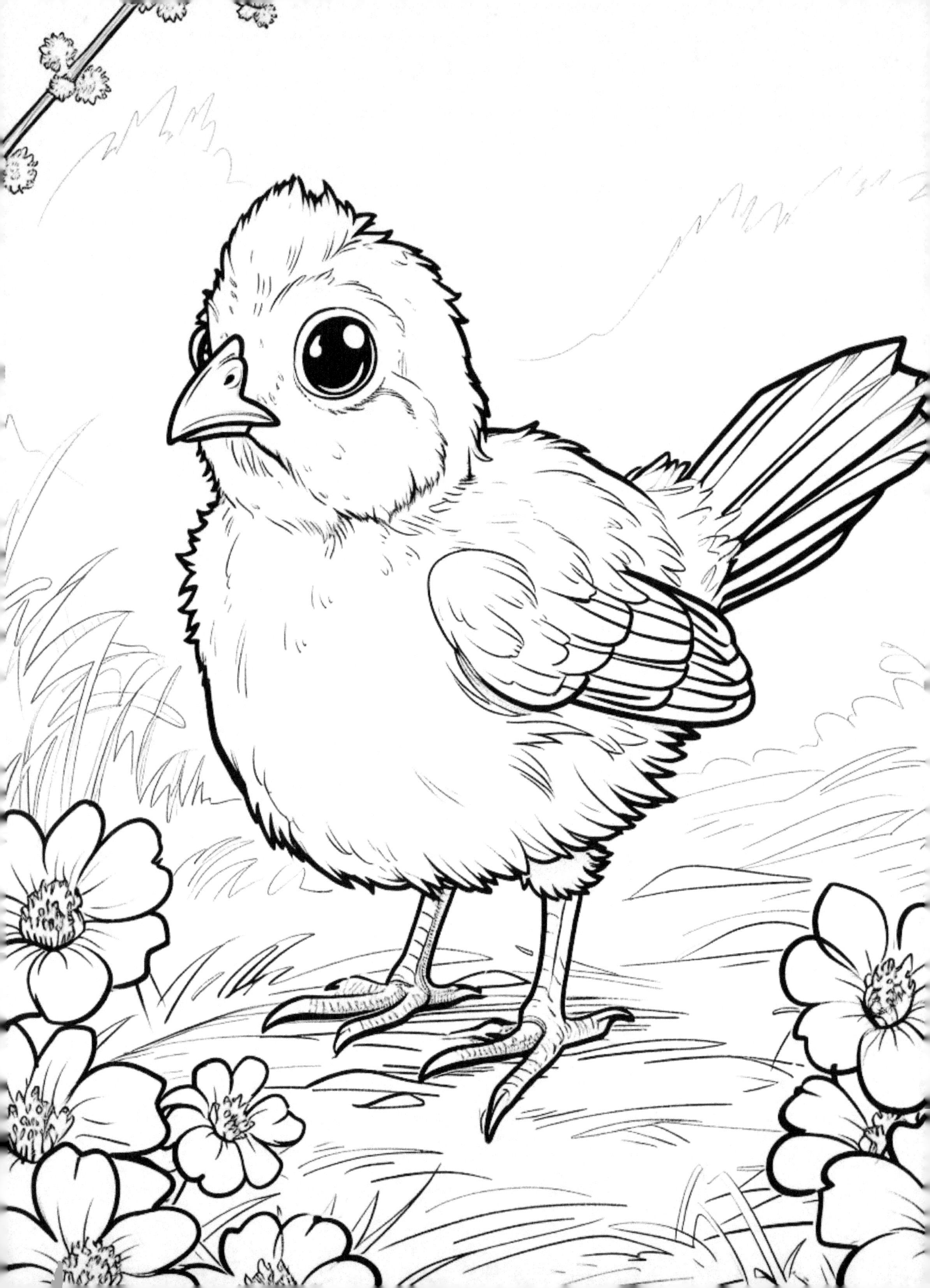

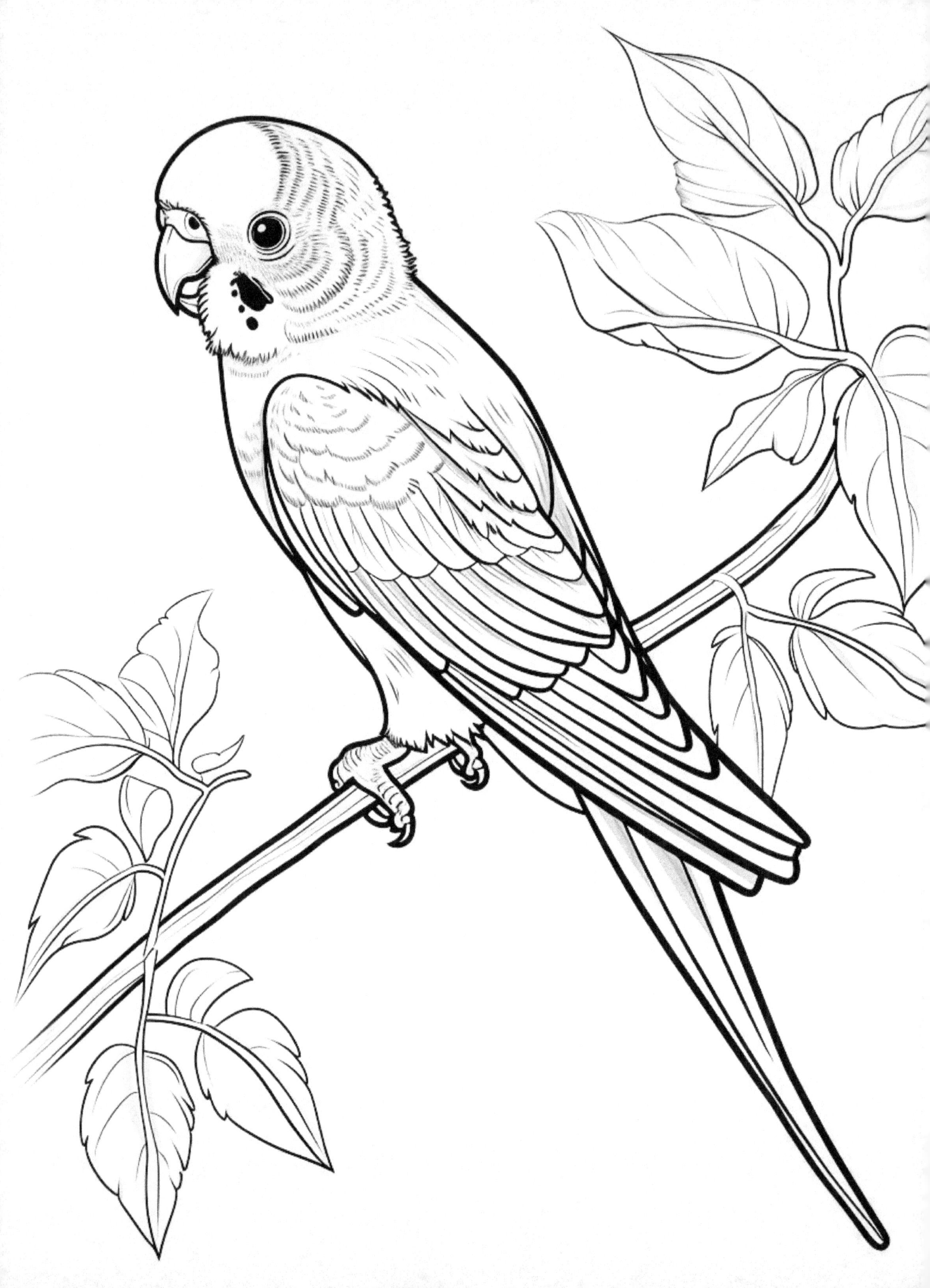

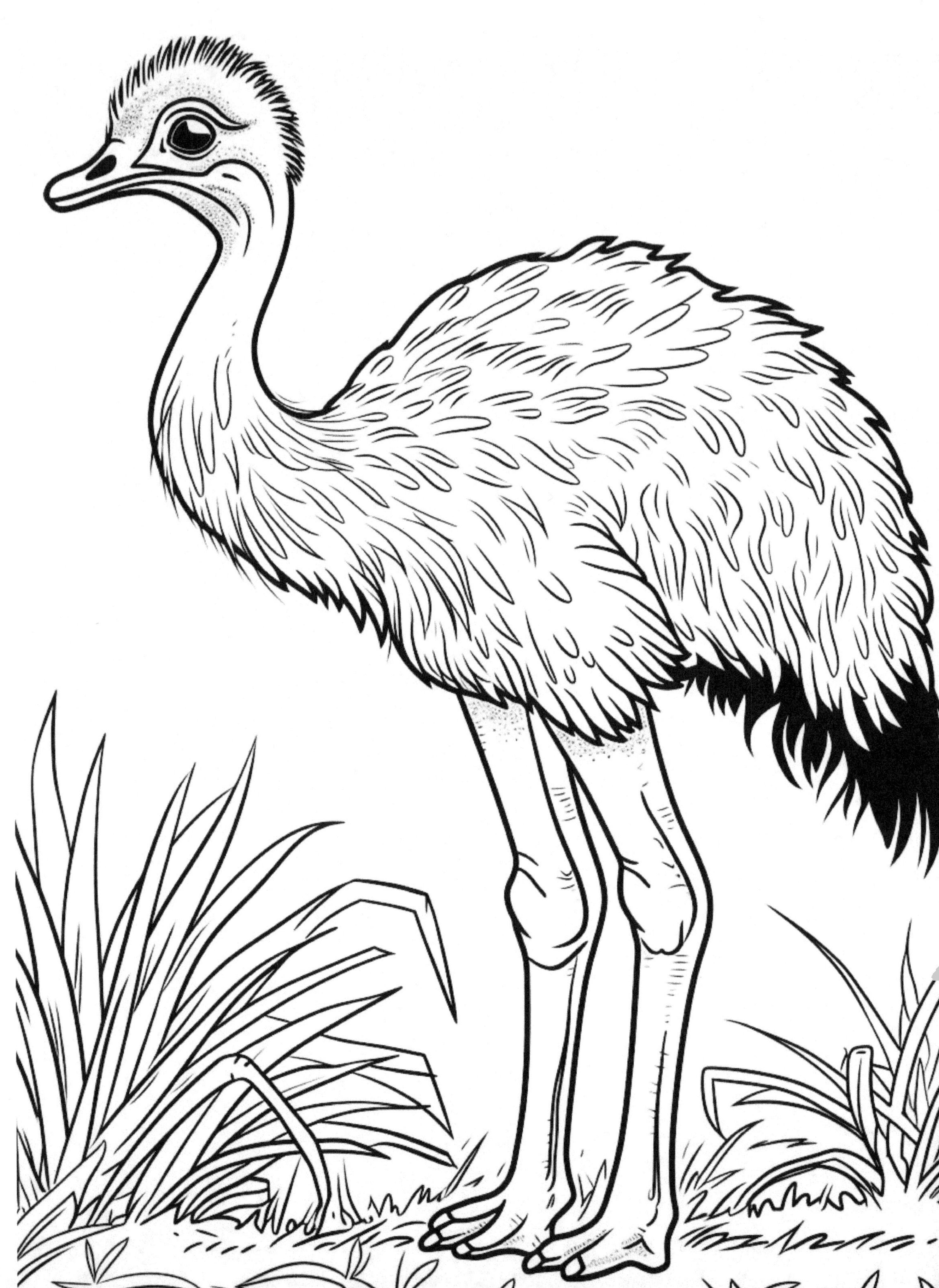

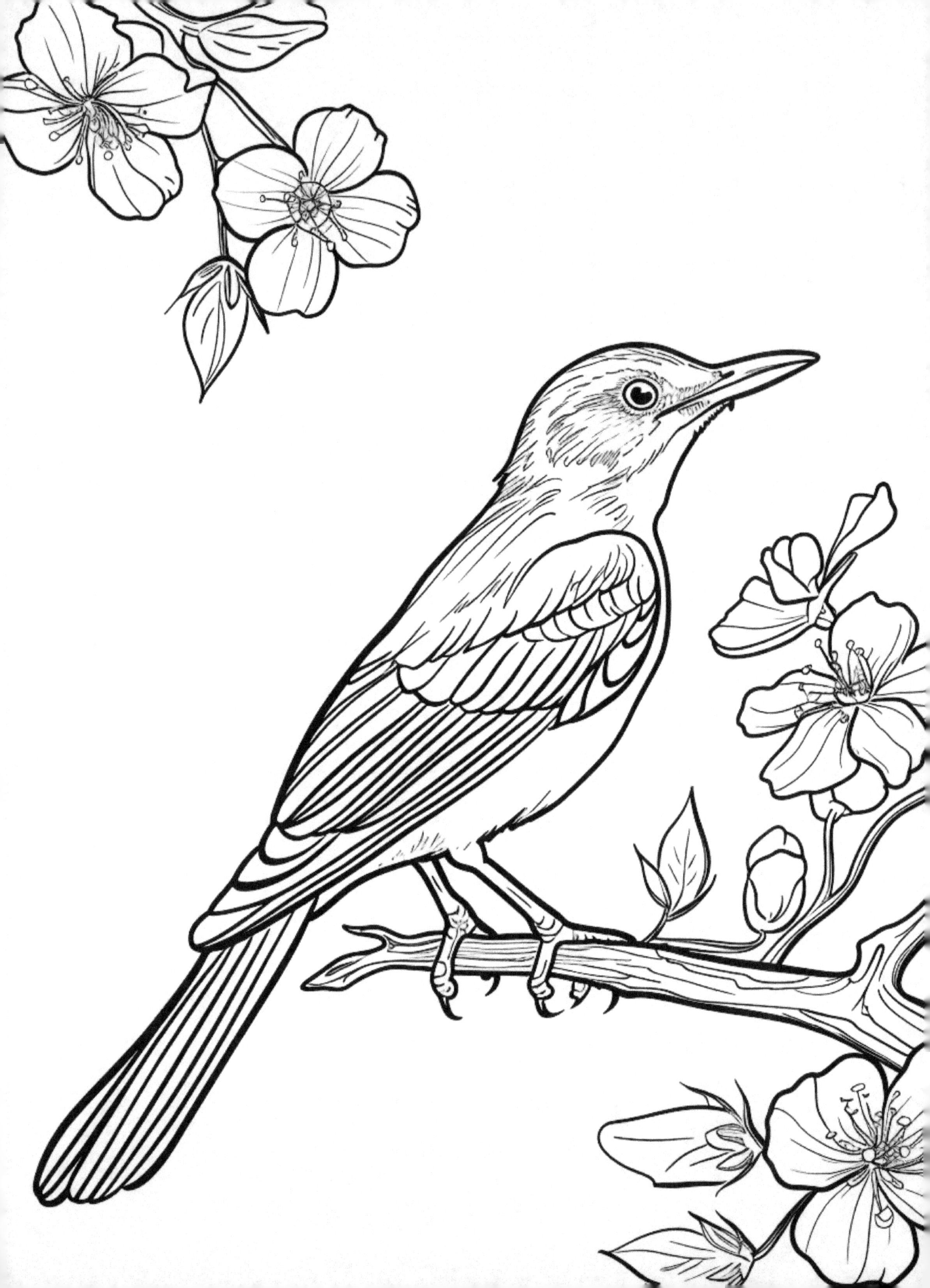

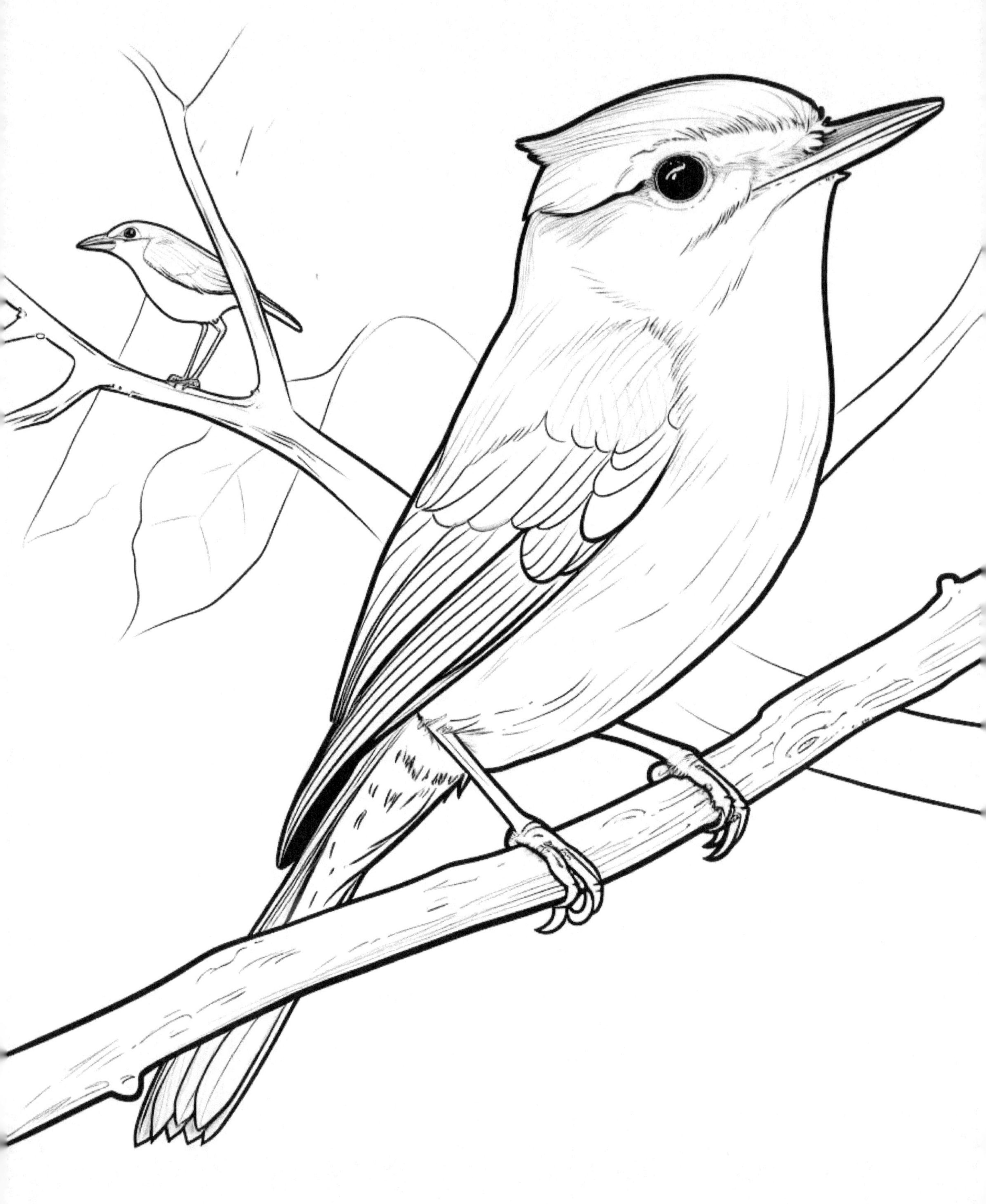

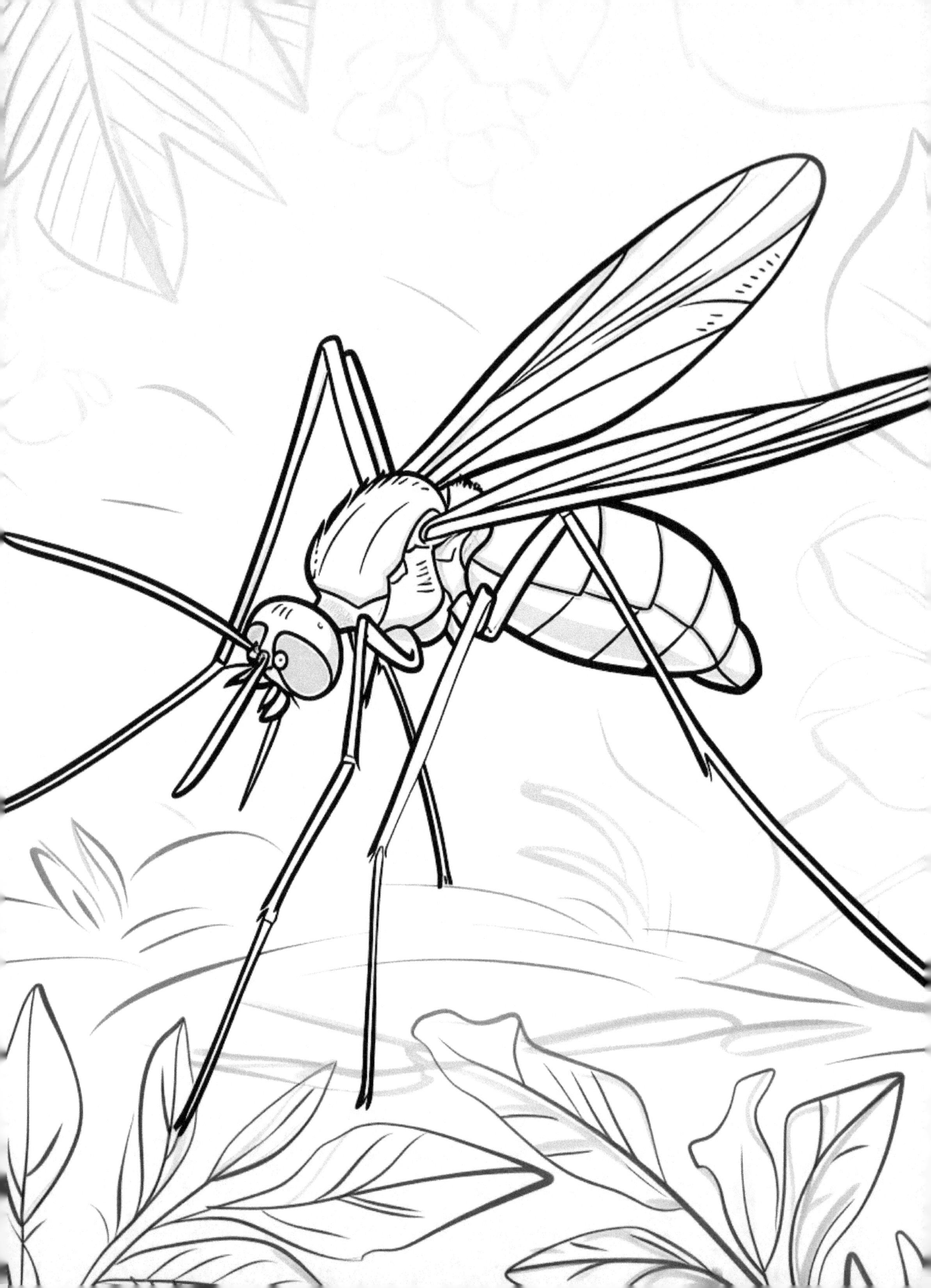

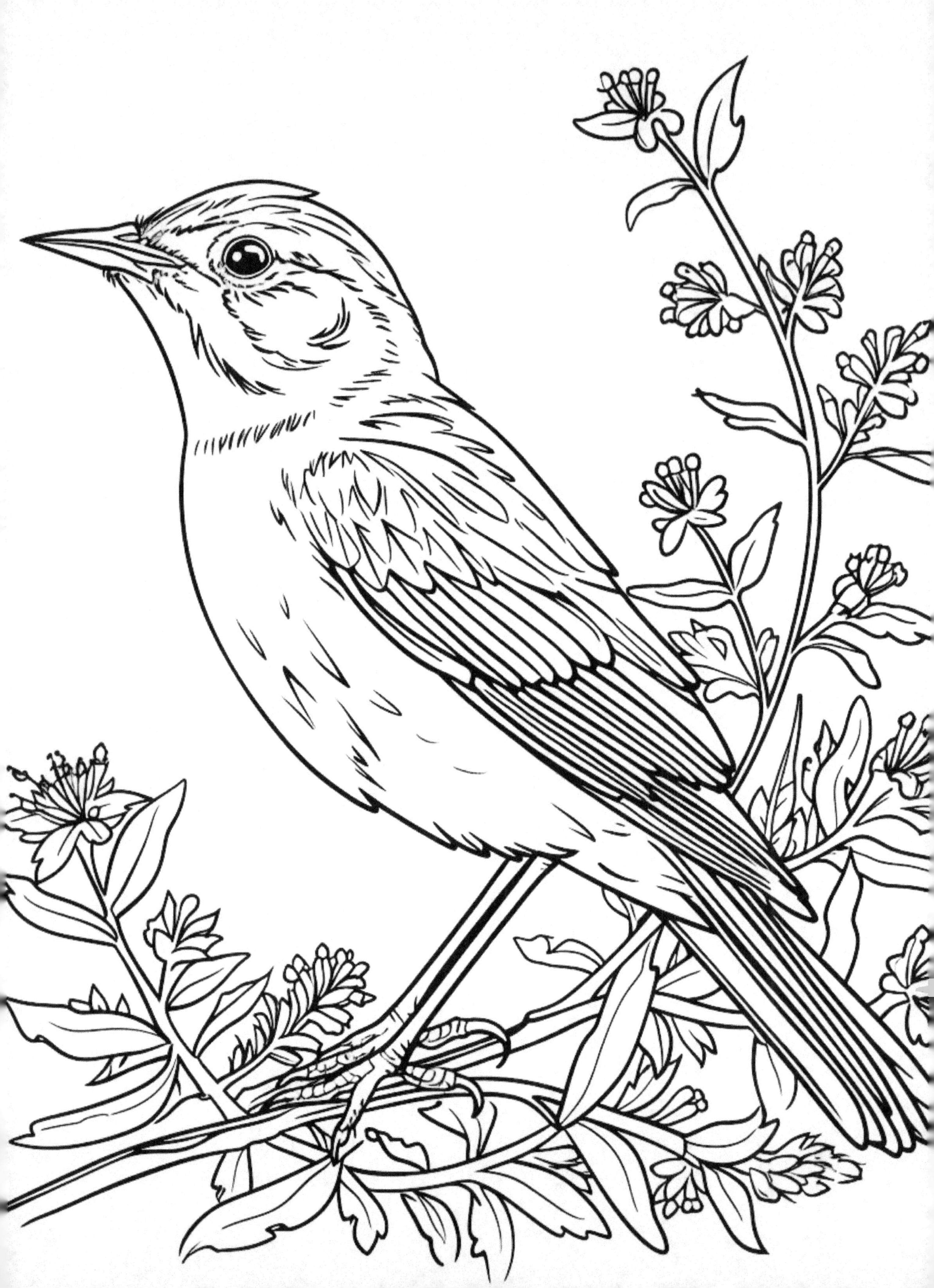

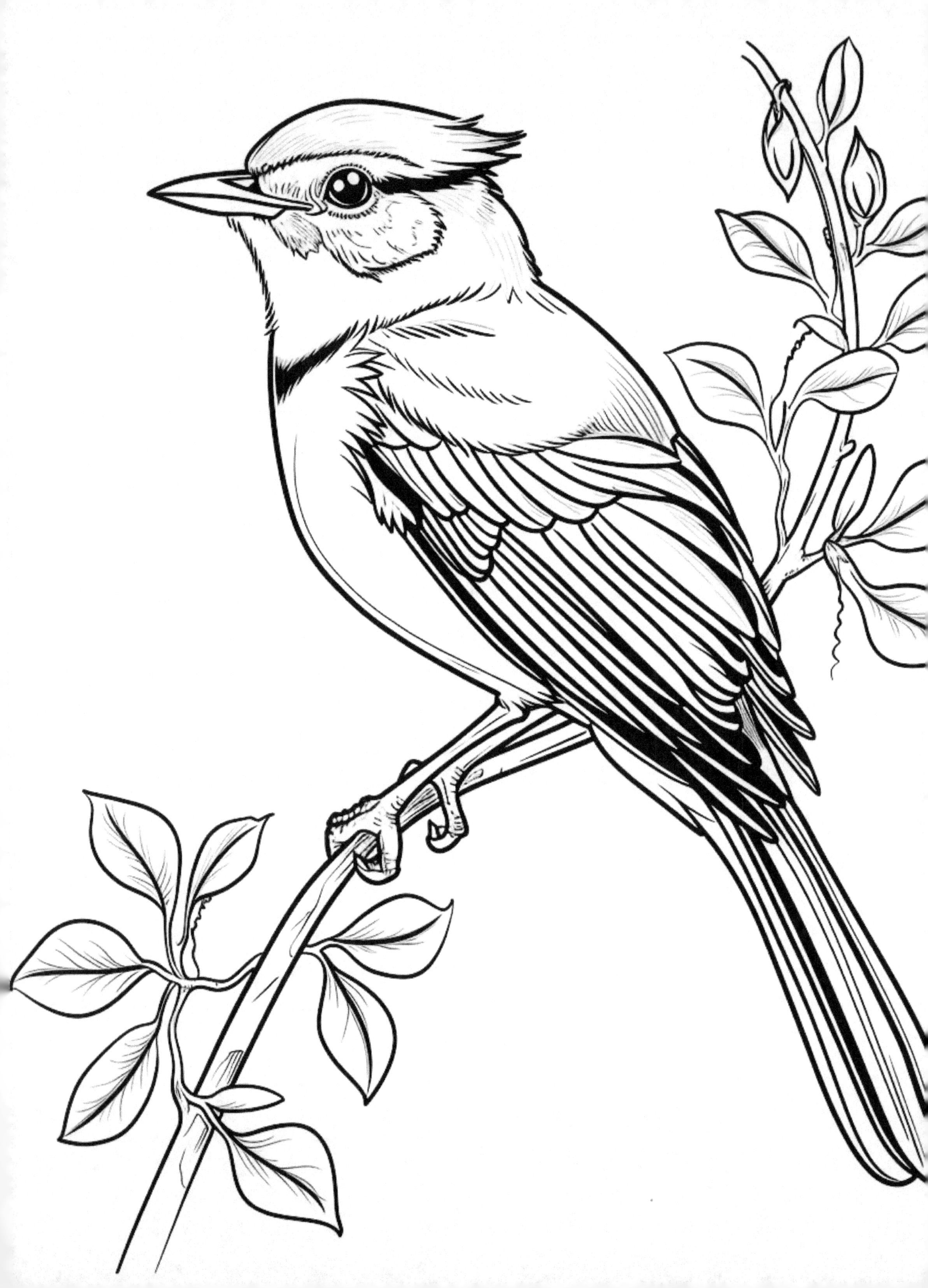

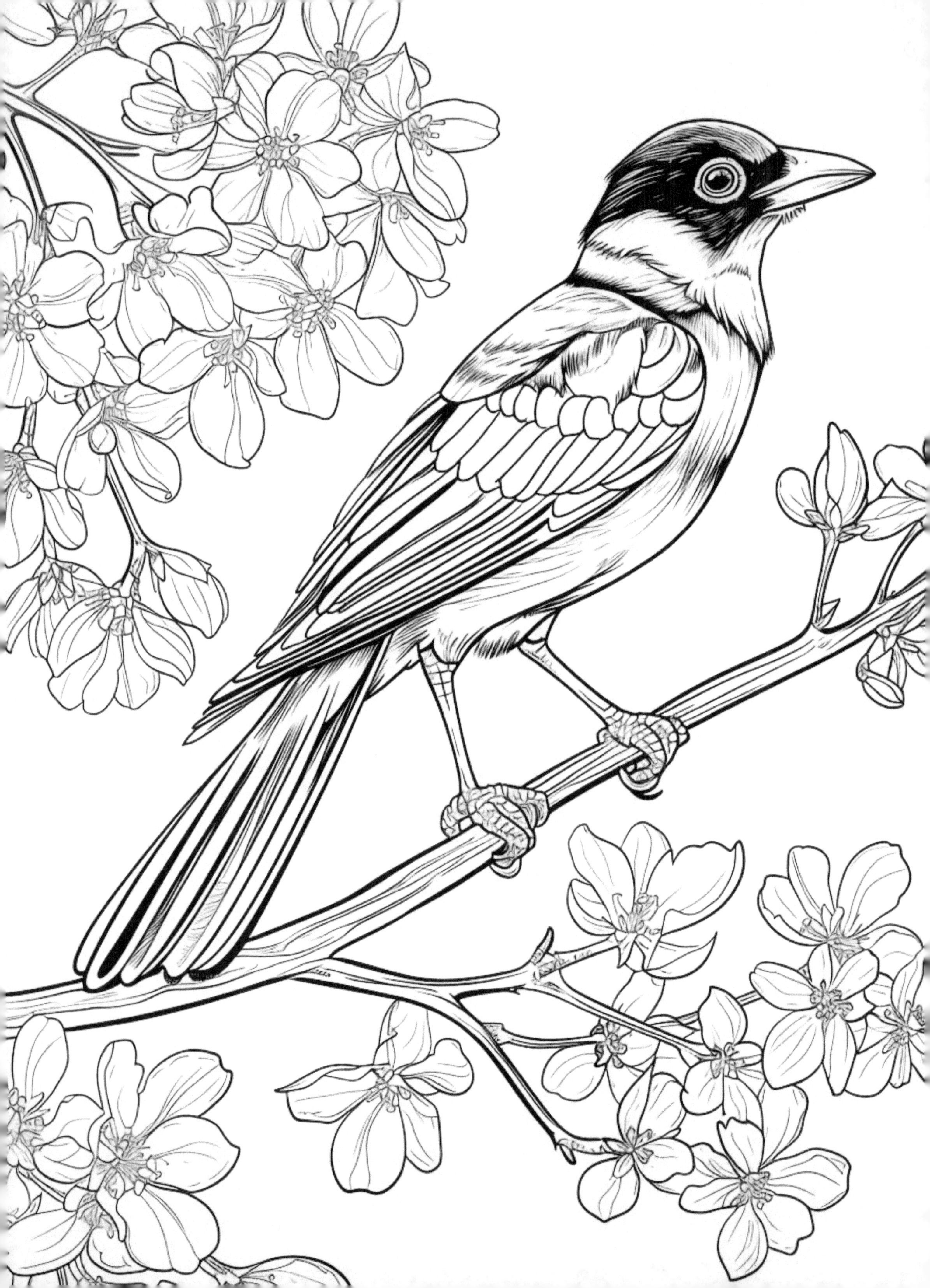

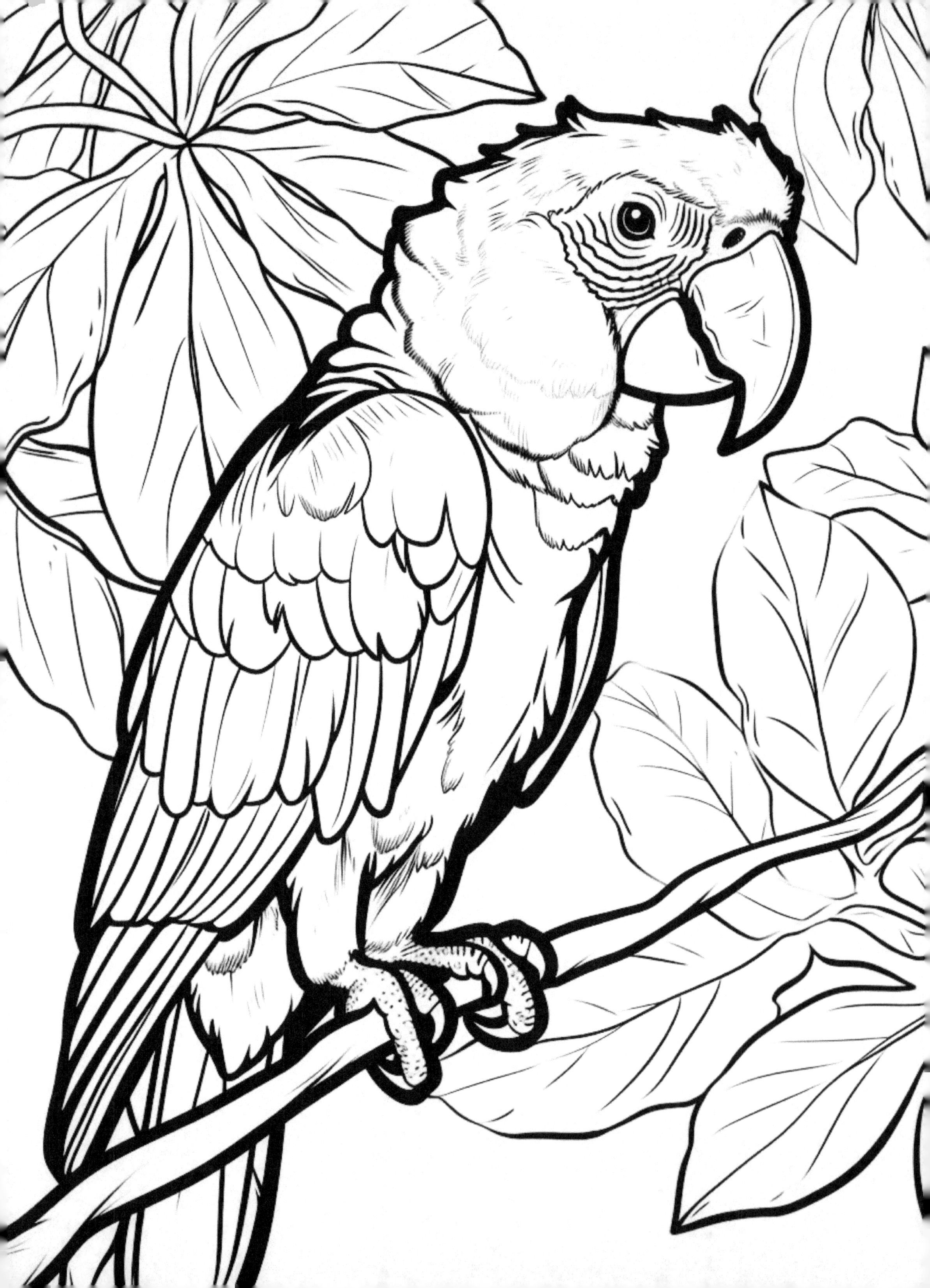

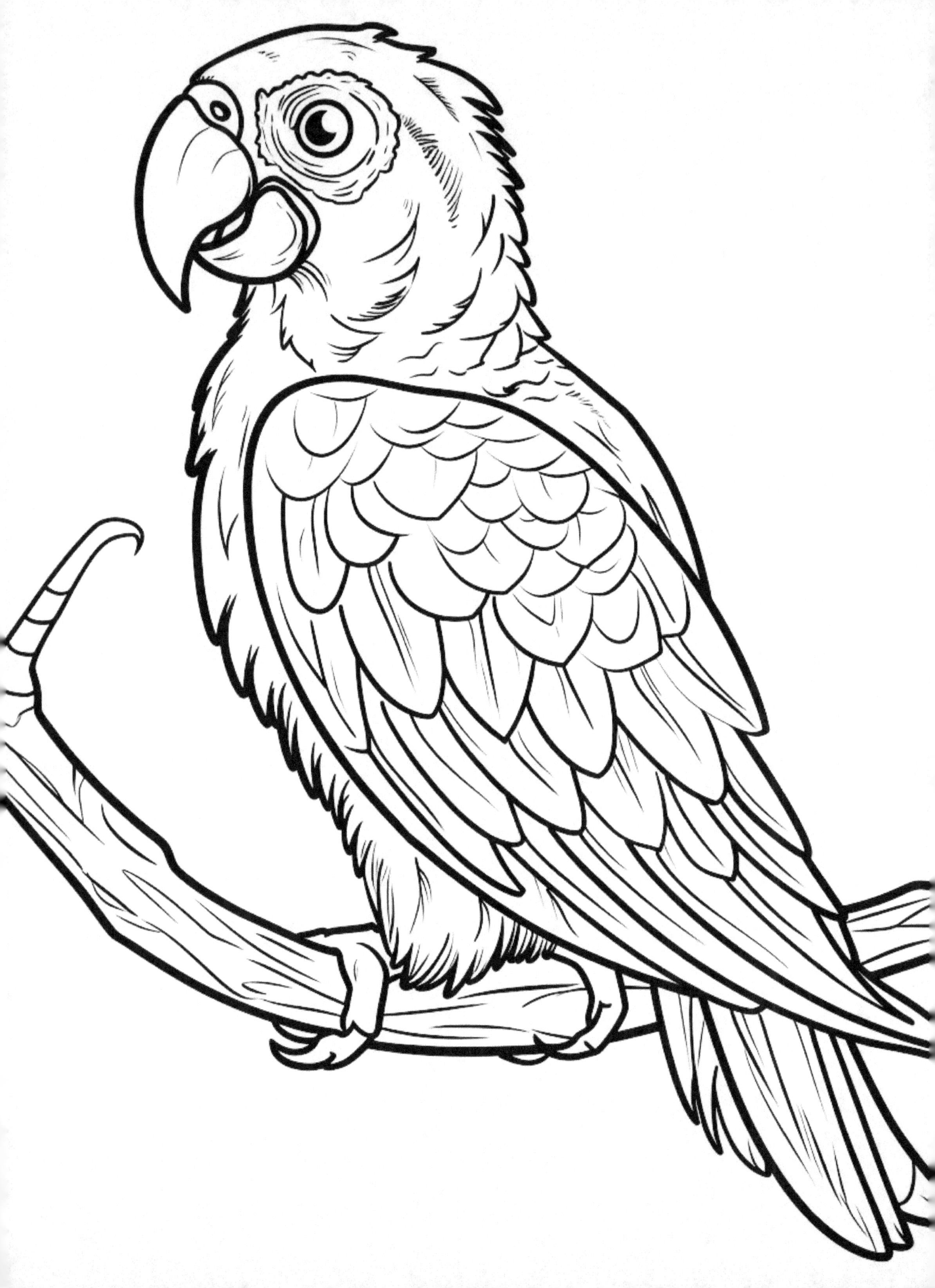

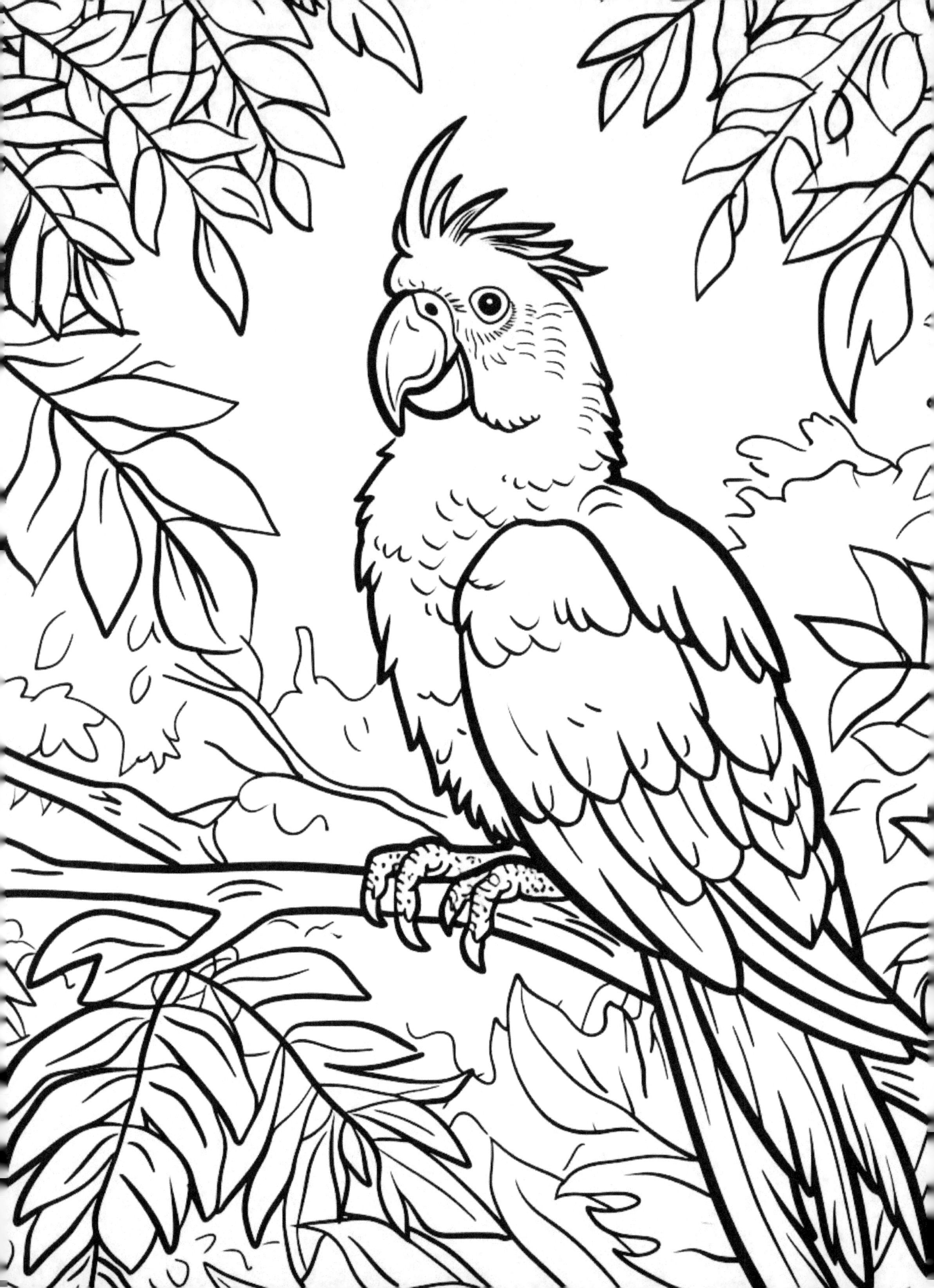

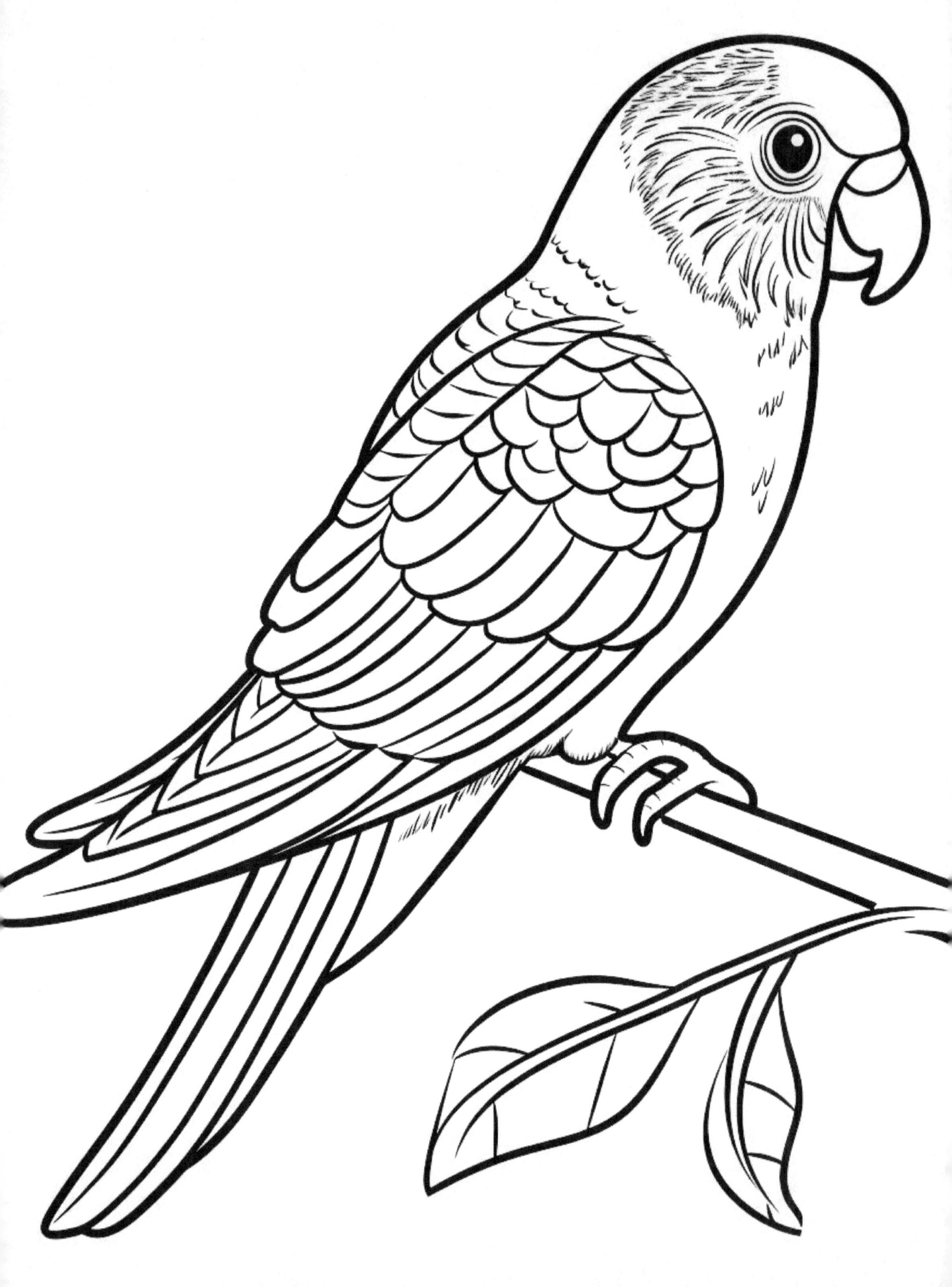

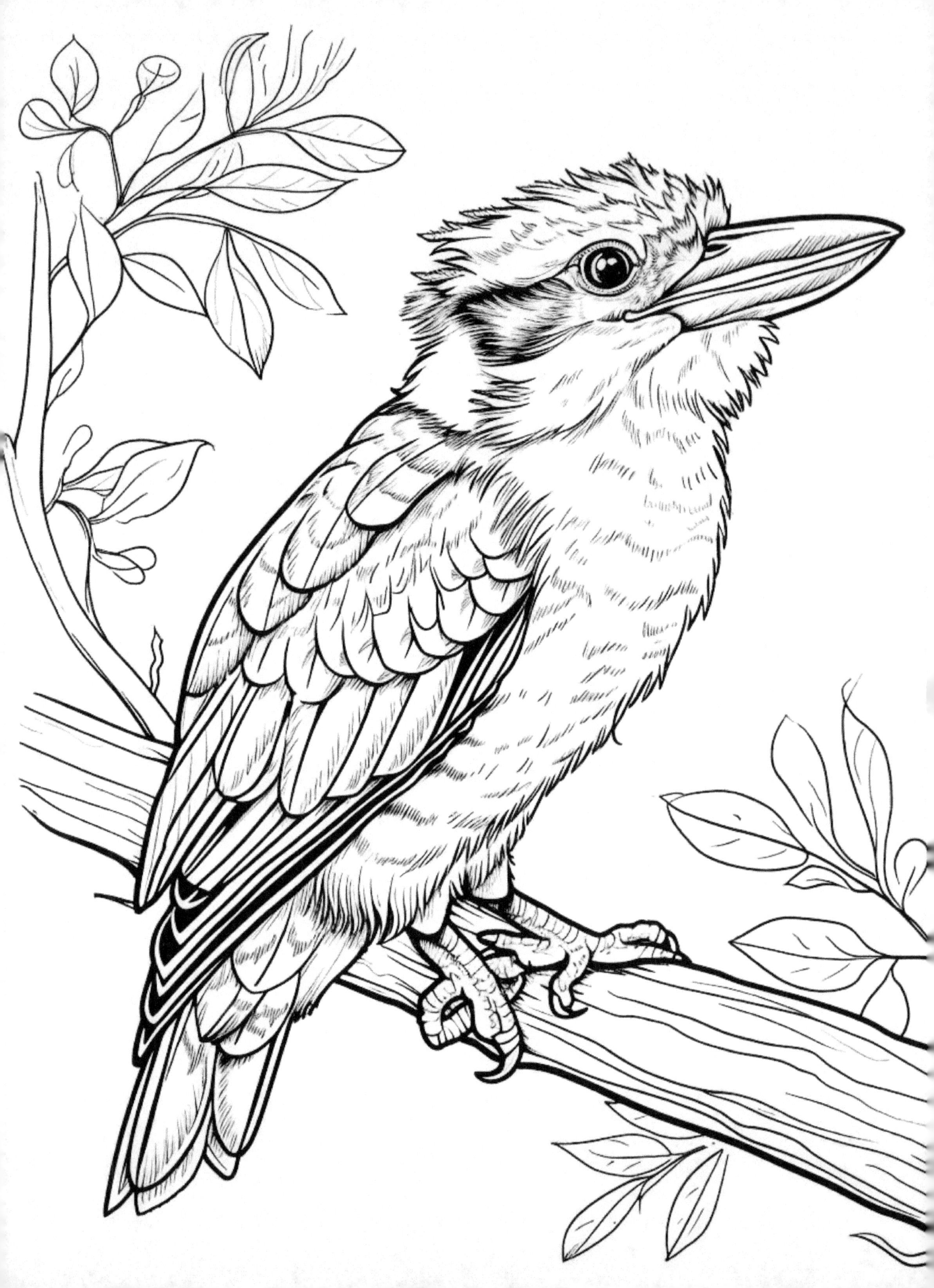

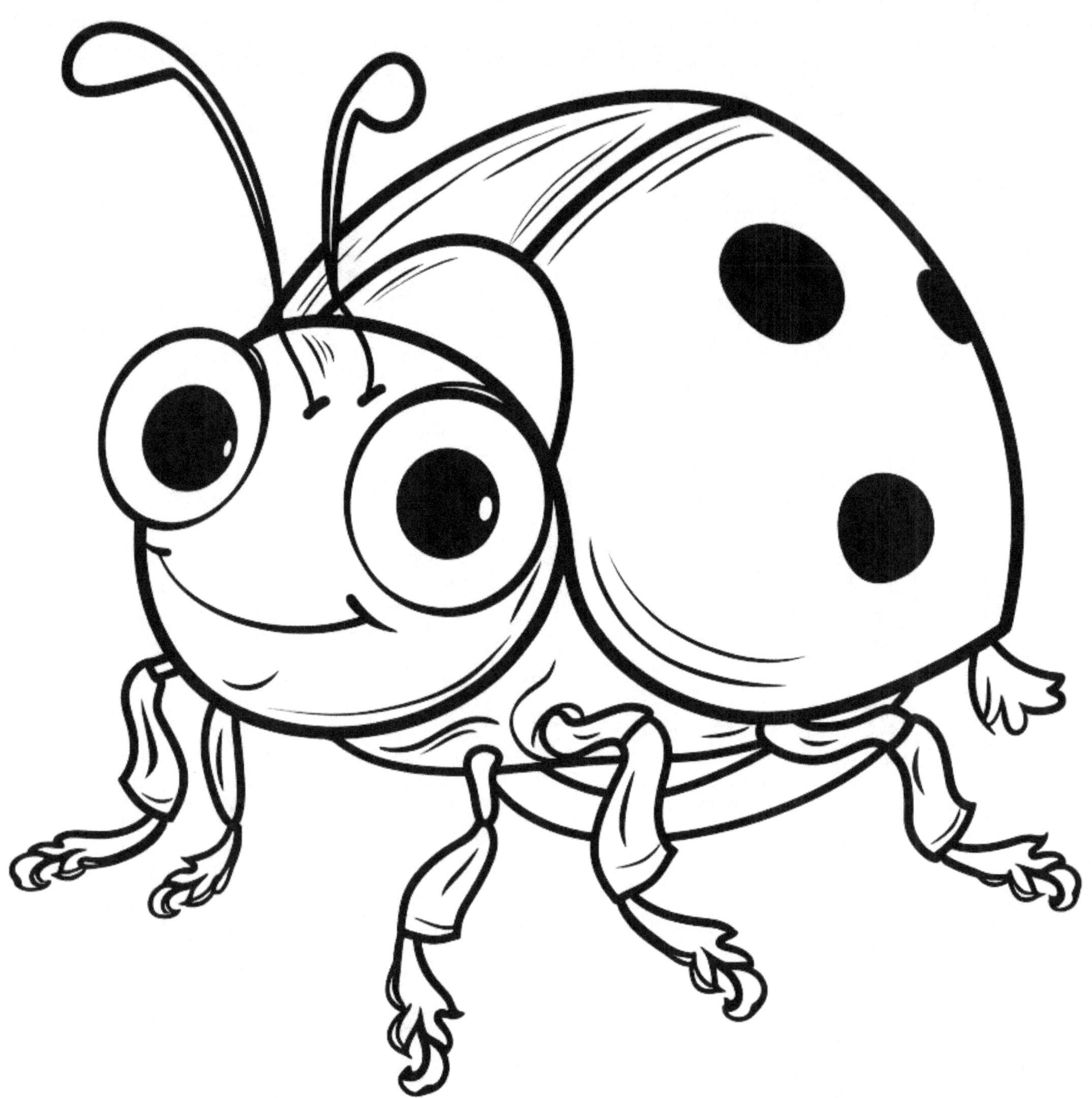

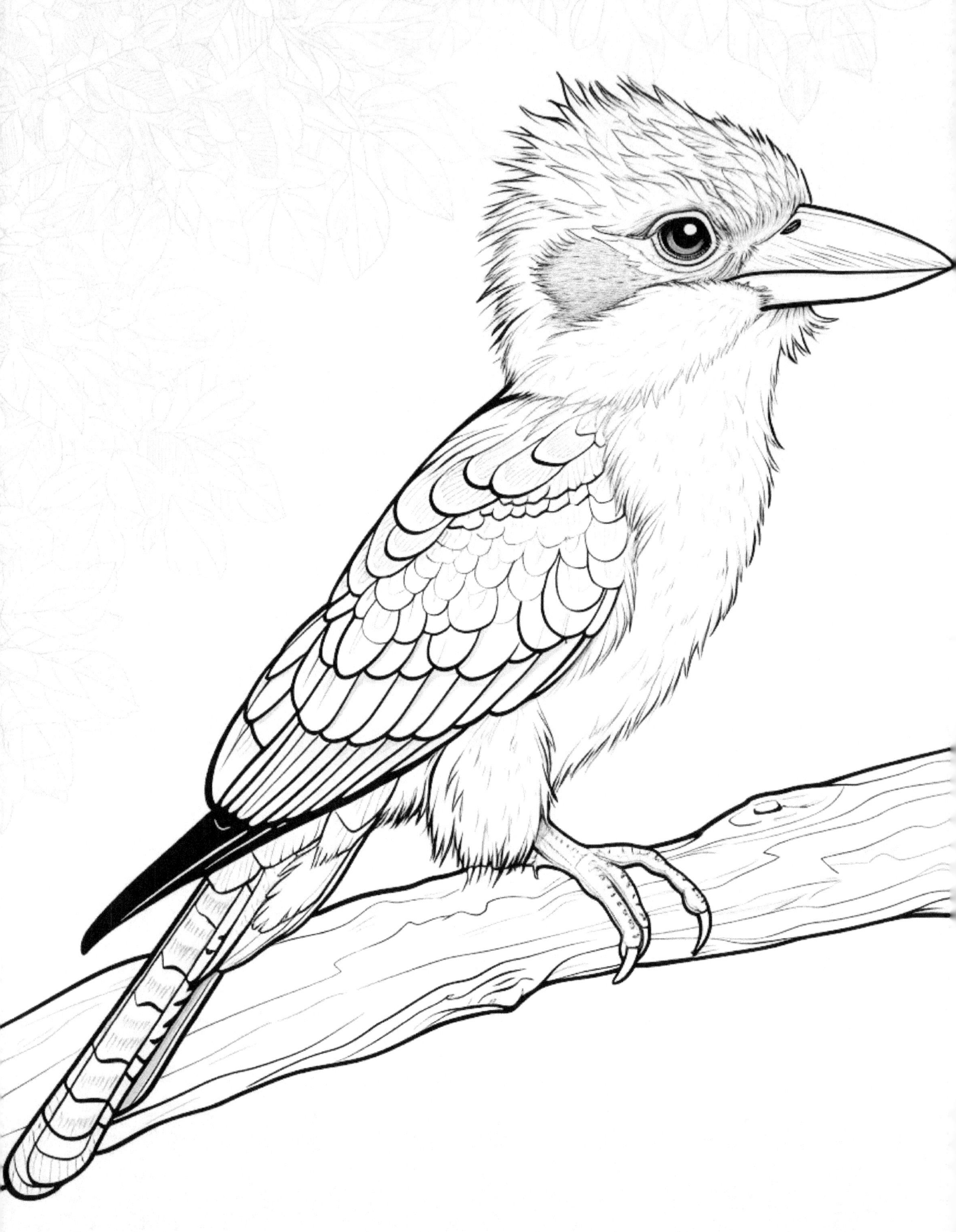

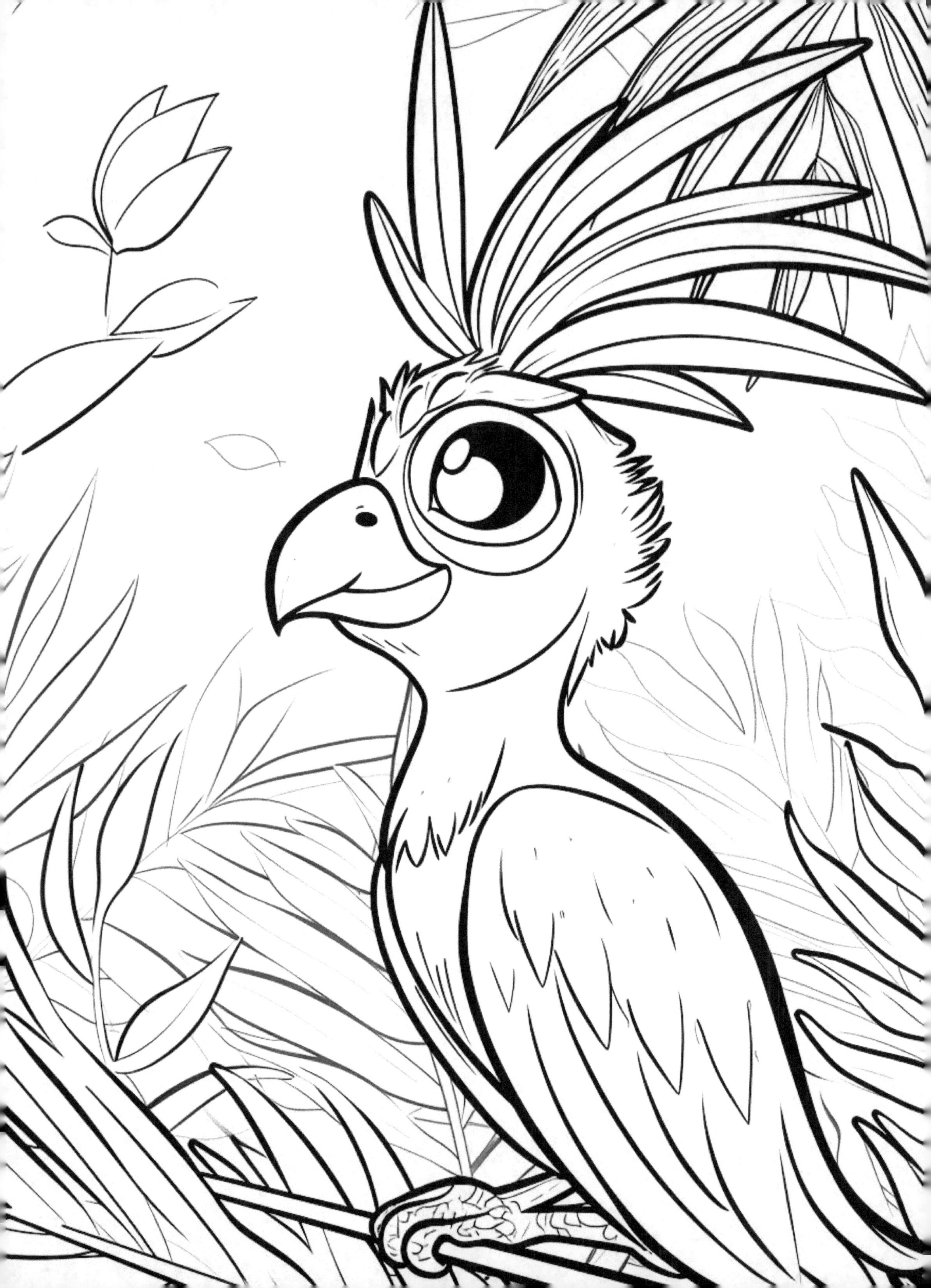

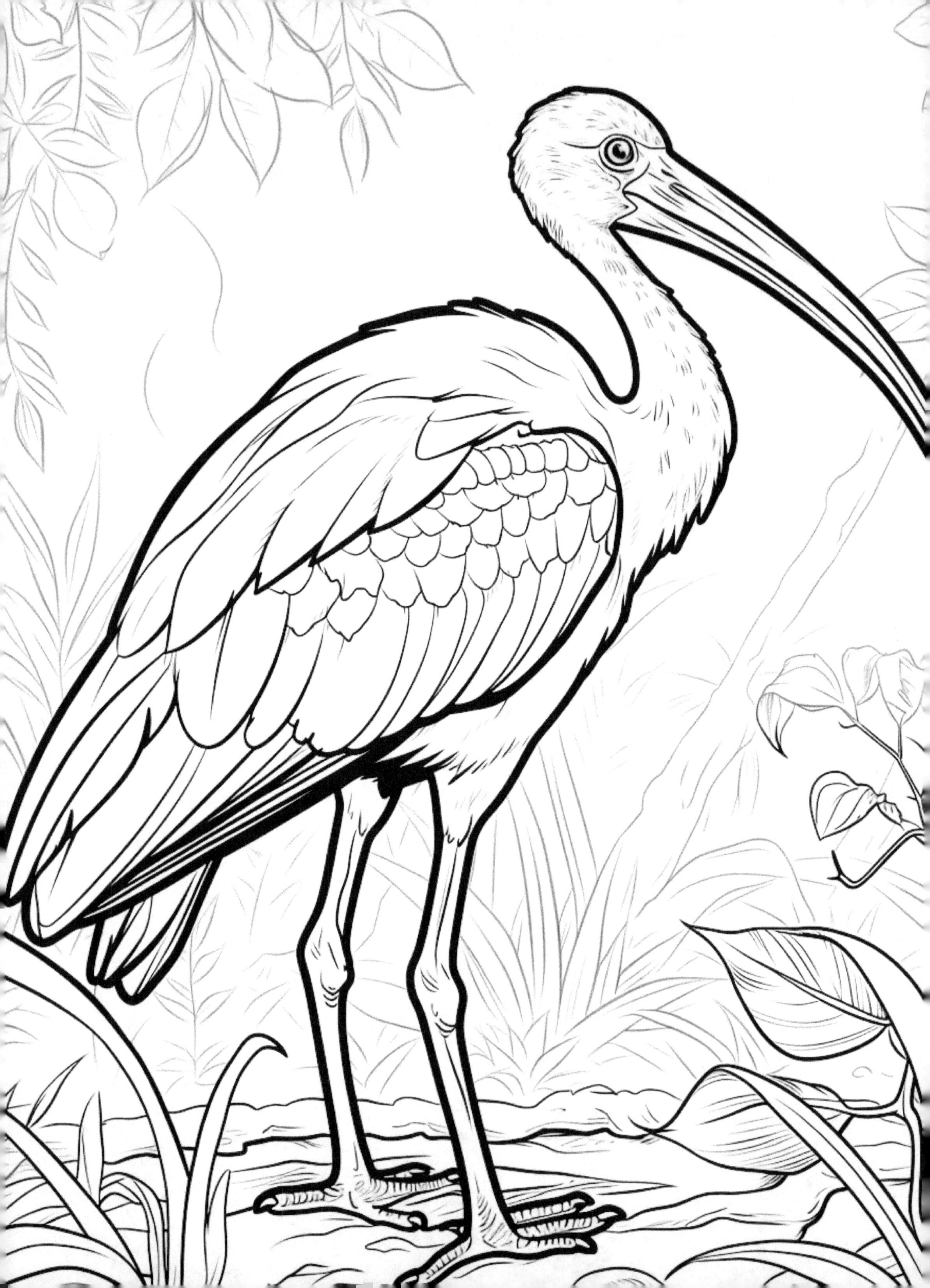

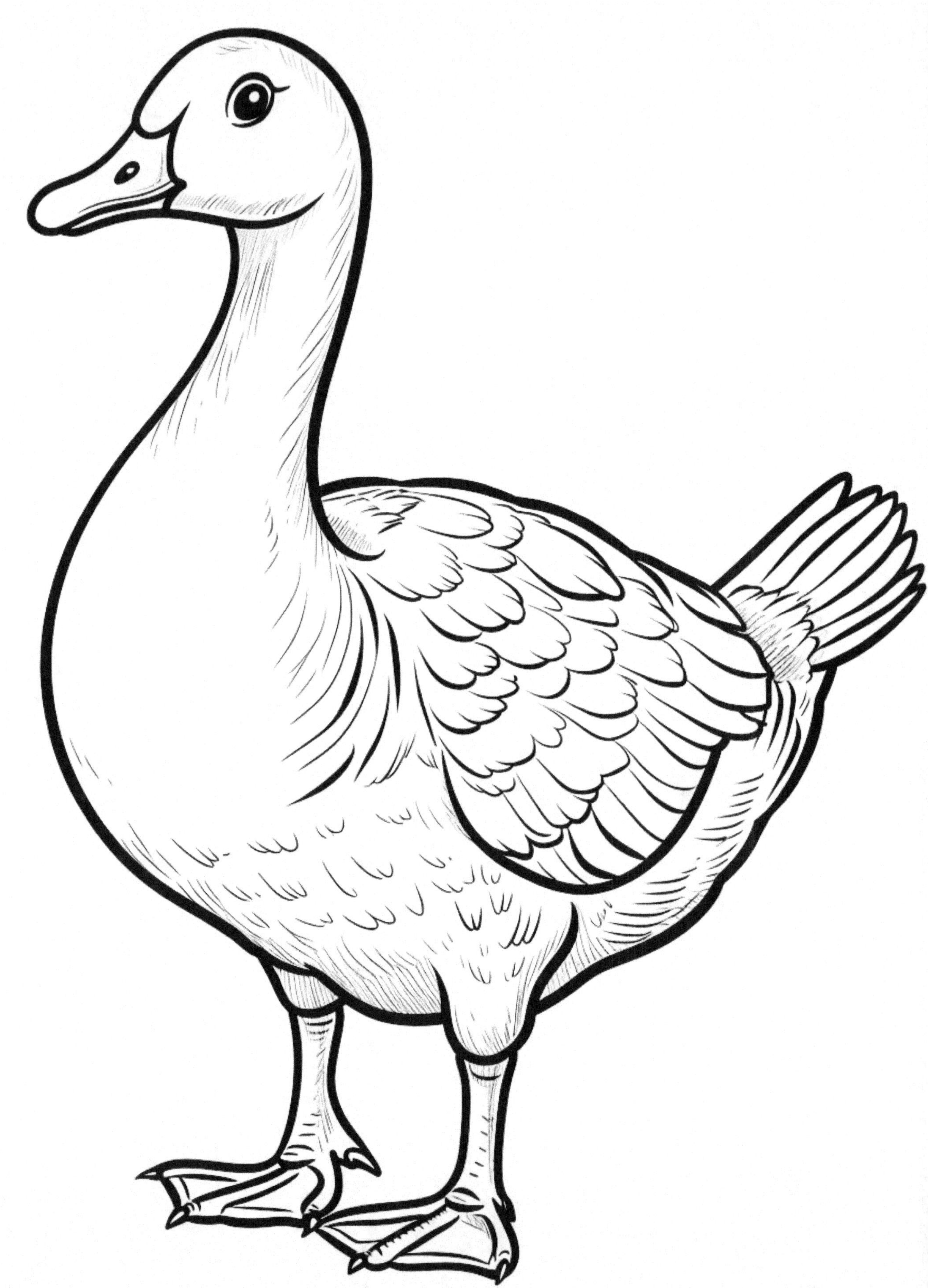

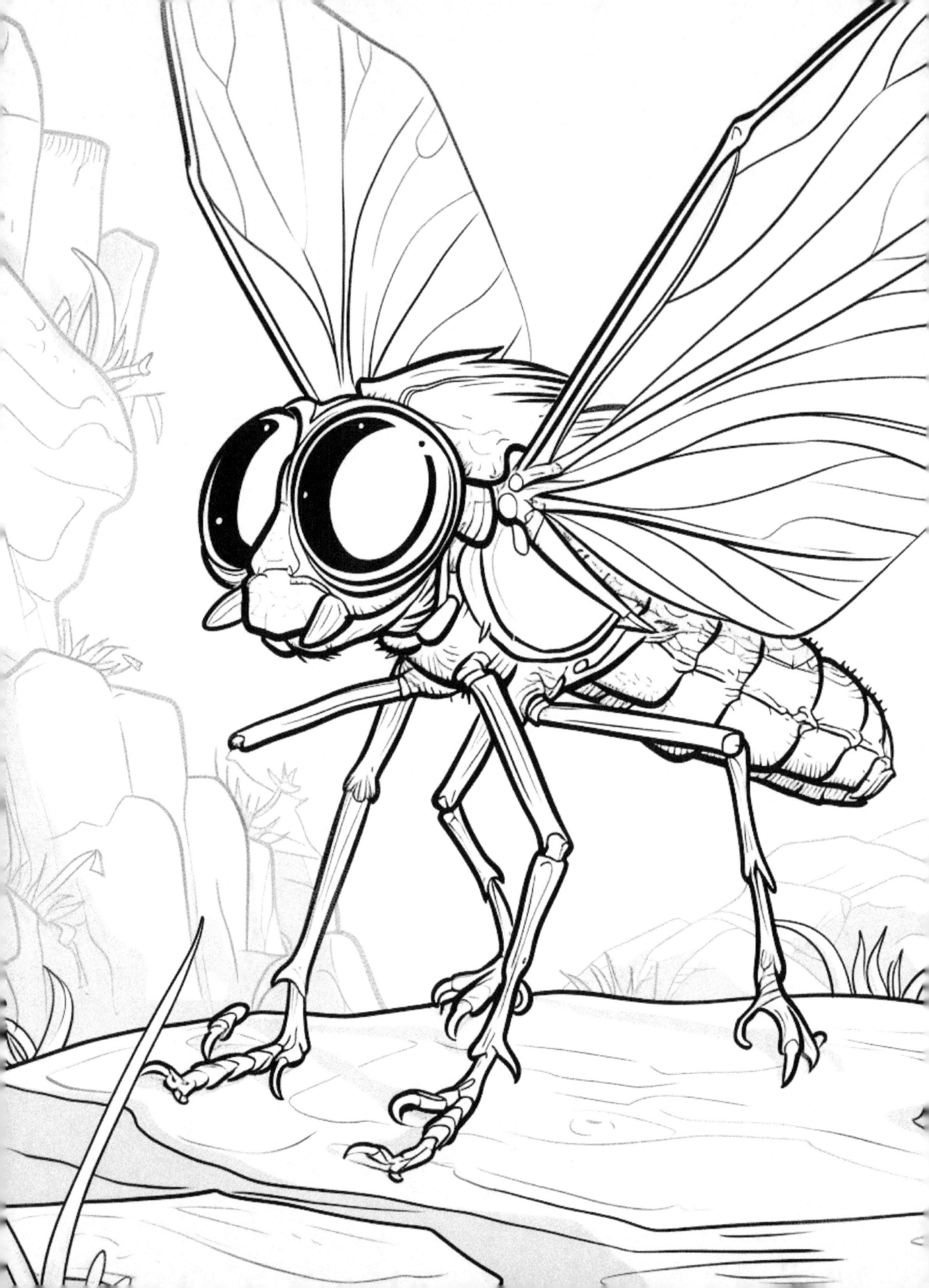

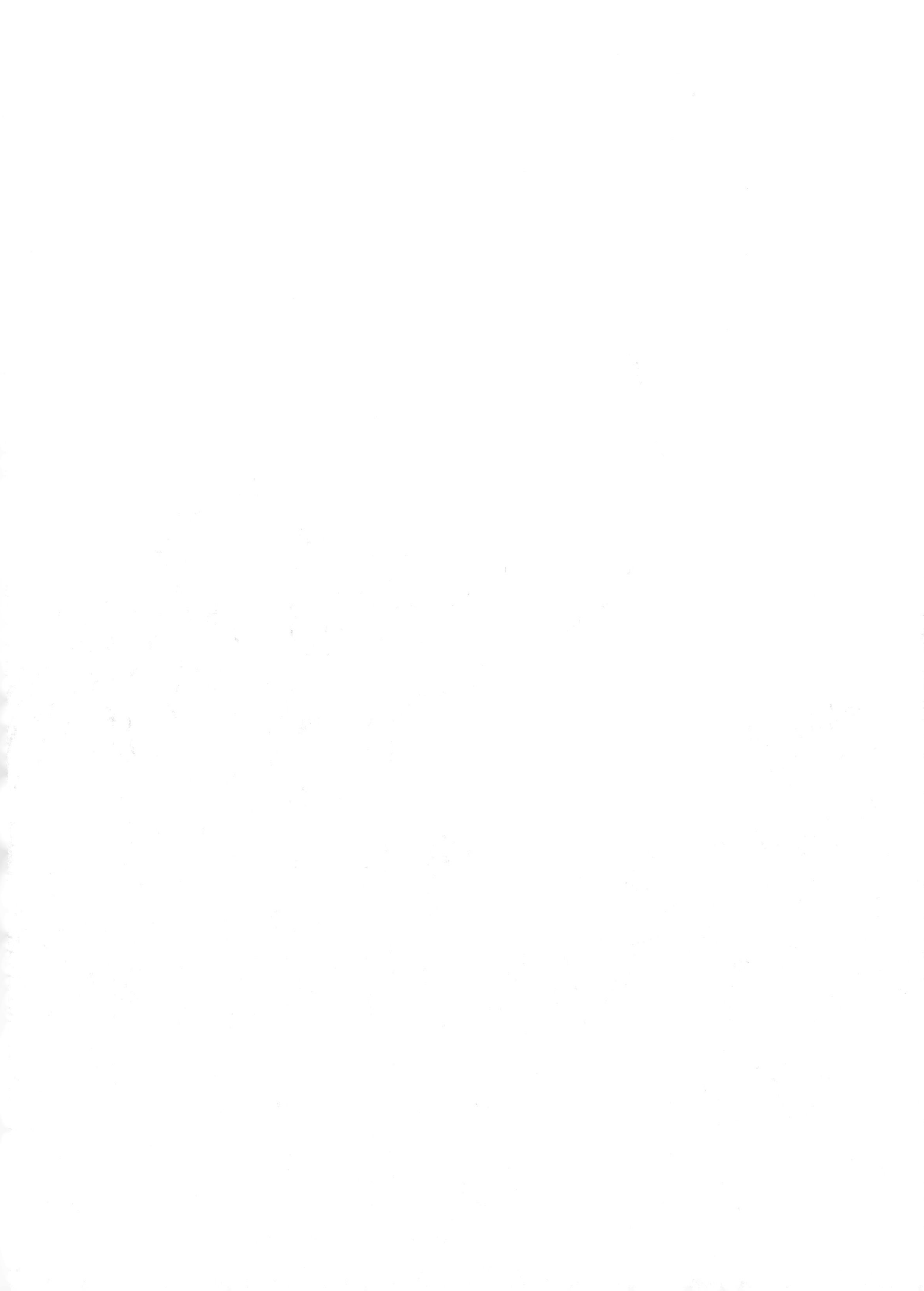

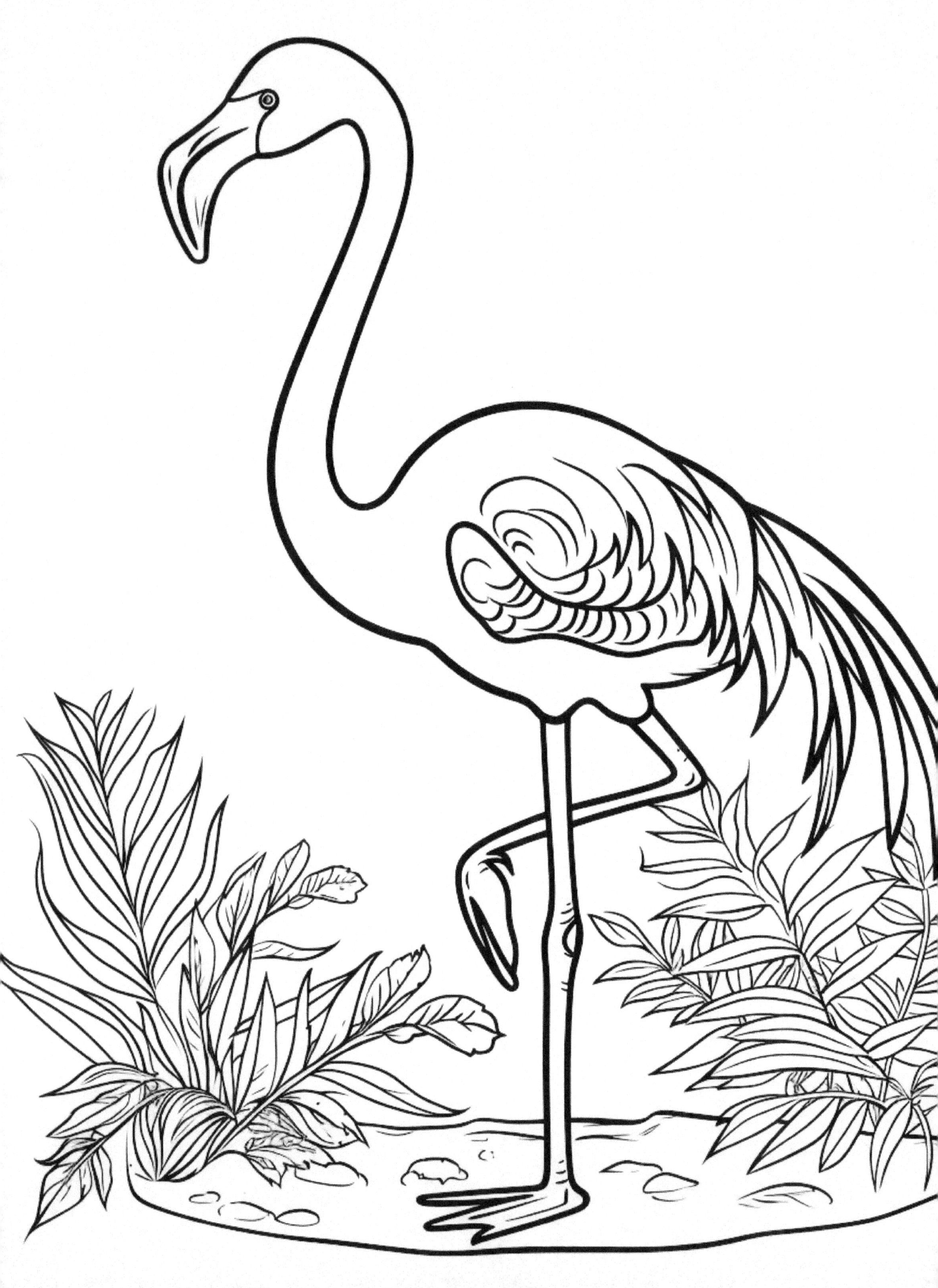

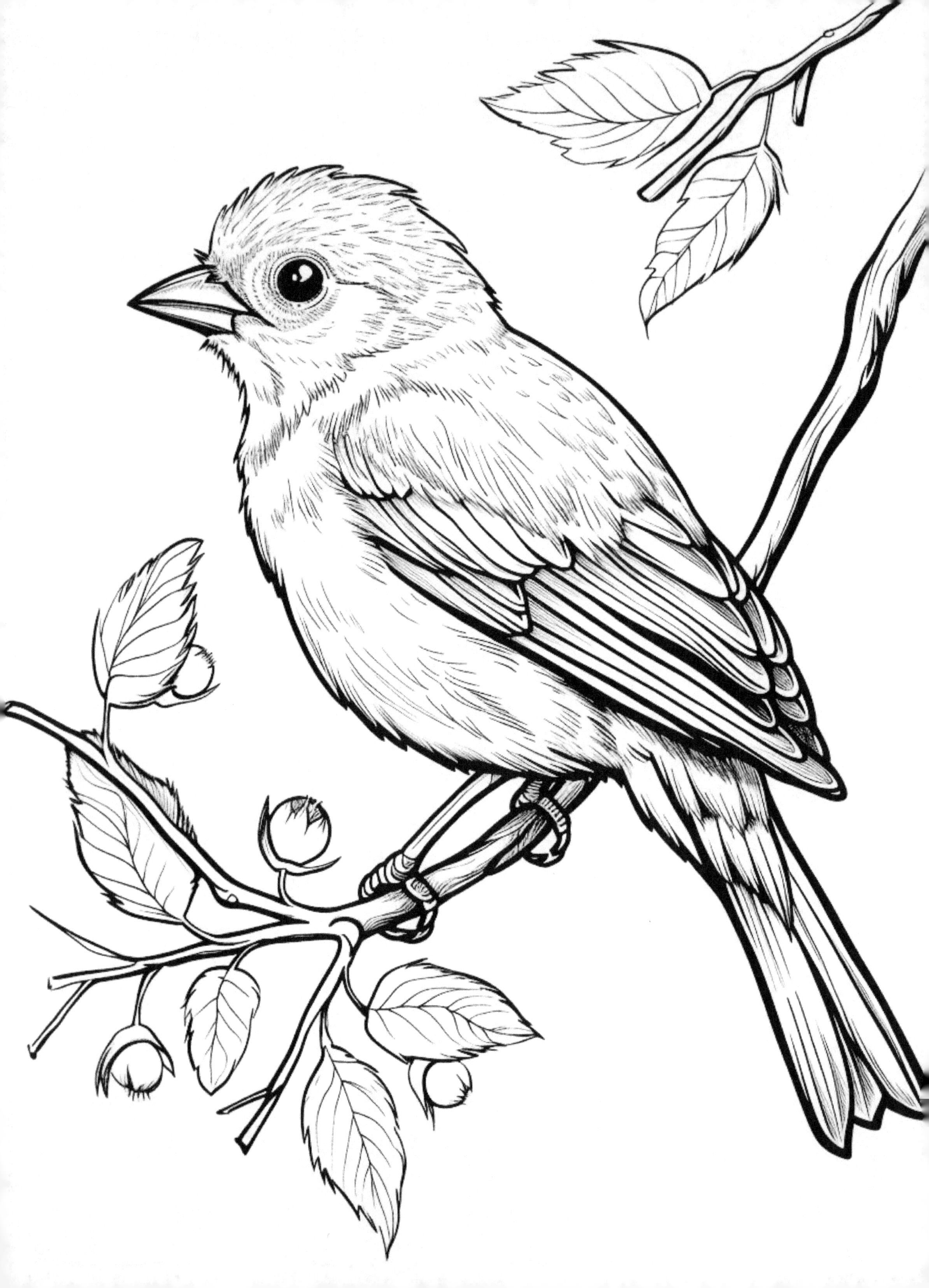

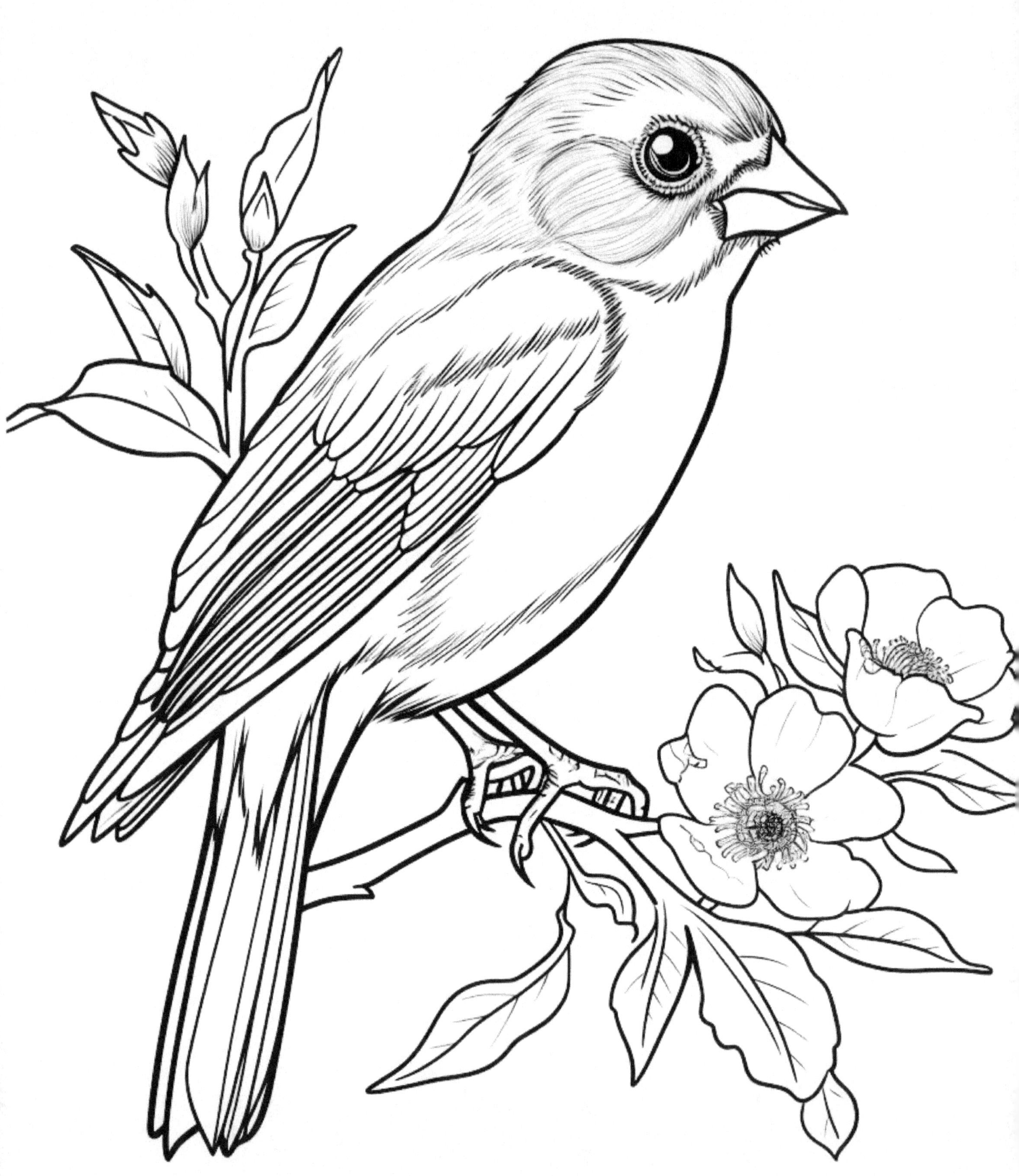

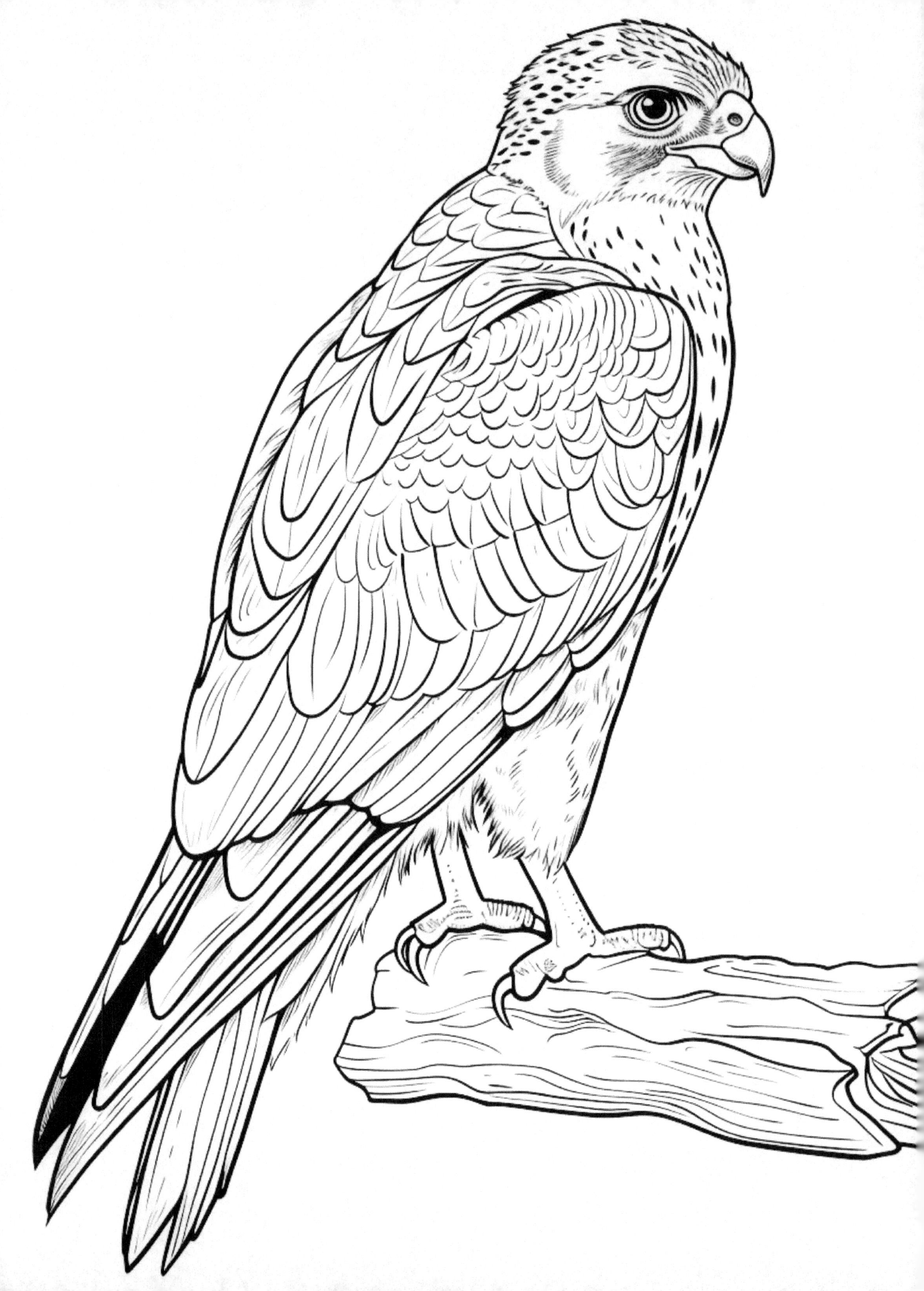

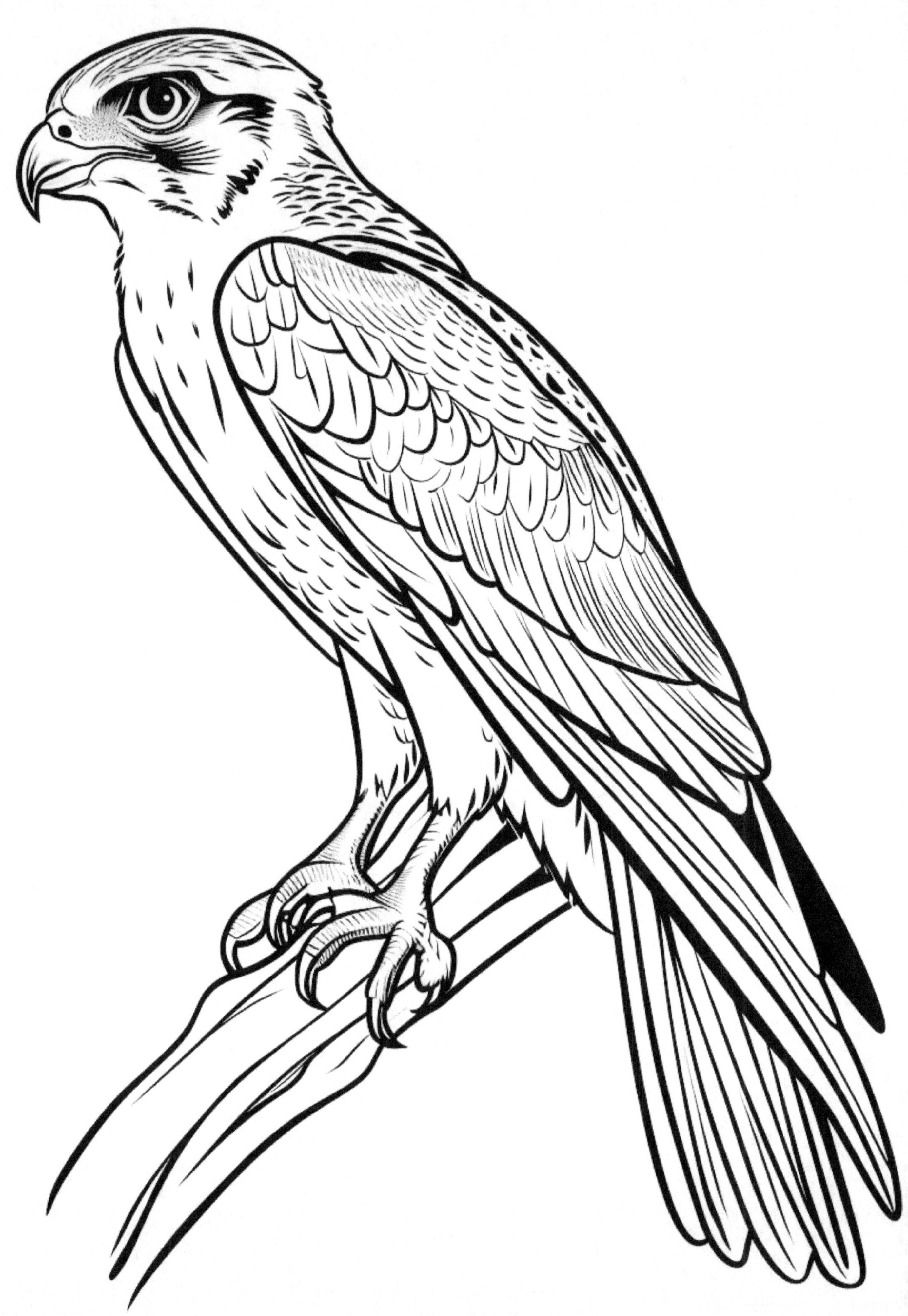

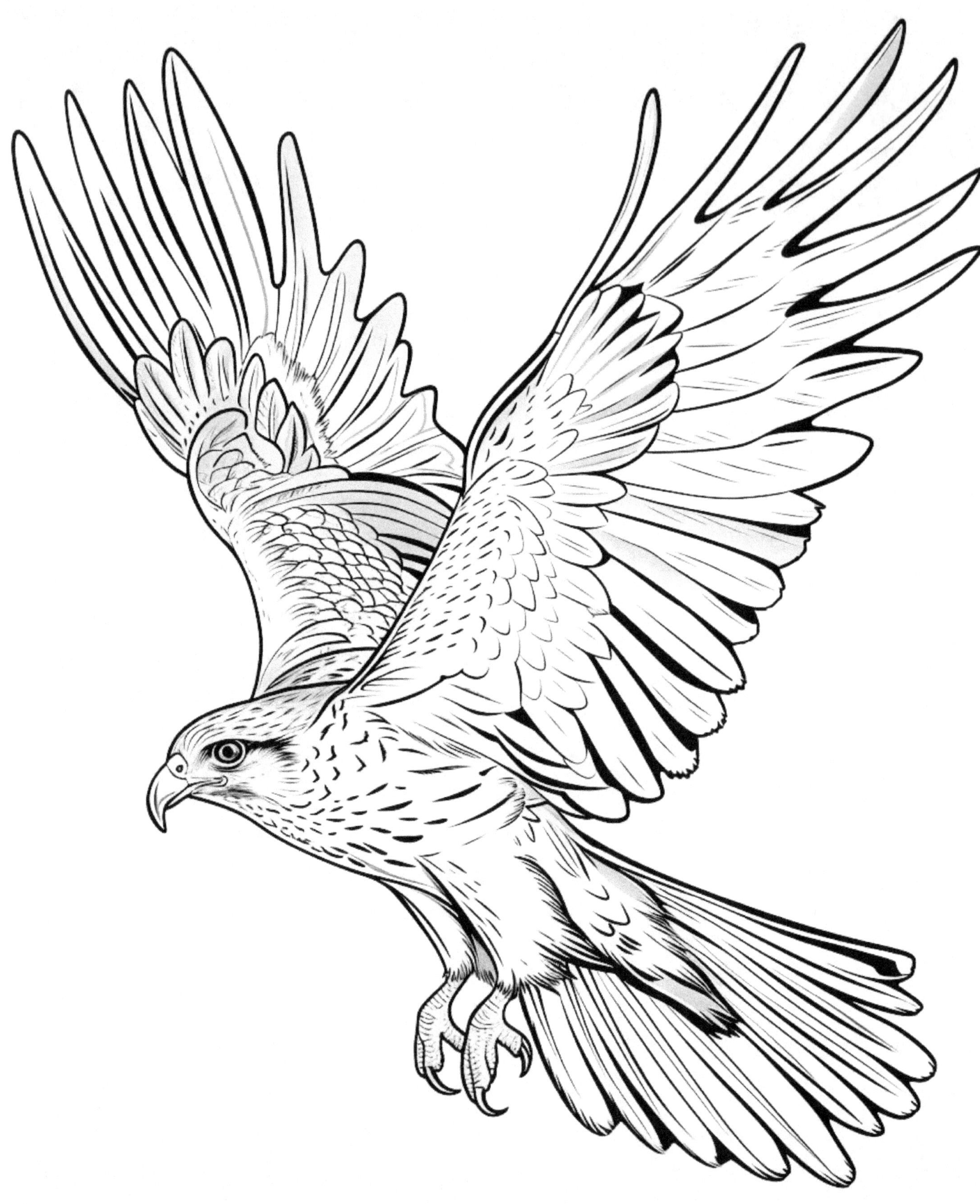

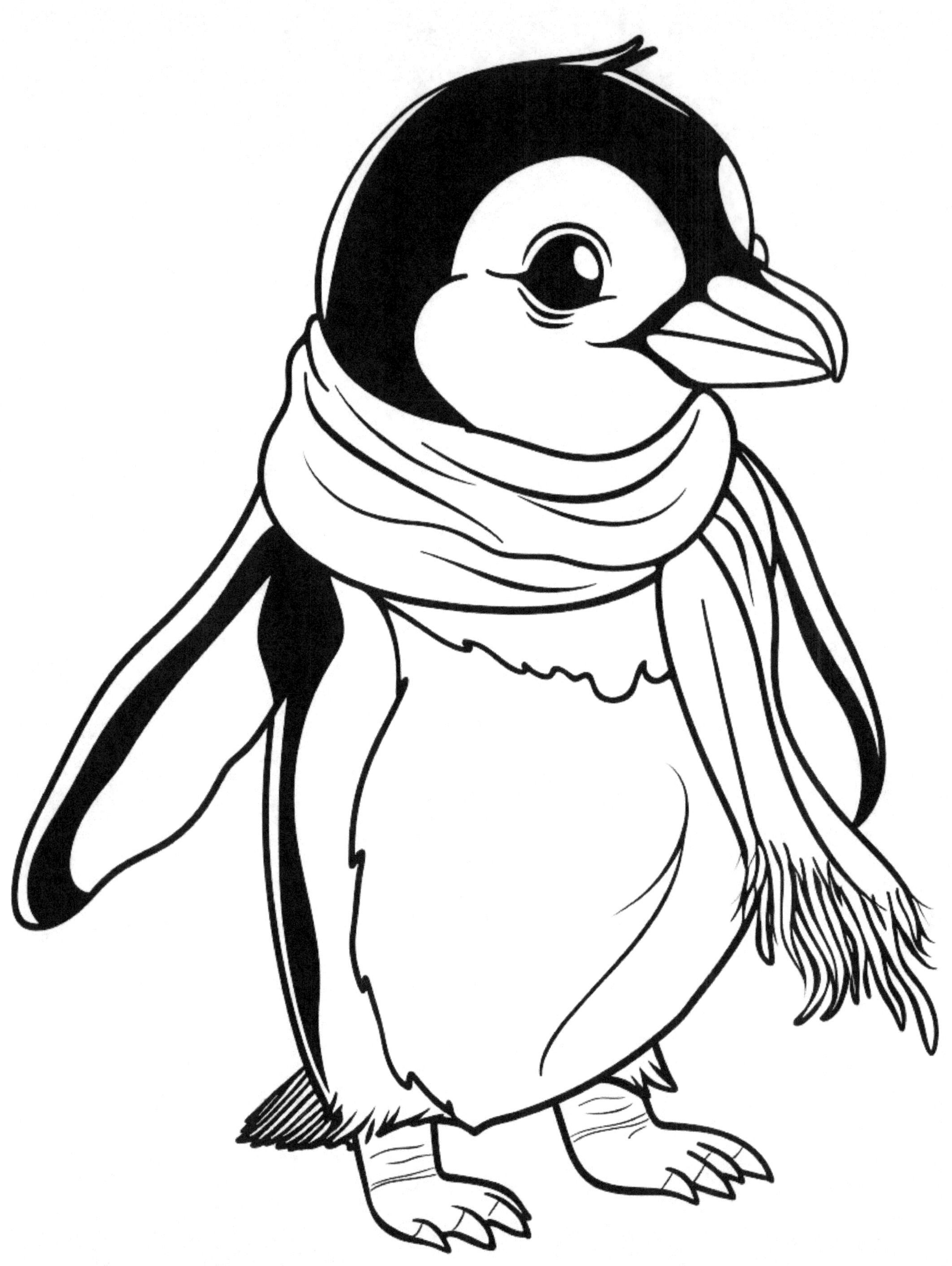

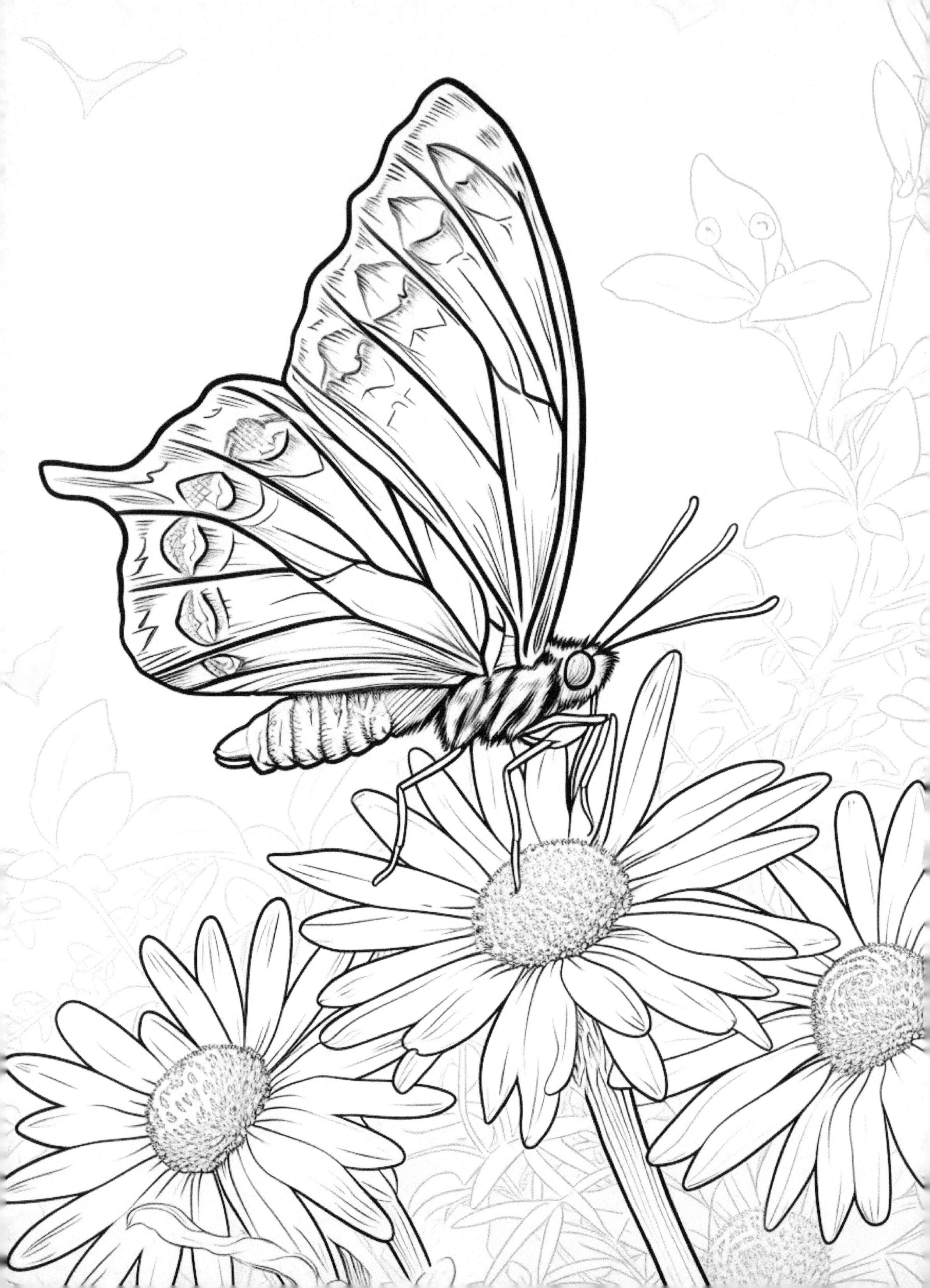

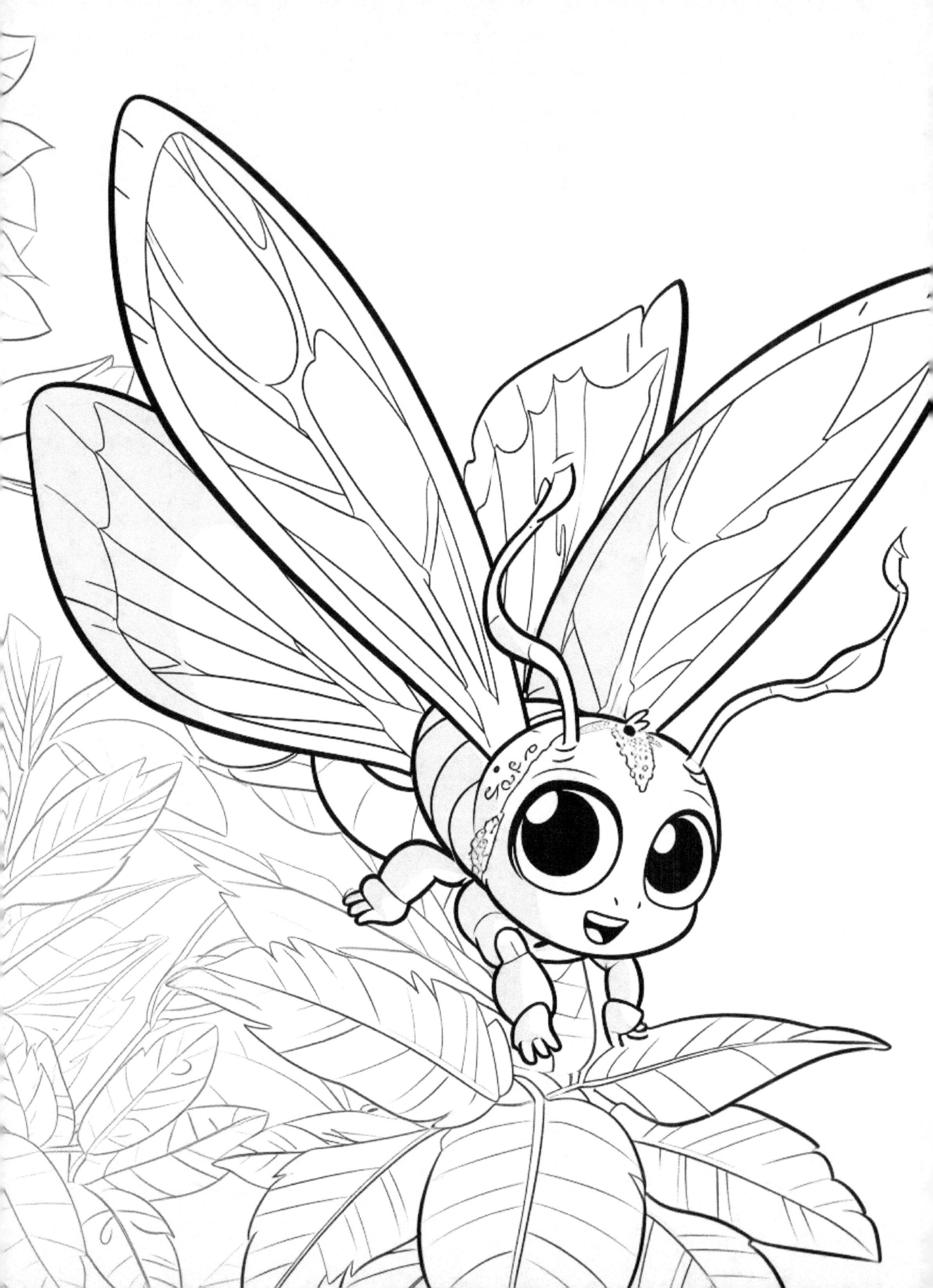

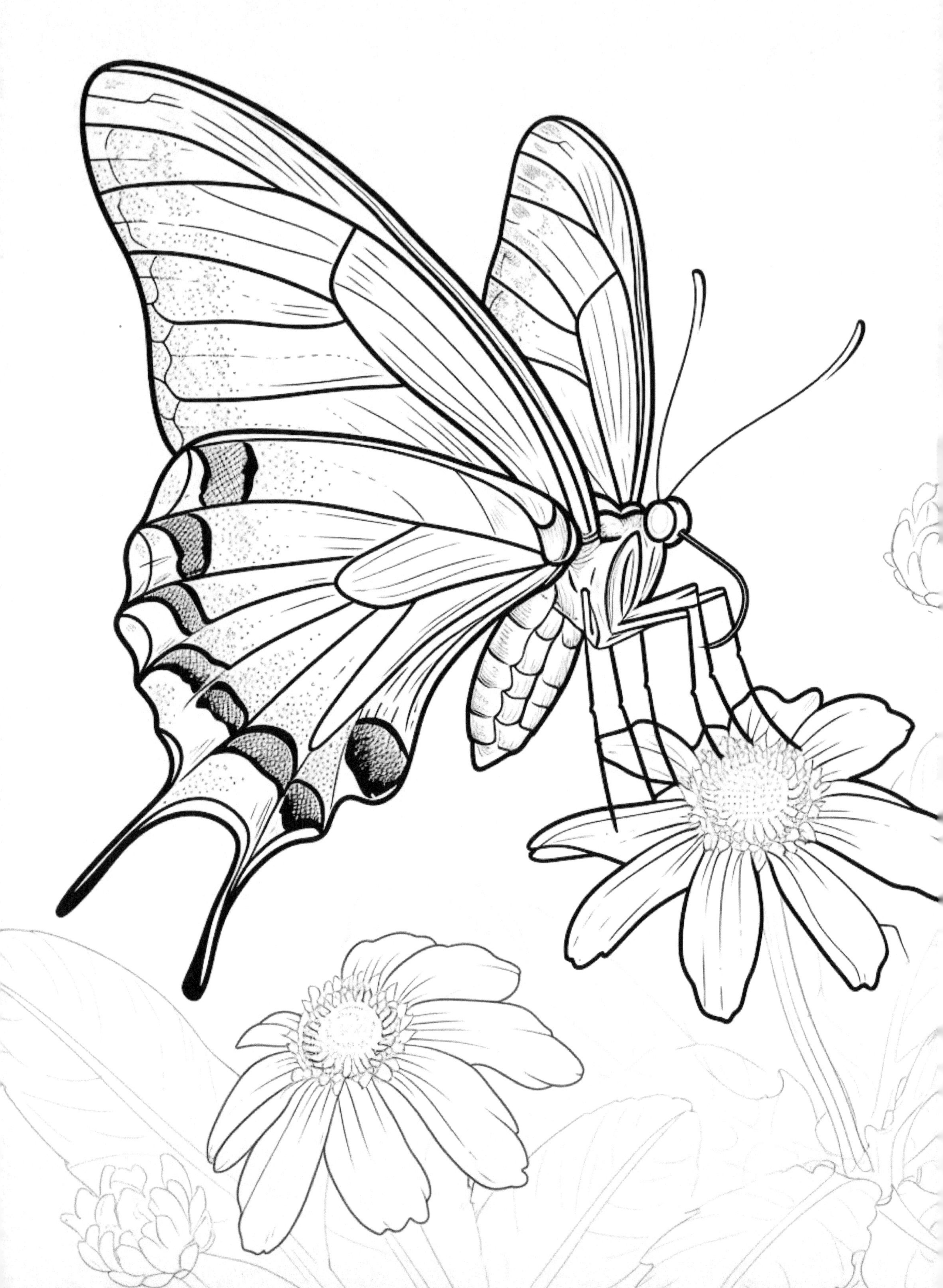

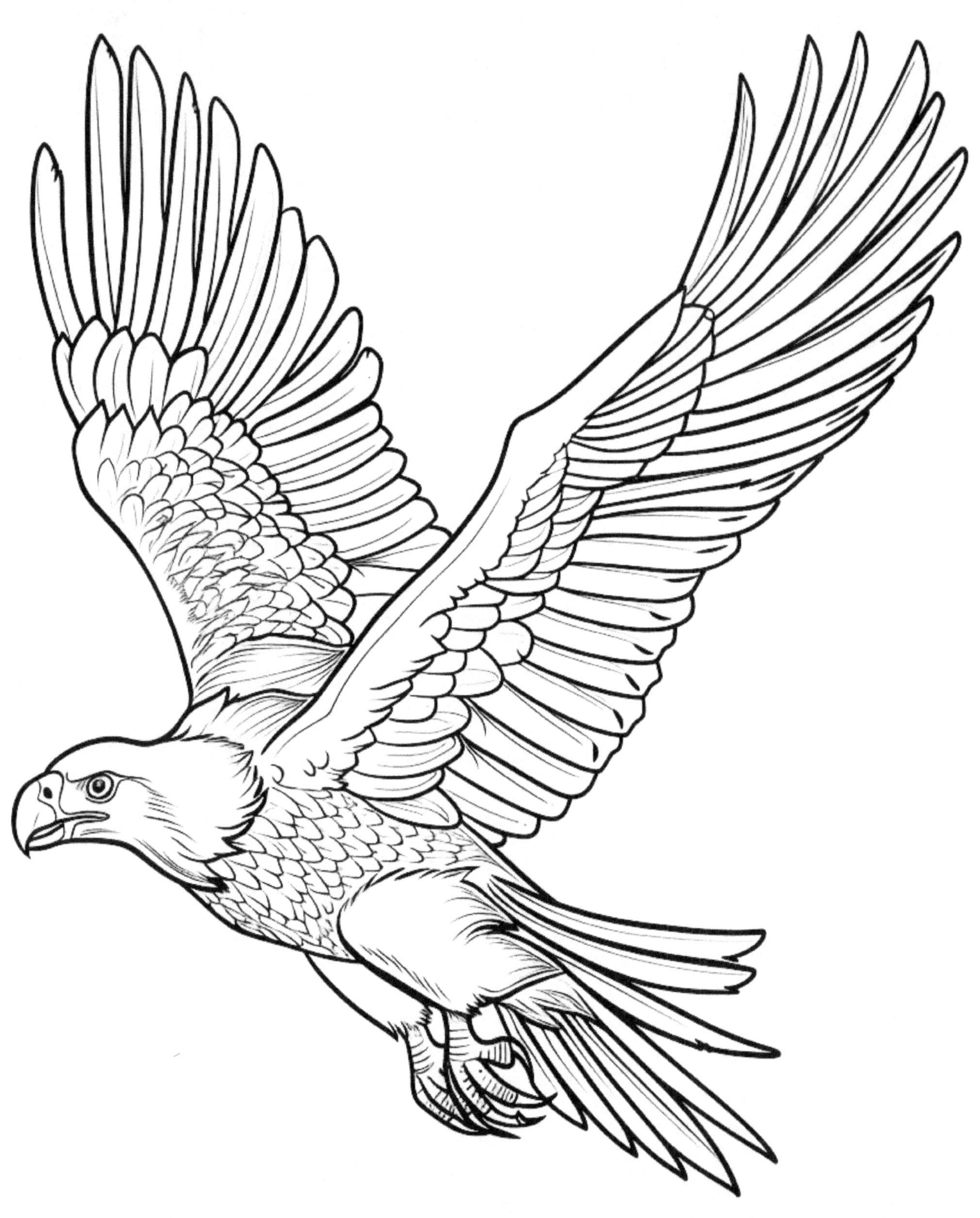

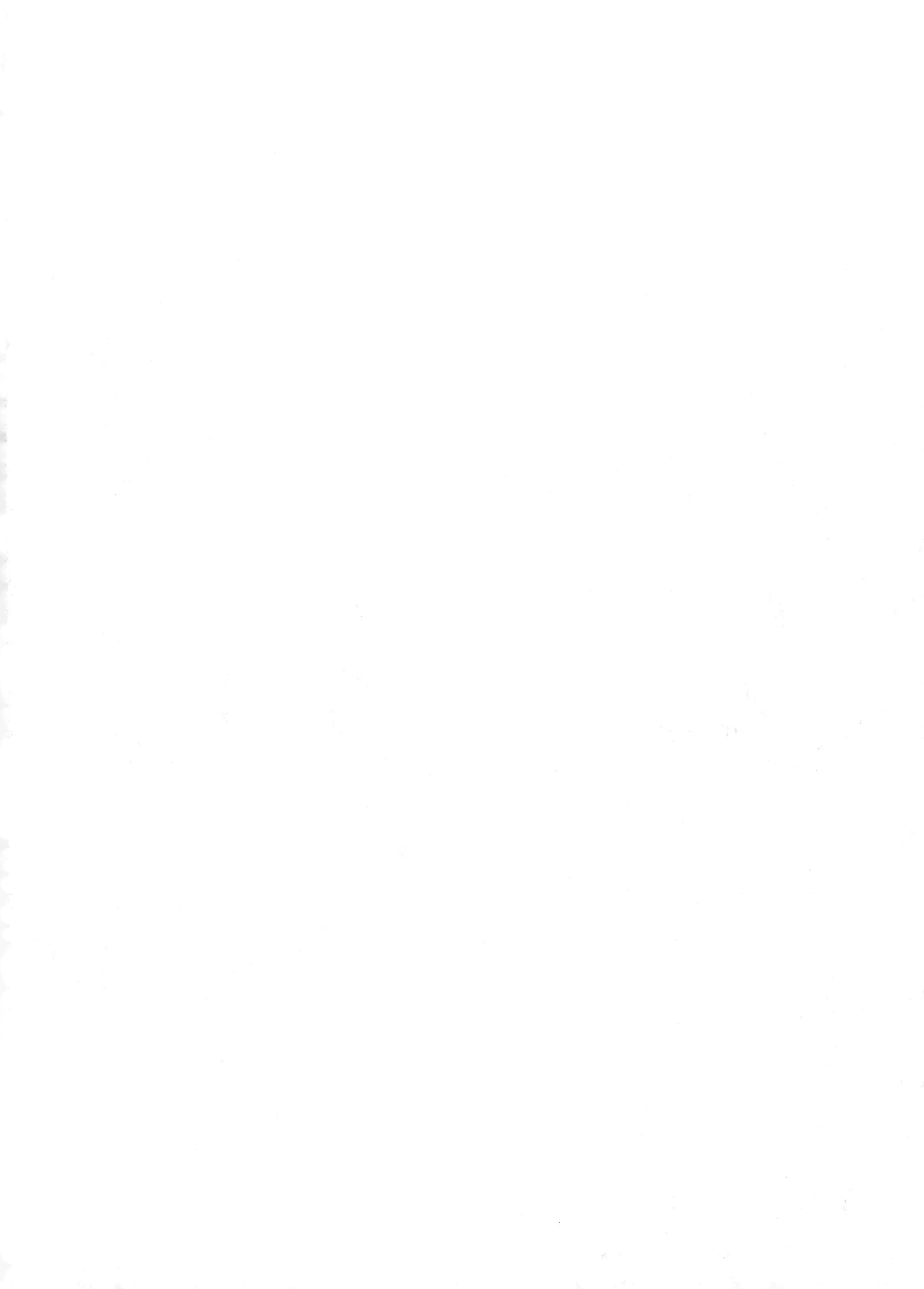

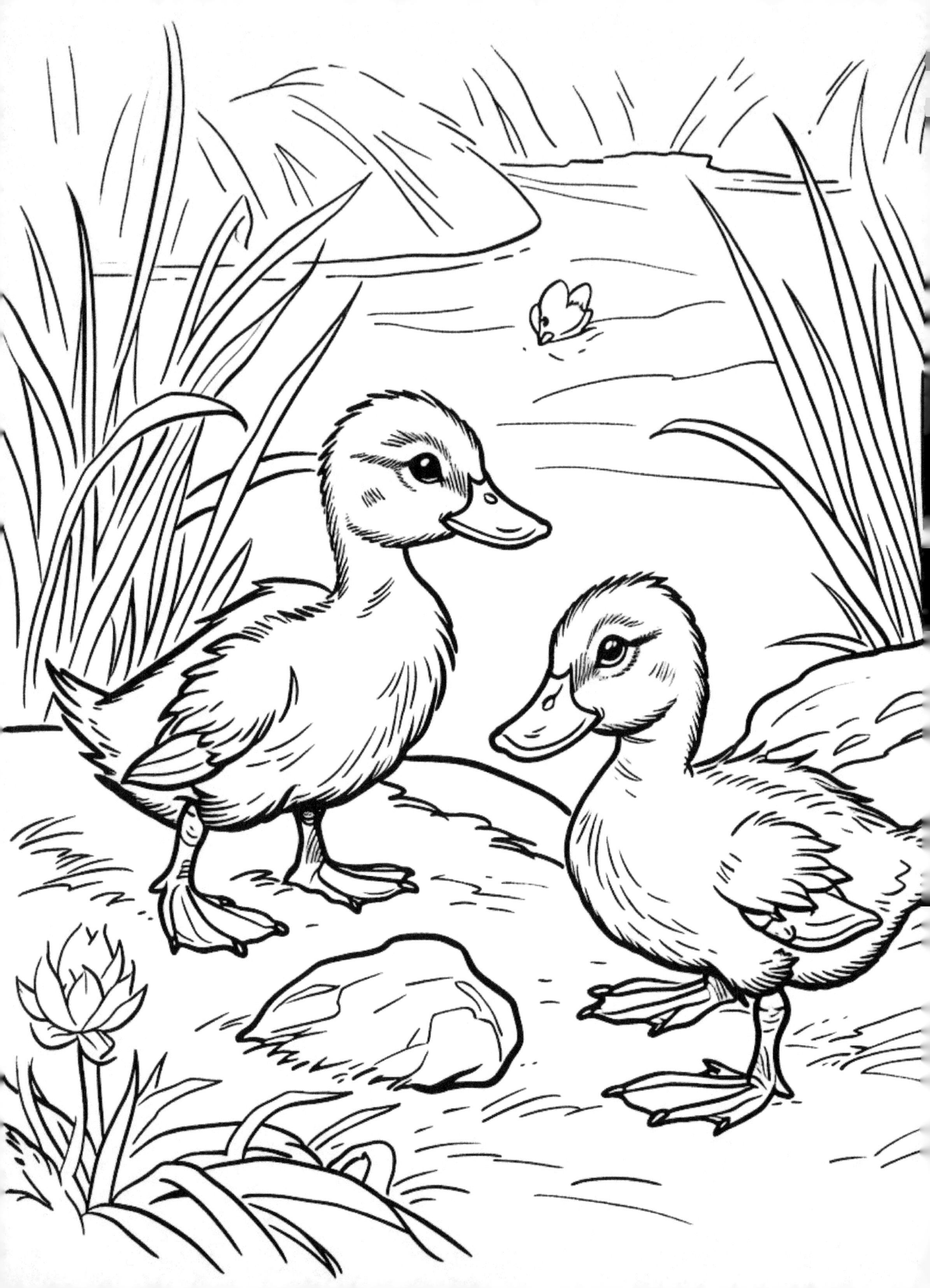

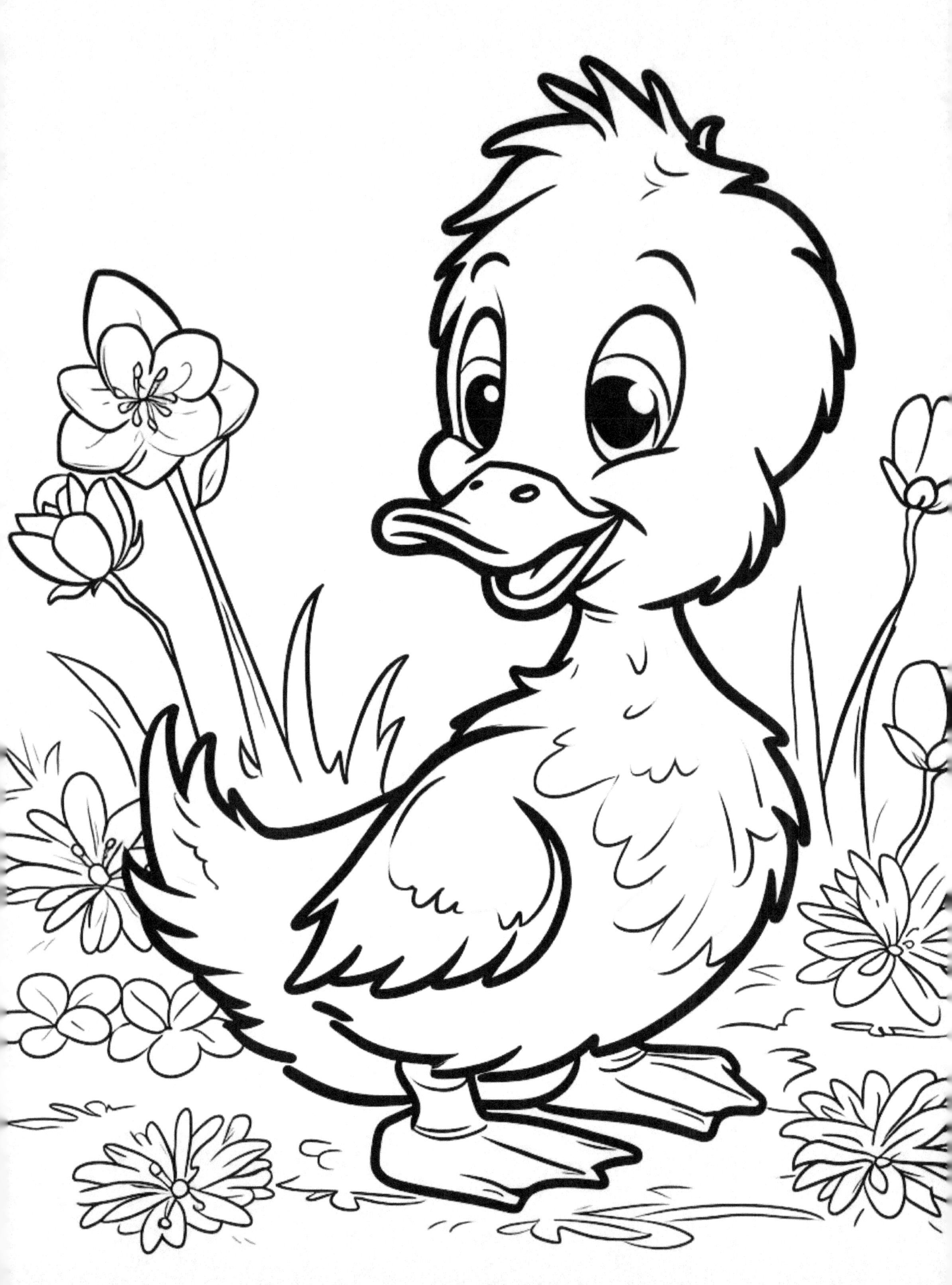

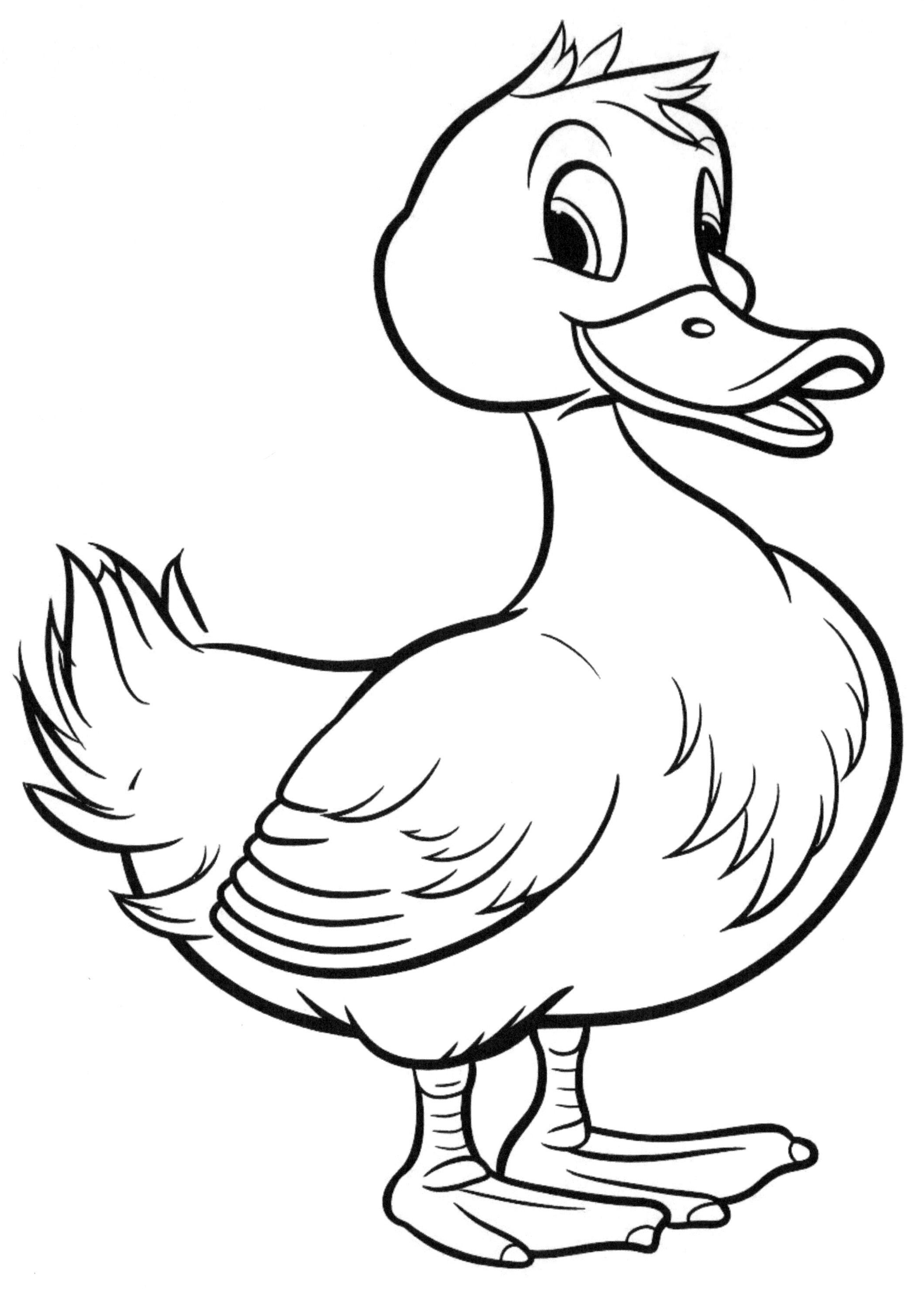

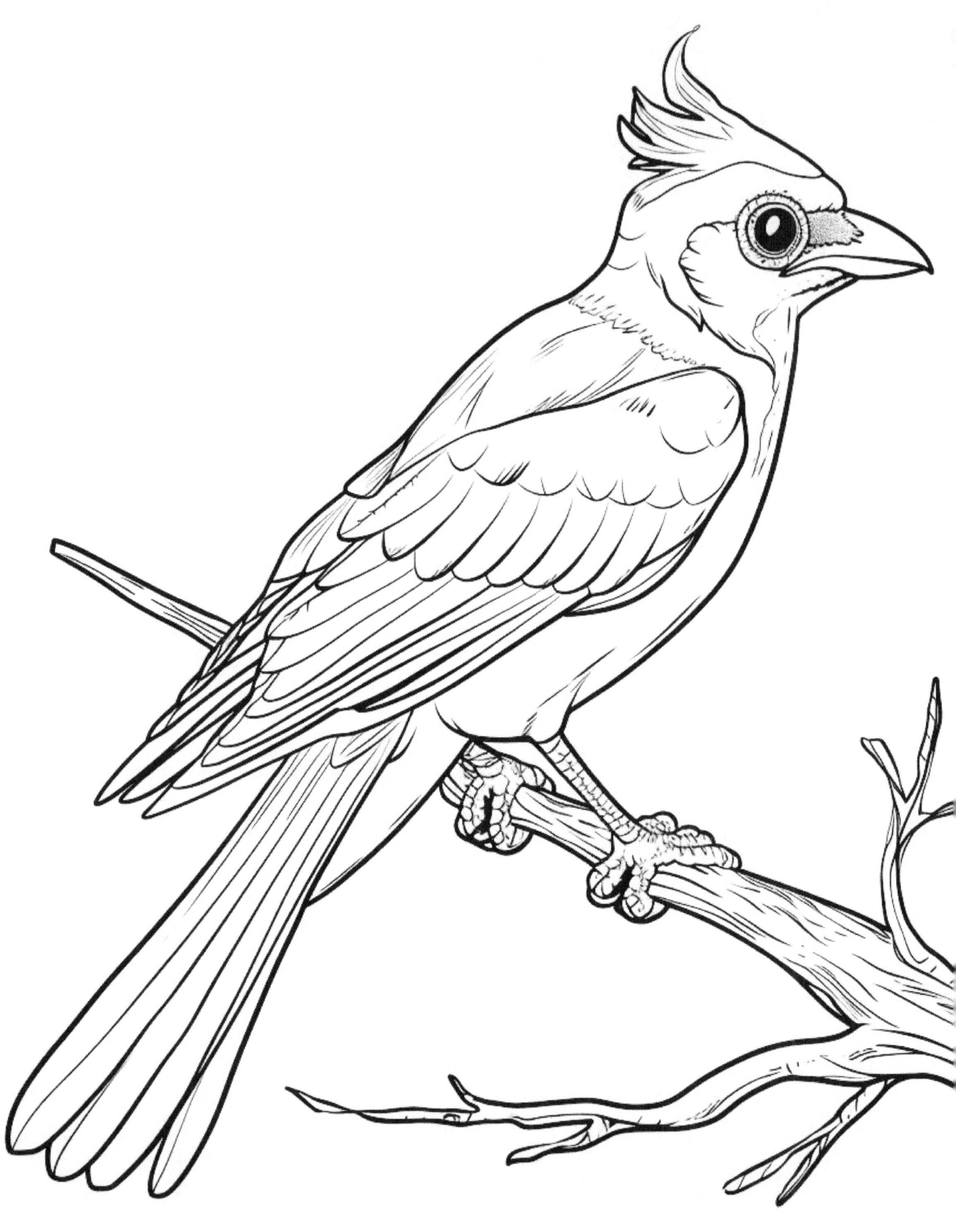

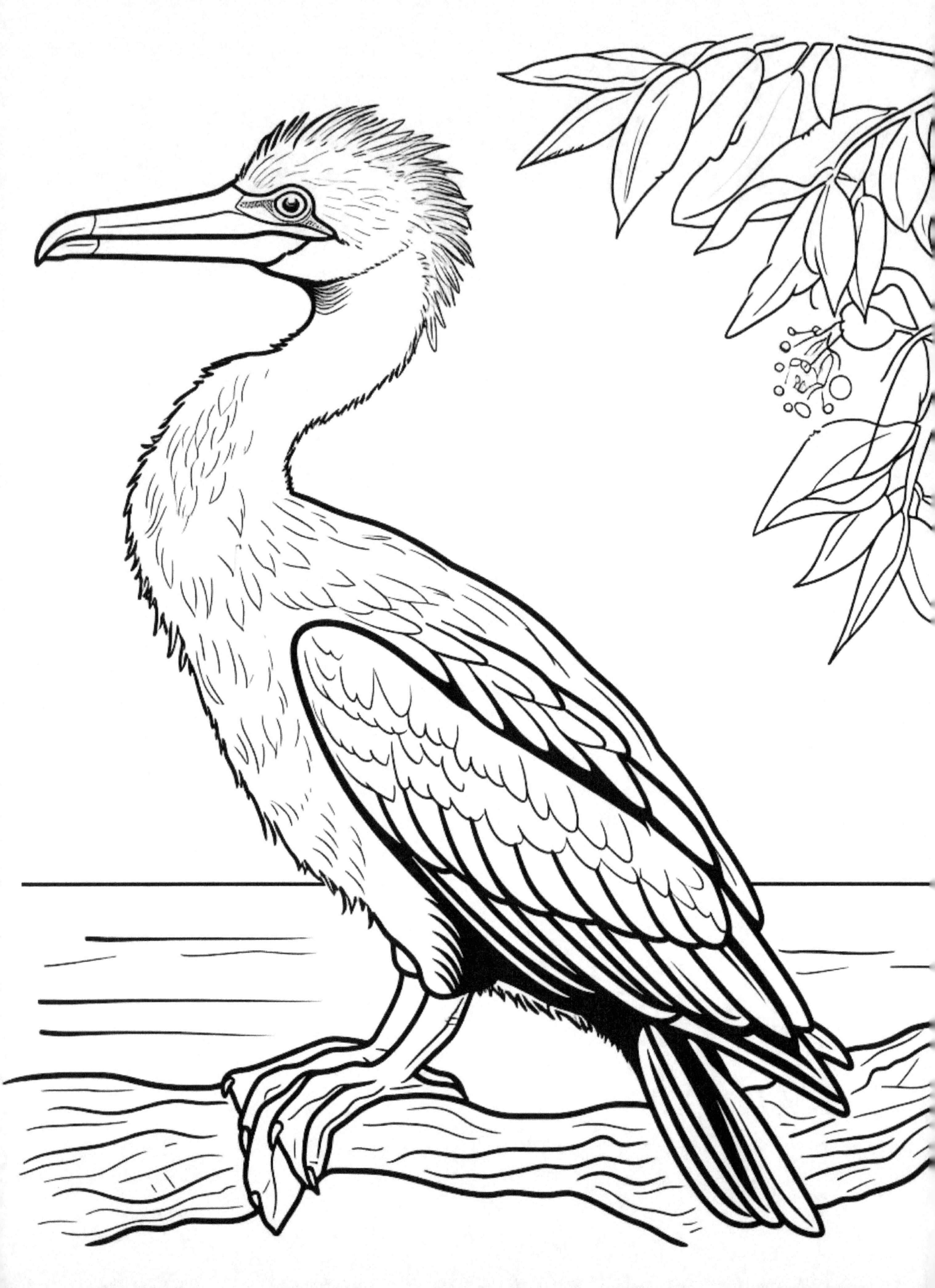

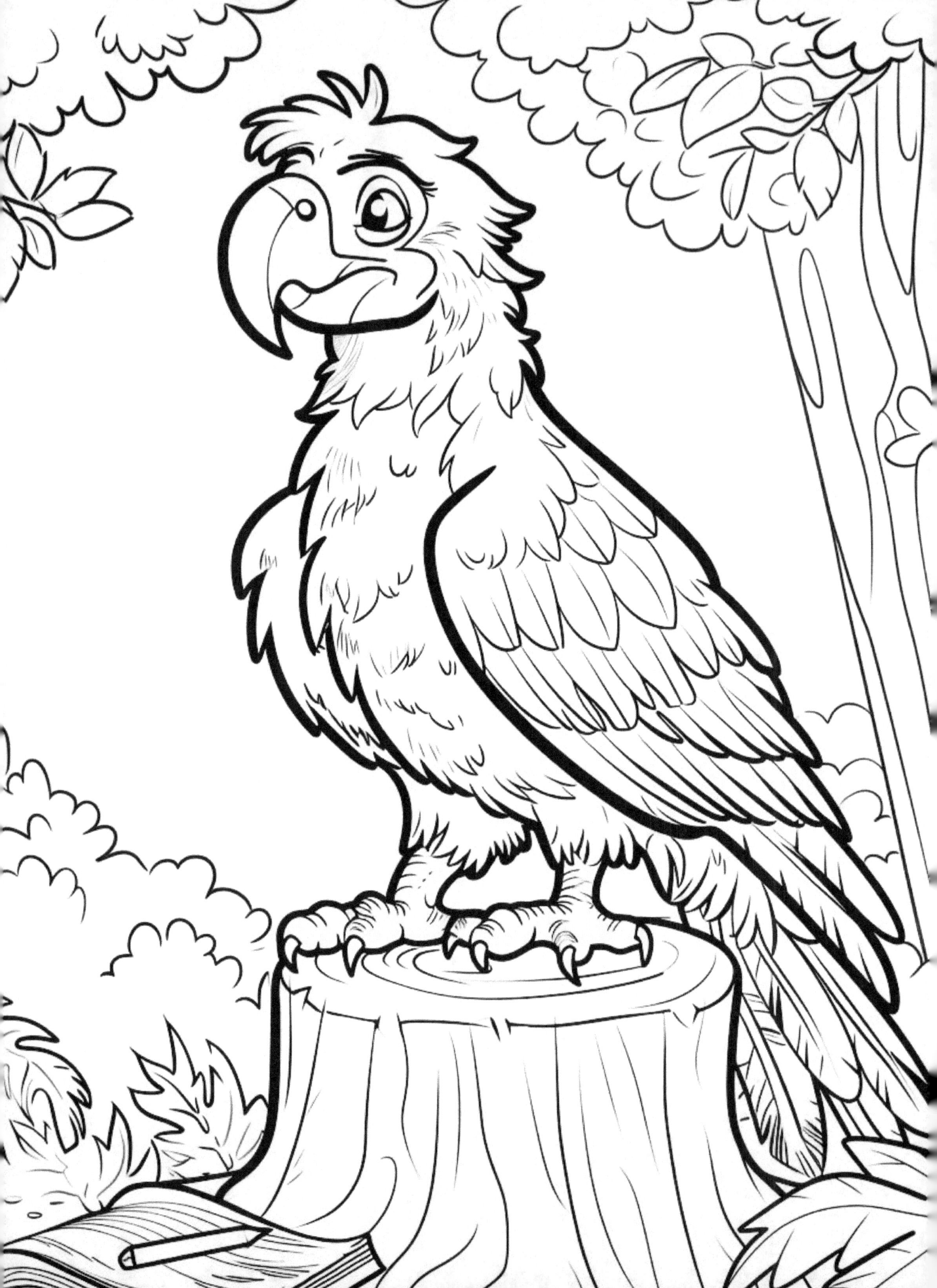

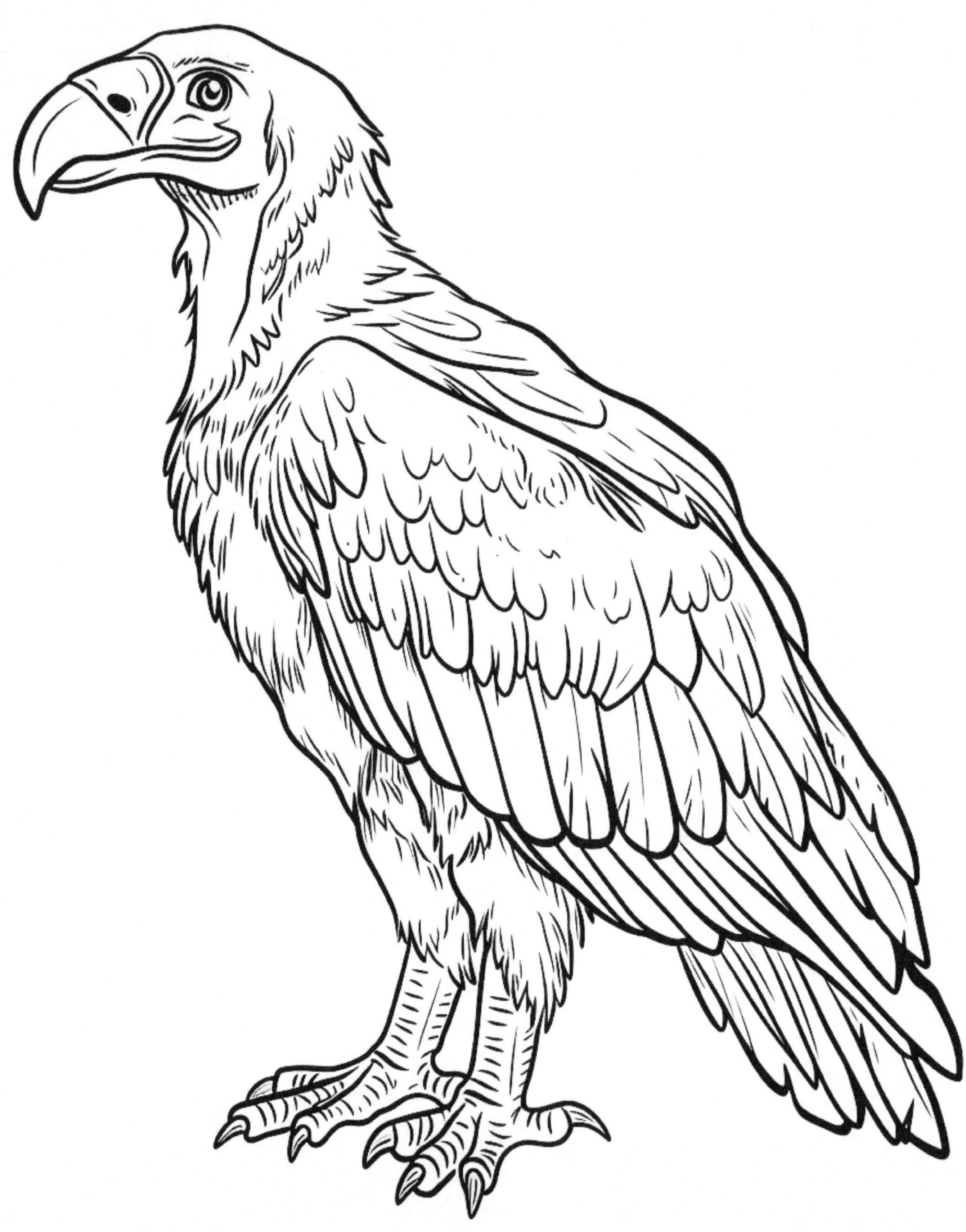

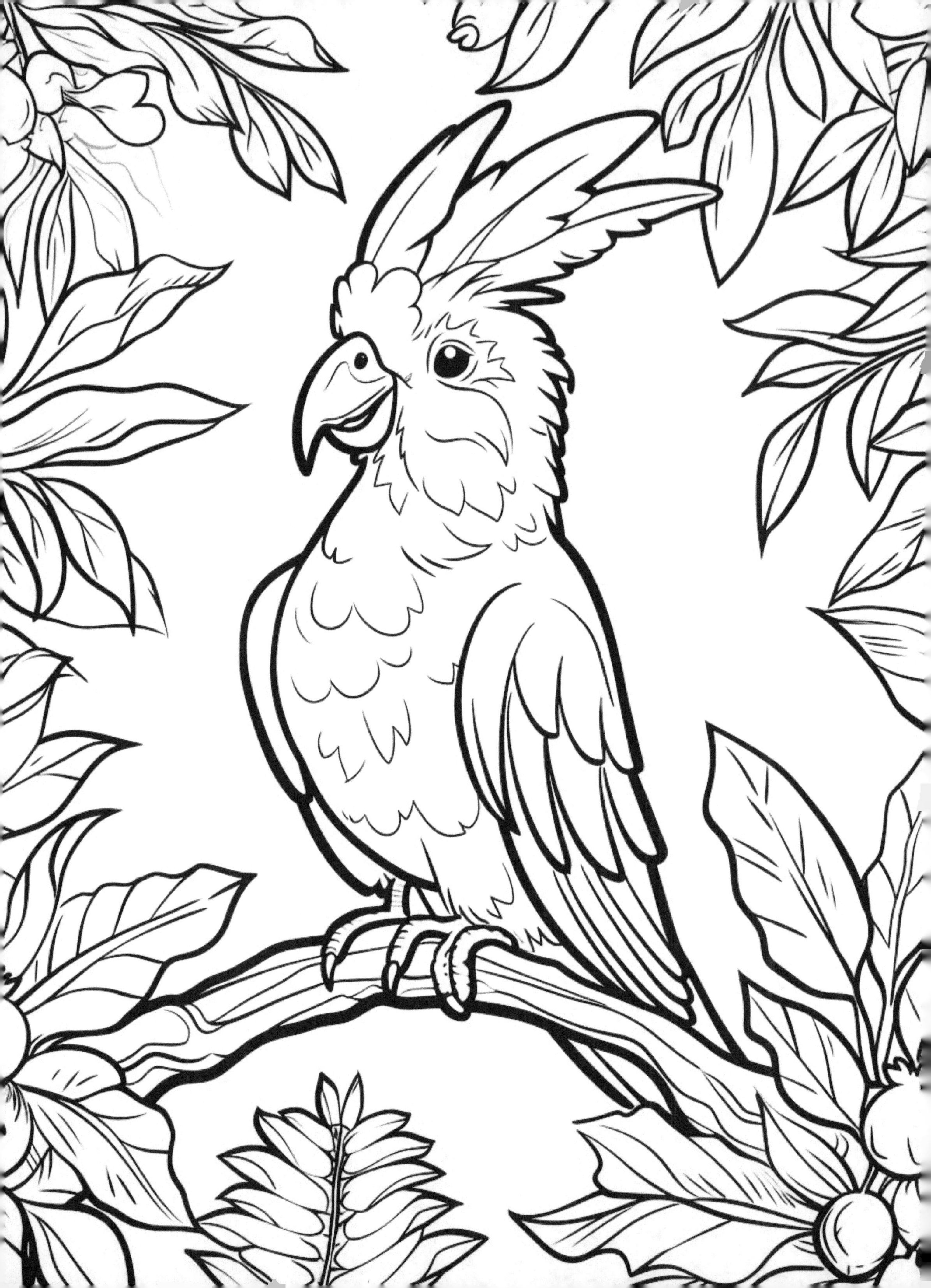

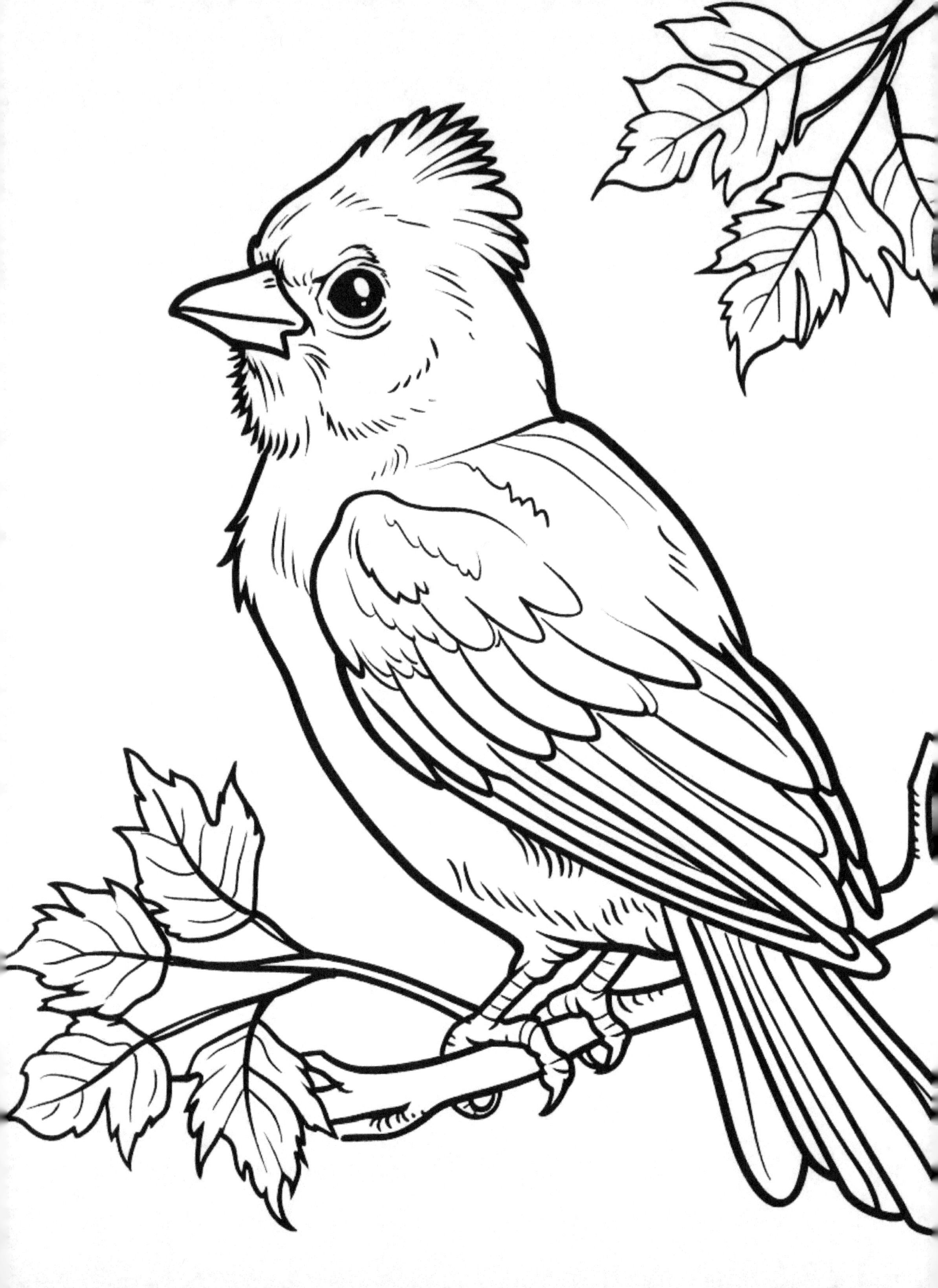

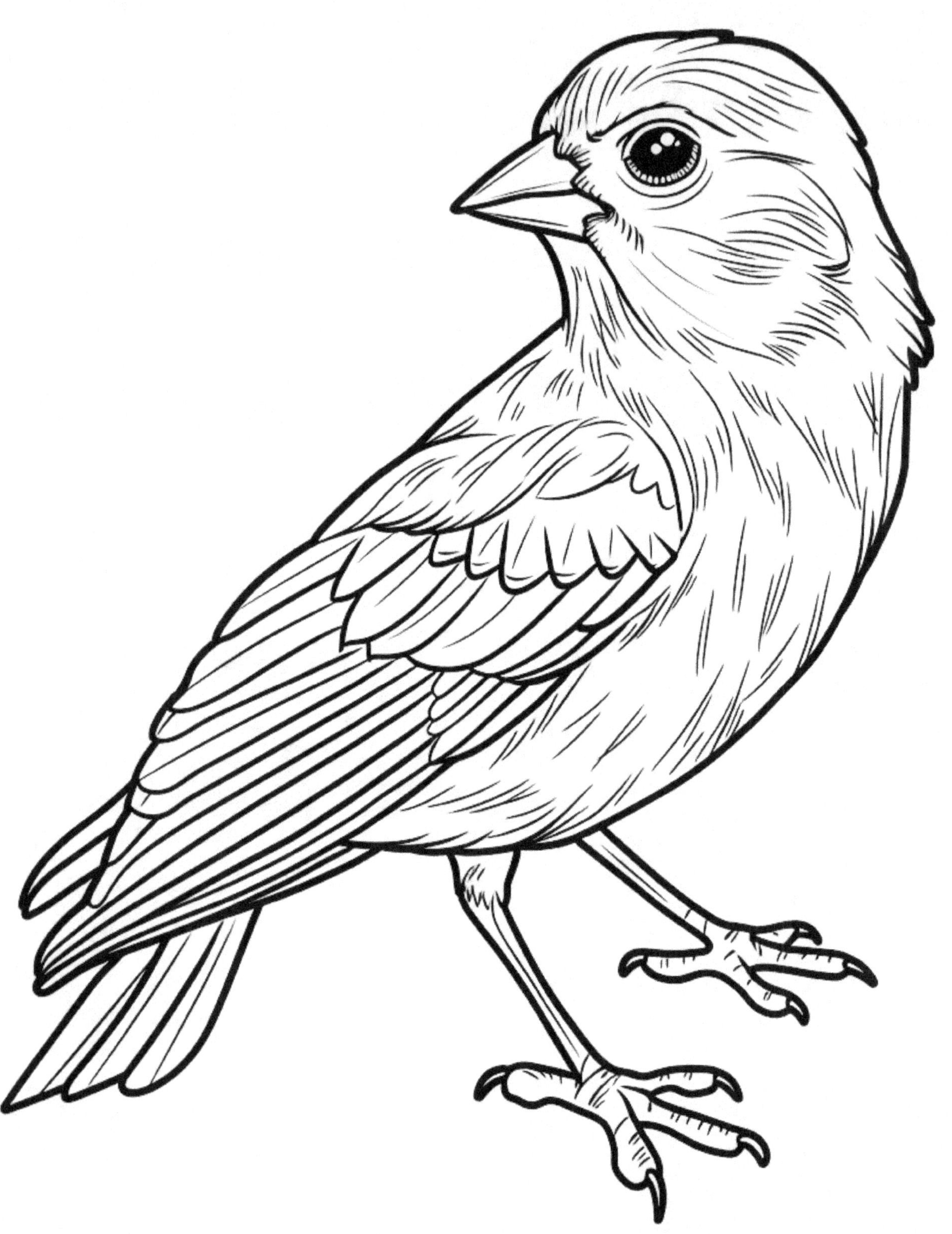

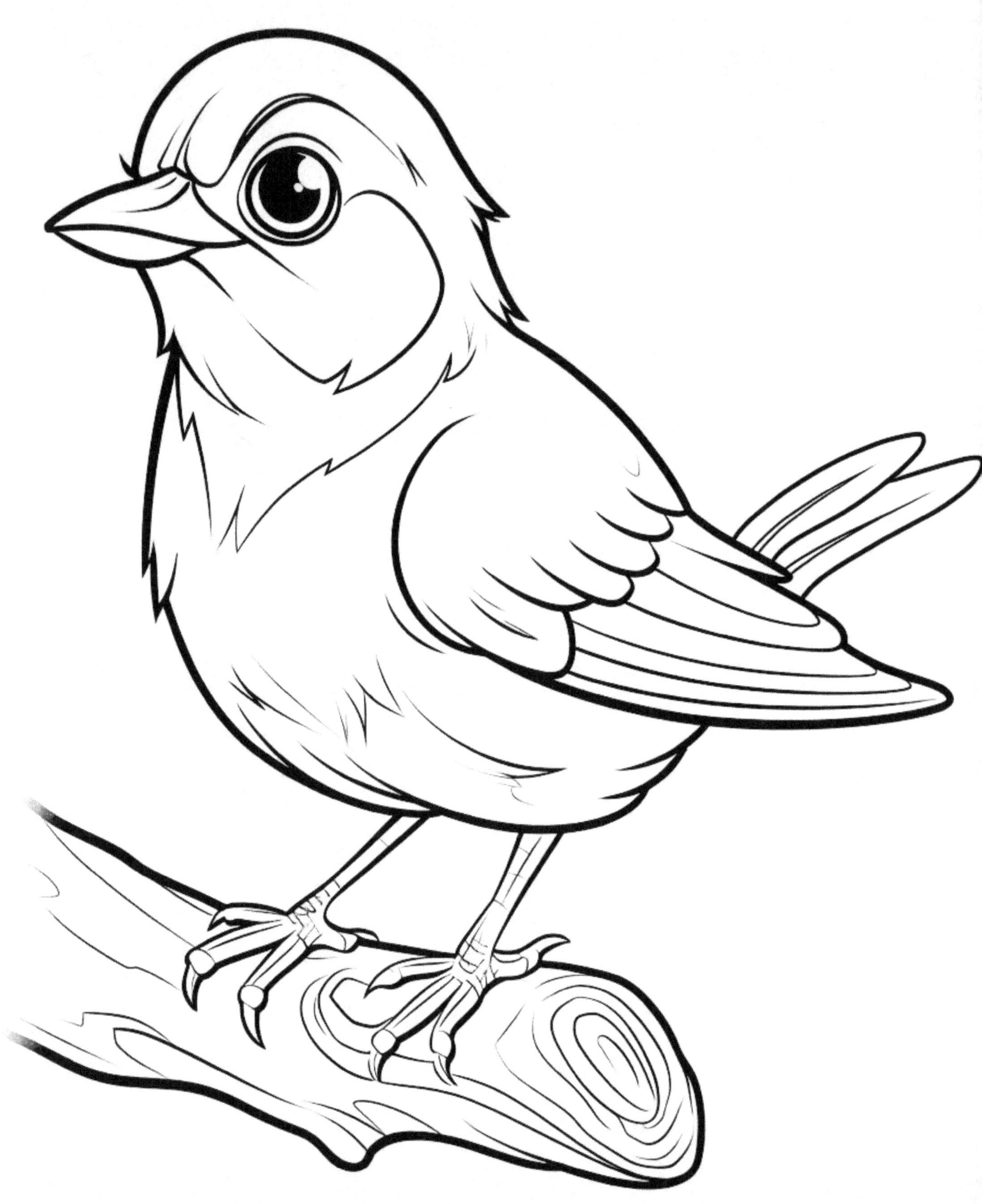

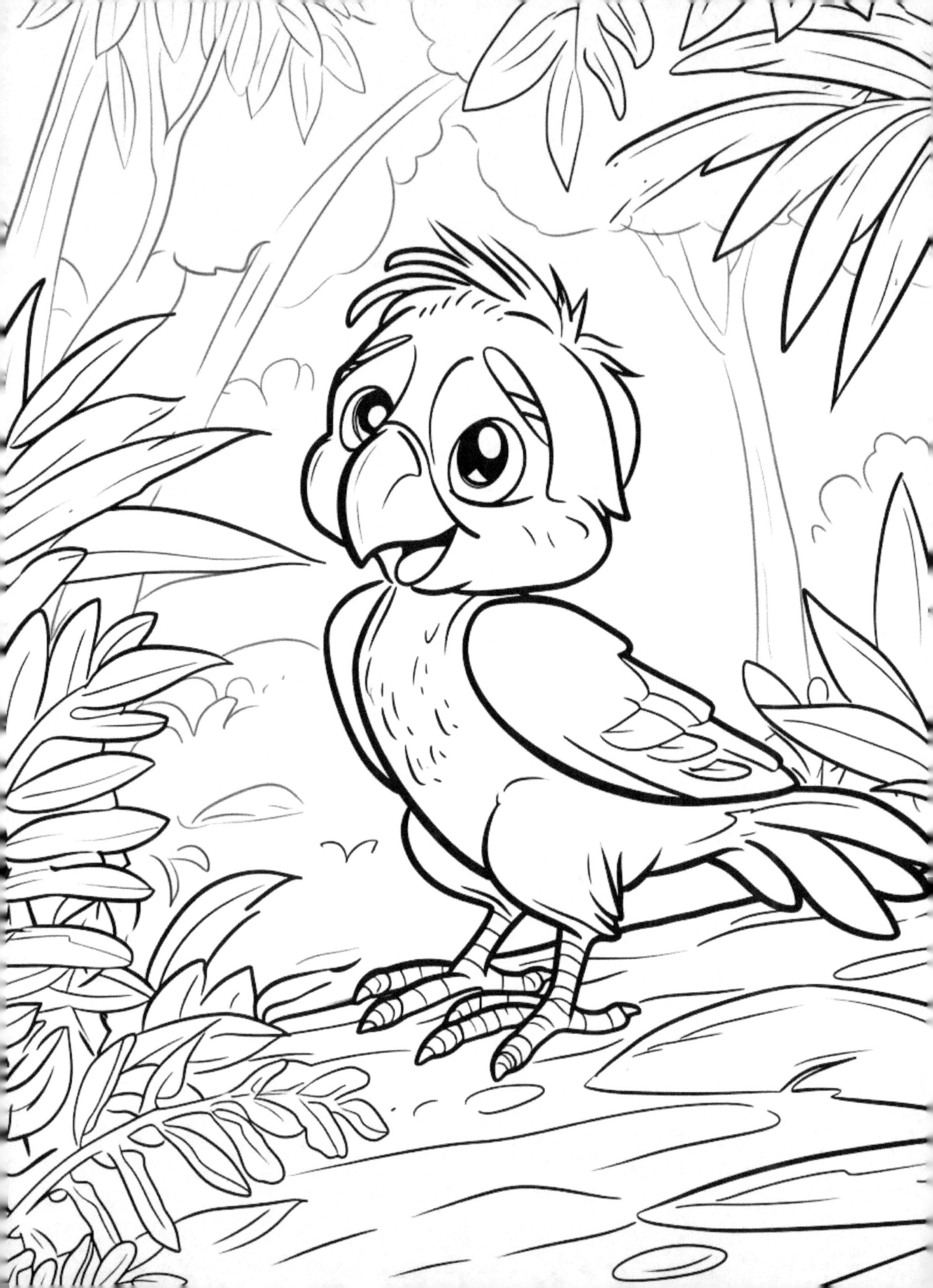

Thank you for joining me on this coloring adventure through the world of birds! I hope you discovered relaxation and joy as you explored the beauty of feathers, beaks, and wings across these pages.

Your creativity has brought these quirky characters to life in your own unique way.
Whether you're a seasoned artist or just starting your coloring journey, I hope this book sparked your imagination and unleashed your inner illustrator.

Remember - each stroke of color you add spreads more beauty into the world.
Wishing you many more hours of relaxing fun and creativity ahead. May your days be filled with inspiration and your creative spirit soar ever higher. Until next time, happy coloring!

With gratitude, Artur Sobolevskij

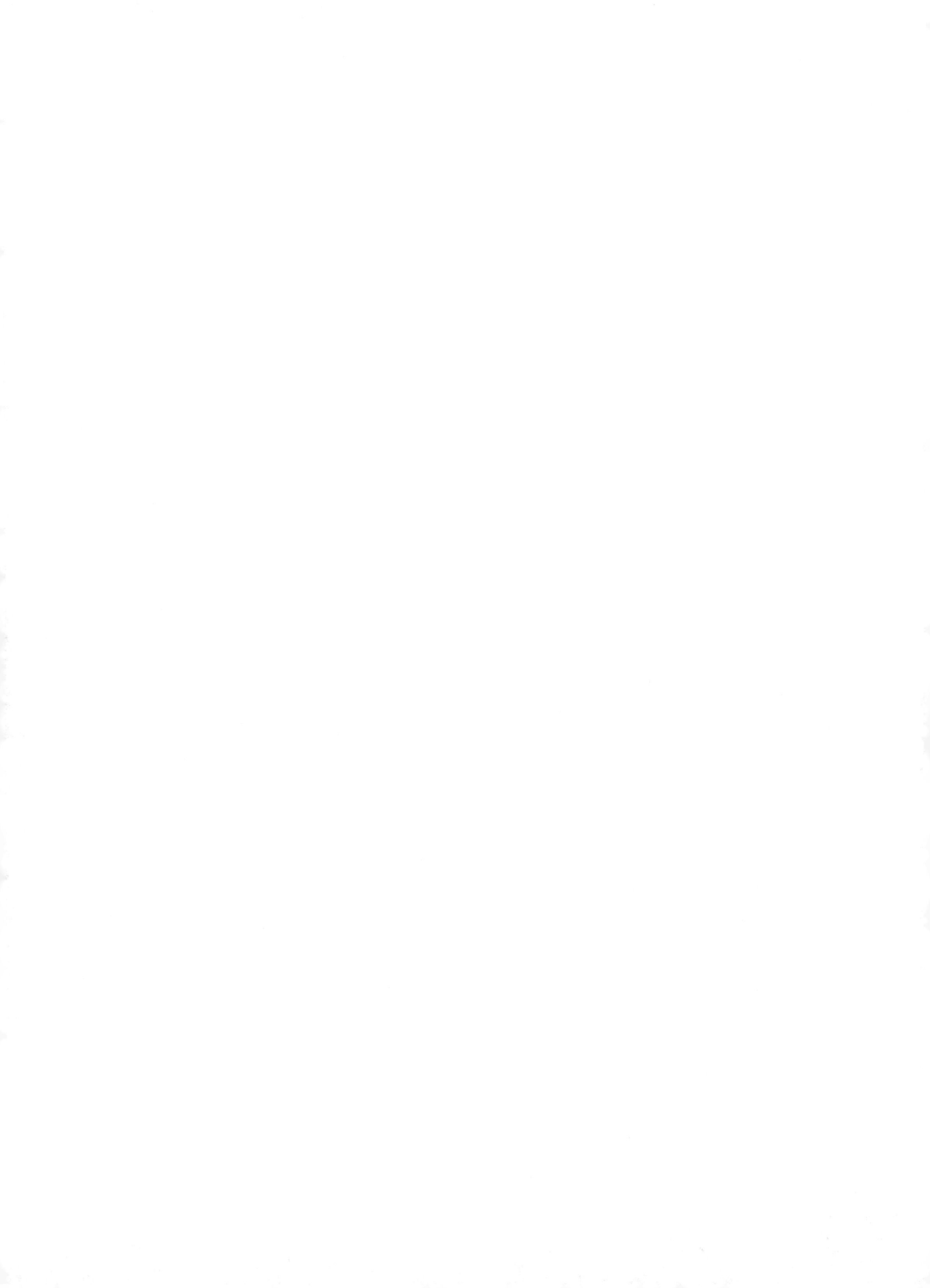